Mrs. Pankhurst
& the Right to Vote

Mrs. Pankhurst & the Right to Vote
The Leader of the Women's Suffrage Movement in Britain

My Own Story
Emmeline Pankhurst

What Forcible Feeding Means
Frank Moxon

Why We are Militant
Speech Given in New York by Mrs. Pankhurst

Beware Suffragists
Cicely Hamilton

Mrs. Pankhurst & the Right to Vote
The Leader of the Women's Suffrage Movement in Britain
My Own Story
By Emmeline Pankhurst
What Forcible Feeding Means
By Frank Moxon
Why We are Militant
Speech Given in New York by Mrs. Pankhurst
Beware Suffragists
By Cicely Hamilton

FIRST EDITION

Leonaur is an imprint of Oakpast Ltd

Copyright in this form © 2016 Oakpast Ltd

ISBN: 978-1-78282-505-0 (hardcover)
ISBN: 978-1-78282-506-7 (softcover)

http://www.leonaur.com

Publisher's Notes

The views expressed in this book are not necessarily those of the publisher.

Contents

Foreword	9
Book 1: The Making of a Militant	11
Book 2: Four Years of Peaceful Militancy	58
Book 3: The Women's Revolution	140
What Forcible Feeding Means	245
Why We are Militant	265
Beware Suffragists	277

MRS. PANKHURST AND THE HUNGER STRIKE

To the Editor of the Manchester Guardian.

Sir,—With your permission, I desire to express my complete agreement with Mrs. Pethick Lawrence's statement in the "Times" of to-day, and to emphasise the fact that the hunger strike was adopted after every other effort had failed to secure the transference of the suffragist prisoners to the First Division, in which Mr. and Mrs. Pethick Lawrence and myself had already been placed. The Second Division prisoners struck against a classification which gave them the status of ordinary criminals; we in the First Division struck because we could not honourably accept treatment denied to our friends.

We did not strike to end or even shorten our term of imprisonment. Had the Home Secretary adopted the obviously right and just course and given equal treatment to all alike, the strike would have ended, and, speaking for myself (and I believe Mr. and Mrs. Lawrence agree with me), I should have been content to remain in prison until the expiration of my sentence. The result of the refusal to do justice is that women, rather than submit to obviously unjust treatment, have faced, and are now facing, death; and in spite of forcible feeding it is made manifest that no prison bars can long deprive a courageous soul of even physical freedom.

Although out of prison, like Mrs. Pethick Lawrence, I desire it to be widely known that until my health is completely restored I shall take no part in suffrage work nor accept responsibility for the agitation as conducted by others.—Yours, &c.,

E. PANKHURST.

Acknowledgment
The author wishes to express her deep obligation to
Rheta Childe Dorr for invaluable editorial services
performed in the preparation of this volume, especially the
American edition.

Foreword

The closing paragraphs of this book were written in the late summer of 1914, when the armies of every great power in Europe were being mobilised for savage, unsparing, barbarous warfare—against one another, against small and unaggressive nations, against helpless women and children, against civilisation itself. How mild, by comparison with the despatches in the daily newspapers, will seem this chronicle of women's militant struggle against political and social injustice in one small corner of Europe. Yet let it stand as it was written, with peace—so-called, and civilisation, and orderly government as the background for heroism such as the world has seldom witnessed. The militancy of men, through all the centuries, has drenched the world with blood, and for these deeds of horror and destruction men have been rewarded with monuments, with great songs and epics. The militancy of women has harmed no human life save the lives of those who fought the battle of righteousness. Time alone will reveal what reward will be allotted to the women.

This we know, that in the black hour that has just struck in Europe, the men are turning to their women and calling on them to take up the work of keeping civilisation alive. Through all the harvest fields, in orchards and vineyards, women are garnering food for the men who fight, as well as for the children left fatherless by war. In the cities the women are keeping open the shops, they are driving trucks and trams, and are altogether attending to a multitude of business.

When the remnants of the armies return, when the commerce of Europe is resumed by men, will they forget the part the women so nobly played? Will they forget in England how women in all ranks of life put aside their own interests and organised, not only to nurse the wounded, care for the destitute, comfort the sick and lonely, but actually to maintain the existence of the nation? Thus far, it must be admitted, there are few indications that the English Government are mindful of the unselfish devotion manifested by the women. Thus far all Government schemes for overcoming unemployment have been directed towards the unemployment of men. The work of women, making garments, etc., has in some cases been taken away.

At the first alarm of war the militants proclaimed a truce, which was answered half-heartedly by the announcement that the Government would release all suffrage prisoners who would give an undertaking "not to commit further crimes or outrages." Since the truce had already been proclaimed, no suffrage prisoner deigned to reply to the Home Secretary's provision.

A few days later, no doubt influenced by representations made to the Government by men and women of every political faith—many of them never having been supporters of revolutionary tactics—Mr. McKenna announced in the House of Commons that it was the intention of the Government, within a few days, to release unconditionally, all suffrage prisoners. So ends, for the present, the war of women against men. As of old, the women become the nurturing mothers of men, their sisters and uncomplaining helpmates. The future lies far ahead, but let this preface and this volume close with the assurance that the struggle for the full enfranchisement of women has not been abandoned; it has simply, for the moment, been placed in abeyance. When the clash of arms ceases, when normal, peaceful, rational society resumes its functions, the demand will again be made. If it is not quickly granted, then once more the women will take up the arms they today, (1914), generously lay down. There can be no real peace in the world until woman, the mother half of the human family, is given liberty in the councils of the world.

Book 1: The Making of a Militant
Mrs. Pankhurst's Own Story

CHAPTER 1

Those men and women are fortunate who are born at a time when a great struggle for human freedom is in progress. It is an added good fortune to have parents who take a personal part in the great movements of their time. I am glad and thankful that this was my case.

One of my earliest recollections is of a great bazaar which was held in my native city of Manchester, the object of the bazaar being to raise money to relieve the poverty of the newly emancipated negro slaves in the United States. My mother took an active part in this effort, and I, as a small child, was entrusted with a lucky bag by means of which I helped to collect money.

Young as I was—I could not have been older than five years—I knew perfectly well the meaning of the words slavery and emancipation. From infancy I had been accustomed to hear pro and con discussions of slavery and the American Civil War. Although the British government finally decided not to recognise the Confederacy, public opinion in England was sharply divided on the questions both of slavery and of secession. Broadly speaking, the propertied classes were pro-slavery, but there were many exceptions to the rule. Most of those who formed the circle of our family friends were opposed to slavery, and my father, Robert Goulden, was always a most ardent abolitionist. He was prominent enough in the movement to be appointed on a committee to meet and welcome Henry Ward Beecher when he arrived in England for a lecture tour.

Mrs. Harriet Beecher Stowe's novel, *Uncle Tom's Cabin*, was so great a favourite with my mother that she used it continually as a source of bedtime stories for our fascinated ears. Those stories, told almost fifty years ago, are as fresh in my mind today as events detailed in the morning's papers. Indeed they are more vivid, because they made a much deeper impression on my consciousness. I can still definitely recall the thrill I experienced every time my mother related the tale of Eliza's race for freedom over the broken ice of the Ohio River, the agonizing pursuit, and the final rescue at the hands of the determined old Quaker. Another thrilling tale was the story of a negro boy's flight from the plantation of his cruel master. The boy had never seen a railroad train, and when, staggering along the unfamiliar railroad track, he heard the roar of an approaching train, the clattering car-wheels seemed to his strained imagination to be repeating over and over again the awful words, "Catch a nigger—catch a nigger—catch a nigger—" This was a terrible story, and throughout my childhood, whenever I rode in a train, I thought of that poor runaway slave escaping from the pursuing monster.

These stories, with the bazaars and the relief funds and subscriptions of which I heard so much talk, I am sure made a permanent impression on my brain and my character. They awakened in me the two sets of sensations to which all my life I have most readily responded: first, admiration for that spirit of fighting and heroic sacrifice by which alone the soul of civilisation is saved; and next after that, appreciation of the gentler spirit which is moved to mend and repair the ravages of war.

I do not remember a time when I could not read, nor any time when reading was not a joy and a solace. As far back as my memory runs I loved tales, especially those of a romantic and idealistic character. *Pilgrim's Progress* was an early favourite, as well as another of Bunyan's visionary romances, which does not seem to be as well known, his *Holy War*. At nine I discovered the *Odyssey* and very soon after that another classic which has remained all my life a source of inspiration. This was Carlyle's *French Revolution*, and I received it with much the same emotion that Keats experienced when he read Chapman's translation of Homer—

> . . . . *like some watcher of the skies,*
> *When a new planet swims into his ken.*

I never lost that first impression, and it strongly affected my attitude toward events which were occurring around my childhood. Manchester is a city which has witnessed a great many stirring episodes, especially of a political character. Generally speaking, its citizens have been liberal in their sentiments, defenders of free speech and liberty of opinion. In the late sixties there occurred in Manchester one of those dreadful events that prove an exception to the rule. This was in connection with the Fenian Revolt in Ireland. There was a Fenian riot, and the police arrested the leaders. These men were being taken to the jail in a prison van.

On the way the van was stopped and an attempt was made to rescue the prisoners. A man fired a pistol, endeavouring to break the lock of the van door. A policeman fell, mortally wounded, and several men were arrested and were charged with murder. I distinctly remember the riot, which I did not witness, but which I heard vividly described by my older brother. I had been spending the afternoon with a young playmate, and my brother had come after tea to escort me home. As we walked through the deepening November twilight he talked excitedly of the riot, the fatal pistol shot, and the slain policeman. I could almost see the man bleeding on the ground, while the crowd swayed and groaned around him.

The rest of the story reveals one of those ghastly blunders which justice not infrequently makes. Although the shooting was done without any intent to kill, the men were tried for murder and three of them were found guilty and hanged. Their execution, which greatly excited the citizens of Manchester, was almost the last, if not the last, public execution permitted to take place in the city. At the time I was a boarding-pupil in a school near Manchester, and I spent my weekends at home. A certain Saturday afternoon stands out in my memory, as on my way home from school I passed the prison where I knew the men had been confined. I saw that a part of the prison wall had been torn away, and in the great gap that remained were evidences of a gallows recently removed. I was transfixed with horror, and over me there swept the sudden conviction that that hanging was a mistake— worse, a crime. It was my awakening to one of the most terrible facts of life—that justice and judgment lie often a world apart.

I relate this incident of my formative years to illustrate the fact that the impressions of childhood often have more to do with character and future conduct than heredity or education. I tell it also to show that my development into an advocate of militancy was largely a sympathetic process. I have not personally suffered from the deprivations, the bitterness and sorrow which bring so many men and women to a realisation of social injustice. My childhood was protected by love and a comfortable home. Yet, while still a very young child, I began instinctively to feel that there was something lacking, even in my own home, some false conception of family relations, some incomplete ideal.

This vague feeling of mine began to shape itself into conviction about the time my brothers and I were sent to school. The education of the English boy, then as now, was considered a much more serious matter than the education of the English boy's sister. My parents, especially my father, discussed the question of my brothers' education as a matter of real importance. My education and that of my sister were scarcely discussed at all. Of course we went to a carefully selected girls' school, but beyond the facts that the head mistress was a gentlewoman and that all the pupils were girls of my own class, nobody seemed concerned. A girl's education at that time seemed to have for its prime object the art of "making home attractive"—presumably to migratory male relatives. It used to puzzle me to understand why I was under such a particular obligation to make home attractive to my brothers. We were on excellent terms of friendship, but it was never suggested to them as a duty that they make home attractive to me. Why not? Nobody seemed to know.

The answer to these puzzling questions came to me unexpectedly one night when I lay in my little bed waiting for sleep to overtake me. It was a custom of my father and mother to make the round of our bedrooms every night before going themselves to bed. When they entered my room that night I was still awake, but for some reason I chose to feign slumber. My father bent over me, shielding the candle flame with his big hand. I cannot know exactly what thought was in his mind as he gazed down at me, but I heard him say, somewhat sadly, "What a pity she wasn't born a lad."

My first hot impulse was to sit up in bed and protest that I didn't want to be a boy, but I lay still and heard my parents' footsteps pass on toward the next child's bed. I thought about my father's remark for many days afterward, but I think I never decided that I regretted my sex. However, it was made quite clear that men considered themselves superior to women, and that women apparently acquiesced in that belief.

I found this view of things difficult to reconcile with the fact that both my father and my mother were advocates of equal suffrage. I was very young when the Reform Act of 1866 was passed, but I very well remember the agitation caused by certain circumstances attending it. This Reform Act, known as the Household Franchise Bill, marked the first popular extension of the ballot in England since 1832. Under its terms, householders paying a minimum of ten pounds a year rental were given the Parliamentary vote. While it was still under discussion in the House of Commons, John Stuart Mill moved an amendment to the bill to include women householders as well as men. The amendment was defeated, but in the act as passed the word "man," instead of the usual "male person," was used. Now, under another act of Parliament it had been decided that the word "man" always included "woman" unless otherwise specifically stated. For example, in certain acts containing rate-paying clauses, the masculine noun and pronoun are used throughout, but the provisions apply to women rate-payers as well as to men. So when the Reform Bill with the word "man" in it became law, many women believed that the right of suffrage had actually been bestowed upon them.

A tremendous amount of discussion ensued, and the matter was finally tested by a large number of women seeking to have their names placed upon the register as voters. In my city of Manchester 3,924 women, out of a total of 4,215 possible women voters, claimed their votes, and their claim was defended in the law courts by eminent lawyers, including my future husband, Dr. Pankhurst. Of course the women's claim was settled adversely in the courts, but the agitation resulted in a strengthening of the woman-suffrage agitation all over the country.

I was too young to understand the precise nature of the affair, but I shared in the general excitement. From reading newspapers aloud to my father I had developed a genuine interest in politics, and the Reform Bill presented itself to my young intelligence as something that was going to do the most wonderful good to the country. The first election after the bill became law was naturally a memorable occasion. It is chiefly memorable to me because it was the first one in which I ever participated. My sister and I had just been presented with new winter frocks, green in colour, and made alike, after the custom of proper British families. Every girl child in those days wore a red flannel petticoat, and when we first put on our new frocks I was struck with the fact that we were wearing red and green—the colours of the Liberal party.

Since our father was a Liberal, of course the Liberal party ought to carry the election, and I conceived a brilliant scheme for helping its progress. With my small sister trotting after me, I walked the better part of a mile to the nearest polling-booth. It happened to be in a rather rough factory district, but we did not notice that. Arrived there, we two children picked up our green skirts to show our scarlet petticoats, and brimful of importance, walked up and down before the assembled crowds to encourage the Liberal vote. From this eminence we were shortly snatched by outraged authority in the form of a nursery-maid. I believe we were sent to bed into the bargain, but I am not entirely clear on this point.

I was fourteen years old when I went to my first suffrage meeting. Returning from school one day, I met my mother just setting out for the meeting, and I begged her to let me go along. She consented, and without stopping to lay my books down I scampered away in my mother's wake. The speeches interested and excited me, especially the address of the great Miss Lydia Becker, who was the Susan B. Anthony of the English movement, a splendid character and a truly eloquent speaker. She was the secretary of the Manchester committee, and I had learned to admire her as the editor of the *Women's Suffrage Journal*, which came to my mother every week. I left the meeting a conscious and confirmed suffragist.

I suppose I had always been an unconscious suffragist. With my temperament and my surroundings I could scarcely have been otherwise. The movement was very much alive in the early seventies, nowhere more so than in Manchester, where it was organised by a group of extraordinary men and women. Among them were Mr. and Mrs. Jacob Bright, who were always ready to champion the struggling cause. Mr. Jacob Bright, a brother of John Bright, was for many years member of Parliament for Manchester, and to the day of his death was an active supporter of woman suffrage. Two especially gifted women, besides Miss Becker, were members of the committee. These were Mrs. Alice Cliff Scatcherd and Miss Wolstentholm, now, (1914), the venerable Mrs. Wolstentholm-Elmy. One of the principal founders of the committee was the man whose wife, in later years, I was destined to become, Dr. Richard Marsden Pankhurst.

When I was fifteen years old I went to Paris, where I was entered as a pupil in one of the pioneer institutions in Europe for the higher education of girls. This school, one of the founders of which was Madame Edmond Adam, who was and is still a distinguished literary figure, was situated in a fine old house in the Avenue de Neuilly. It was under the direction of Mlle. Marchef-Girard, a woman distinguished in education, and who afterward was appointed government inspector of schools in France. Mlle. Marchef-Girard believed that girls' education should be quite as thorough and even more practical than the education boys were receiving at that time. She included chemistry and other sciences in her courses, and in addition to embroidery she had her girls taught bookkeeping. Many other advanced ideas prevailed in this school, and the moral discipline which the pupils received was, to my mind, as valuable as the intellectual training. Mlle. Marchef-Girard held that women should be given the highest ideals of honour. Her pupils were kept to the strictest principles of truth-telling and candour. Myself she understood and greatly benefited by an implicit trust which I am sure I could not have betrayed, even had I felt for her less real affection.

My roommate in this delightful school was an interesting young girl of my own age, Noemie Rochefort, daughter of that great Republican, Communist, journalist, and swordsman, Henri Rochefort. This was very shortly after the Franco-Prussian War, and memories of the Empire's fall and of the bloody and disastrous Commune were very keen in Paris. Indeed my roommate's illustrious father and many others were then in exile in New Caledonia for participation in the Commune. My friend Noemie was torn with anxiety for her father. She talked of him constantly, and many were the blood-curdling accounts of daring and of patriotism to which I listened.

Henri Rochefort was, in fact, one of the moving spirits of the Republican movement in France, and after his amazing escape in an open boat from New Caledonia, he lived through many years of political adventures of the most lively and picturesque character. His daughter and I remained warm friends long after our schooldays ended, and my association with her strengthened all the liberal ideas I had previously acquired.

I was between eighteen and nineteen when I finally returned from school in Paris and took my place in my father's home as a finished young lady. I sympathised with and worked for the woman-suffrage movement, and came to know Dr. Pankhurst, whose work for woman suffrage had never ceased. It was Dr. Pankhurst who drafted the first enfranchisement bill, known as the Women's Disabilities Removal Bill, and introduced into the House of Commons in 1870 by Mr. Jacob Bright. The bill advanced to its second reading by a majority vote of thirty-three, but it was killed in committee by Mr. Gladstone's peremptory orders. Dr. Pankhurst, as I have already said, with another distinguished barrister, Lord Coleridge, acted as counsel for the Manchester women, who tried in 1868 to be placed on the register as voters. He also drafted the bill giving married women absolute control over their property and earnings, a bill which became law in 1882.

My marriage with Dr. Pankhurst took place in 1879.

I think we cannot be too grateful to the group of men and women who, like Dr. Pankhurst, in those early days lent the weight of their honoured names to the suffrage movement in the trials of its struggling youth. These men did not wait until the movement became popular, nor did they hesitate until it was plain that women were roused to the point of revolt. They worked all their lives with those who were organising, educating, and preparing for the revolt which was one day to come. Unquestionably those pioneer men suffered in popularity for their feminist views. Some of them suffered financially, some politically. Yet they never wavered.

My married life lasted through nineteen happy years. Often I have heard the taunt that suffragists are women who have failed to find any normal outlet for their emotions, and are therefore soured and disappointed beings. This is probably not true of any suffragist, and it is most certainly not true of me. My home life and relations have been as nearly ideal as possible in this imperfect world. About a year after my marriage my daughter Christabel was born, and in another eighteen months my second daughter Sylvia came. Two other children followed, and for some years I was rather deeply immersed in my domestic affairs.

I was never so absorbed with home and children, however, that I lost interest in community affairs. Dr. Pankhurst did not desire that I should turn myself into a household machine. It was his firm belief that society as well as the family stands in need of women's services. So while my children were still in their cradles I was serving on the executive committee of the Women's Suffrage Society, and also on the executive board of the committee which was working to secure the Married Women's Property Act. This act having passed in 1882, I threw myself into the suffrage work with renewed energy. A new Reform Act, known as the County Franchise Bill, extending the suffrage to farm labourers, was under discussion, and we believed that our years of educational propaganda work had prepared the country to support us in a demand for a women's suffrage amendment to the bill.

For several years we had been holding the most splendid meetings in cities all over the kingdom. The crowds, the enthusiasm, the generous response to appeals for support, all these seemed to justify us in our belief that women's suffrage was near. In fact, in 1884, when the County Franchise Bill came before the country, we had an actual majority in favour of suffrage in the House of Commons.

But a favourable majority in the House of Commons by no means insures the success of any measure. I shall explain this at length when I come to our work of opposing candidates who have avowed themselves suffragists, a course which has greatly puzzled our American friends. The Liberal party was in power in 1884, and a great memorial was sent to the prime minister, the Right Honourable William E. Gladstone, asking that a women's suffrage amendment to the County Franchise Bill be submitted to the free and unbiased consideration of the House. Mr. Gladstone curtly refused, declaring that if a women's suffrage amendment should be carried, the government would disclaim responsibility for the bill. The amendment was submitted nevertheless, but Mr. Gladstone would not allow it to be freely discussed, and he ordered Liberal members to vote against it. What we call a whip was sent out against it, a note virtually commanding party members to be on hand at a certain hour to vote against the women's amendment. Undismayed, the women tried to have an independent suffrage bill introduced, but Mr. Gladstone so arranged Parliamentary business that the bill never even came up for discussion.

I am not going to write a history of the woman suffrage movement in England prior to 1903, when the Women's Social and Political Union was organised. That history is full of repetitions of just such stories as the one I have related. Gladstone was an implacable foe of woman suffrage. He believed that women's work and politics lay in service to men's parties. One of the shrewdest acts of Mr. Gladstone's career was his disruption of the suffrage organisation in England. He accomplished this by substituting "something just as good," that something being Women's Liberal Associations. Beginning in 1881 in Bristol, these associations spread rapidly through the country and, in 1887, became a National Women's Liberal Federation. The promise of the Federation was that by allying themselves with men in party politics, women would soon earn the right to vote. The avidity with which the women swallowed this promise, left off working for themselves, and threw themselves into the men's work was amazing.

The Women's Liberal Federation is an organisation of women who believe in the principles of the Liberal party. (The somewhat older Primrose League is a similar organisation of women who adhere to Conservative party principles.) Neither of these organisations have woman suffrage for their object. They came into existence to uphold party ideas and to work for the election of party candidates.

I am told that women in America have recently allied themselves with political parties, believing, just as we did, that such action would break down opposition to suffrage by showing the men that women possess political ability, and that politics is work for women as well as men. Let them not be deceived. I can assure the American women that our long alliance with the great parties, our devotion to party programmes, our faithful work at elections, never advanced the suffrage cause one step. The men accepted the services of the women, but they never offered any kind of payment.

As far as I am concerned, I did not delude myself with any false hopes in the matter. I was present when the Women's Liberal Federation came into existence. Mrs. Gladstone presided, offering the meeting many consolatory words for the absence of "our great leader," Mr. Gladstone, who of course had no time to waste on a gathering of women. At Mrs. Jacob Bright's request I joined the Federation. At this stage of my development I was a member of the Fabian Society, and I had considerable faith in the permeating powers of its mild socialism. But I was already fairly convinced of the futility of trusting to political parties. Even as a child I had begun to wonder at the *naïve* faith of party members in the promises of their leaders. I well remember my father returning home from political meetings, his face aglow with enthusiasm. "What happened, father?" I would ask, and he would reply triumphantly, "Ah! We passed the resolution."

"Then you'll get your measure through the next session," I predicted.

"I won't say that," was the usual reply. "Things don't always move as quickly as that. But we passed the resolution."

Well, the suffragists, when they were admitted into the Women's Liberal Federation must have felt that they had passed their resolution. They settled down to work for the party and to prove that they were as capable of voting as the recently enfranchised farm labourers. Of course a few women remained loyal to suffrage. They began again on the old educational lines to work for the cause. Not one woman took counsel with herself as to how and why the agricultural labourers had won their franchise. They had won it, as a matter of fact, by burning hay-ricks, rioting, and otherwise demonstrating their strength in the only way that English politicians can understand. The threat to march a hundred thousand men to the House of Commons unless the bill was passed played its part also in securing the agricultural labourer his political freedom. But no woman suffragist noticed that.

As for myself, I was too young politically to learn the lesson then. I had to go through years of public work before I acquired the experience and the wisdom to know how to wring concessions from the English Government. I had to hold public office. I had to go behind the scenes in the government schools, in the workhouses and other charitable institutions; I had to get a close-hand view of the misery and unhappiness of a man-made world, before I reached the point where I could successfully revolt against it. It was almost immediately after the collapse of the woman suffrage movement in 1884 that I entered upon this new phase of my career.

Chapter 2

In 1885, a year after the failure of the third women's suffrage bill, my husband, Dr. Pankhurst, stood as the Liberal candidate for Parliament in Rotherline, a riverside constituency of London. I went through the campaign with him, speaking and canvassing to the best of my ability. Dr. Pankhurst was a popular candidate, and unquestionably would have been returned but for the opposition of the Home-Rulers. Parnell was in command, and his settled policy was opposition to all government candidates. So, in spite of the fact that Dr. Pankhurst was a staunch upholder of home rule, the Parnell forces were solidly opposed to him, and he was defeated. I remember expressing considerable indignation, but my husband pointed out to me that Parnell's policy was absolutely right. With his small party he could never hope to win home rule from a hostile majority, but by constant obstruction he could in time wear out the government, and force it to surrender. That was a valuable political lesson, one that years later I was destined to put into practice.

The following year found us living in London, and, as usual, interesting ourselves with labour matters and other social movements. This year was memorable for a great strike of women working in the Bryant and May match factories. I threw myself into this strike with enthusiasm, working with the girls and with some women of prominence, among these the celebrated Mrs. Annie Besant. The strike was a successful one, the girls winning substantial improvements in their working conditions.

It was a time of tremendous unrest, of labour agitations, of strikes and lockouts. It was a time also when a most stupid reactionary spirit seemed to take possession of the government and the authorities. The Salvation Army, the Socialists, the trade-unionists—in fact, all bodies holding outdoor meetings—were made special objects of attack. As a protest against this policy a Law and Liberty League was formed in London, and an immense Free Speech meeting was held in Trafalgar Square, John Burns and Cunningham Graham being the principal speakers. I was present at this meeting, which resulted in a bloody riot between the police and the populace. The Trafalgar Square Riot is historic, and to it Mr. John Burns owes, in large part, his subsequent rise to political eminence. Both John Burns and Cunningham Graham served prison sentences for the part they played in the riot, but they gained fame, and they did much to establish the right of free speech for English men. English women are still contending for that right.

In 1890 my last child was born in London. I now had a family of five young children, and for a time I was less active in public work. On the retirement of Mrs. Annie Besant from the London School Board I had been asked to stand as candidate for the vacancy, but although I should have enjoyed the work, I decided not to accept this invitation. The next year, however, a new suffrage association, the Women's Franchise League, was formed, and I felt it my duty to become affiliated with it The League was preparing a new suffrage bill, the provisions of which I could not possibly approve, and I joined with old friends, among whom were Mrs. Jacob Bright, Mrs. Wolstentholm-Elmy, who was a member of the London School Board, and Mrs. Stanton Blatch, then resident in England, in an effort to substitute the original bill drafted by Dr. Pankhurst.

As a matter of fact, neither of the bills was introduced into Parliament that year. Mr. (now, 1914, Lord) Haldane, who had the measure in charge, introduced one of his own drafting. It was a truly startling bill, royally inclusive in its terms. It not only enfranchised all women, married and unmarried, of the householding classes, but it made them eligible to all offices under the Crown. The bill was never taken seriously by the government, and indeed it was never intended that it should be, as we were later made to understand. I remember going with Mrs. Stanton Blatch to the law courts to see Mr. Haldane, and to protest against the introduction of a measure that had not the remotest chance of passing.

"All, that bill," said Haldane, "is for the future."

All their woman suffrage bills are intended for the future, a future so remote as to be imperceptible. We were beginning to understand this even in 1891. However, as long as there was a bill, we determined to support it. Accordingly, we canvassed the members, distributed a great deal of literature, and organised and addressed meetings. We not only made speeches ourselves, but we induced friendly members of Parliament to go on our platforms. One of these meetings, held in an East End Radical club, was addressed by Mr. Haldane and a young man who accompanied him. This young man, Sir Edward Grey, then in the beginning of his career, made an eloquent plea for woman's suffrage. That Sir Edward Grey should, later in life, become a bitter foe of woman's suffrage need astonish no one. I have known many young Englishmen who began their political life as suffrage speakers and who later became anti-suffragists or traitorous "friends" of the cause. These young and aspiring statesmen have to attract attention in some fashion, and the espousal of advanced causes, such as labour or women's suffrage, seems an easy way to accomplish that end.

Well, our speeches and our agitation did nothing at all to assist Mr. Haldane's impossible bill. It never advanced beyond the first reading.

Our London residence came to an end in 1893. In that year we returned to our Manchester home, and I again took up the work of the Suffrage Society. At my suggestion the members began to organise their first out-of-door meetings, and we continued these until we succeeded in working up a great meeting that filled Free Trade Hall, and overflowed into and crowded a smaller hall near at hand. This marked the beginning of a campaign of propaganda among working people, an object which I had long desired to bring about.

And now began a new and, as I look back on it, an absorbingly interesting stage of my career. I have told how our leaders in the Liberal Party had advised the women to prove their fitness for the Parliamentary franchise by serving in municipal offices, especially the unsalaried offices. A large number of women had availed themselves of this advice, and were serving on Boards of Guardians, on school boards, and in other capacities. My children now being old enough for me to leave them with competent nurses, I was free to join these ranks. A year after my return to Manchester I became a candidate for the Board of Poor Law Guardians. Several weeks before, I had contested unsuccessfully for a place on the school board. This time, however, I was elected, heading the poll by a very large majority.

For the benefit of American readers I shall explain something of the operation of our English Poor Law. The duty of the law is to administer an act of Queen Elizabeth, one of the greatest reforms effected by that wise and humane monarch. When Elizabeth came to the throne she found England, the Merrie England of contemporary poets, in a state of appalling poverty. Hordes of people were literally starving to death, in wretched hovels, in the streets, and at the very gates of the palace. The cause of all this misery was the religious reformation under Henry VIII, and the secession from Rome of the English Church. King Henry, it is known, seized all the Church lands, the abbeys and the convents, and gave them as rewards to those nobles and favourites who had supported his policies. But in taking over the Church's property the Protestant nobles by no means assumed the Church's ancient responsibilities of lodging wayfarers, giving alms, nursing the sick, educating youths, and caring for the young and the superannuated. When the monks and the nuns were turned out of their convents these duties devolved on no one. The result, after the brief reign of Edward VI and the bloody one of Queen Mary, was the social anarchy inherited by Elizabeth.

This great queen and great woman, perceiving that the responsibility for the poor and the helpless rightfully rests on the community, caused an act to be passed creating in the parishes public bodies to deal with local conditions of poverty. The Board of Poor Law Guardians disburses for the poor the money coming from the Poor Rates (taxes), and some additional moneys allowed by the local government board, the president of which is a Cabinet Minister. Mr. John Burns is the present incumbent of the office. The Board of Guardians has control of the institution we call the workhouse. You have, I believe, almshouses, or poorhouses, but they are not quite so extensive as our workhouses, which are all kinds of institutions in one. We had, in my workhouse, a hospital with nine hundred beds, a school with several hundred children, a farm, and many workshops.

When I came into office I found that the law in our district, Chorlton, was being very harshly administered. The old board had been made up of the kind of men who are known as rate savers. They were guardians, not of the poor but of the rates, and, as I soon discovered, not very astute guardians even of money. For instance, although the inmates were being very poorly fed, a frightful waste of food was apparent. Each inmate was given each day a certain weight of food, and bread formed so much of the ration that hardly anyone consumed all of his portion. In the farm department pigs were kept on purpose to consume this surplus of bread, and as pigs do not thrive on a solid diet of stale bread the animals fetched in the market a much lower price than properly fed farm pigs. I suggested that, instead of giving a solid weight of bread in one lump, the loaf be cut in slices and buttered with margarine, each person being allowed all that he cared to eat. The rest of the board objected, saying that our poor charges were very jealous of their rights, and would suspect in such an innovation an attempt to deprive them of a part of their ration.

This was easily overcome by the suggestion that we consult the inmates before we made the change. Of course the poor people consented, and with the bread that we saved we made puddings with milk and currants, to be fed to the old people of the workhouse. These old folks I found sitting on backless forms, or benches. They had no privacy, no possessions, not even a locker. The old women were without pockets in their gowns, so they were obliged to keep any poor little treasures they had in their bosoms. Soon after I took office we gave the old people comfortable Windsor chairs to sit in, and in a number of ways we managed to make their existence more endurable.

These, after all, were minor benefits. But it does gratify me when I look back and remember what we were able to do for the children of the Manchester workhouse. The first time I went into the place I was horrified to see little girls seven and eight years old on their knees scrubbing the cold stones of the long corridors. These little girls were clad, summer and winter, in thin cotton frocks, low in the neck and short sleeved. At night they wore nothing at all, night dresses being considered too good for paupers. The fact that bronchitis was epidemic among them most of the time had not suggested to the guardians any change in the fashion of their clothes. There was a school for the children, but the teaching was of the poorest order. They were forlorn enough, these poor innocents, when I first met them. In five years' time we had changed the face of the earth for them. We had bought land in the country and had built a cottage system home for the children, and we had established for them a modern school with trained teachers. We had even secured for them a gymnasium and a swimming-bath. I may say that I was on the building committee of the board, the only woman member.

Whatever may be urged against the English Poor Law system, I maintain that under it no stigma of pauperism need be applied to workhouse children. If they are treated like paupers of course they will be paupers, and they will grow up paupers, permanent burdens on society; but if they are regarded merely as children under the guardianship of the state, they assume quite another character. Rich children are not pauperized by being sent to one or another of the free public schools with which England is blest. Yet a great many of those schools, now exclusively used for the education of upper middle-class boys, were founded by legacies left to educate the poor—girls as well as boys. The English Poor Law, properly administered, ought to give back to the children of the destitute what the upper classes have taken from them, a good education on a self-respecting basis.

The trouble is, as I soon perceived after taking office, the law cannot, in existing circumstances, do all the work, even for children, that it was intended to do. We shall have to have new laws, and it soon became apparent to me that we can never hope to get them until women have the vote. During the time I served on the board, and for years since then, women guardians all over the country have striven in vain to have the law reformed in order to ameliorate conditions which break the hearts of women to see, but which apparently affect men very little. I have spoken of the little girls I found scrubbing the workhouse floors. There were others at the hateful labour who aroused my keenest pity. I found that there were pregnant women in that workhouse, scrubbing floors, doing the hardest kind of work, almost until their babies came into the world. Many of them were unmarried women, very, very young, mere girls.

These poor mothers were allowed to stay in the hospital after confinement for a short two weeks. Then they had to make a choice of staying in the workhouse and earning their living by scrubbing and other work, in which case they were separated from their babies; or of taking their discharges. They could stay and be paupers, or they could leave—leave with a two-weeks-old baby in their arms, without hope, without home, without money, without anywhere to go. What became of those girls, and what became of their hapless infants? That question was at the basis of the women guardians' demand for a reform of one part of the Poor Law.

That section deals with the little children who are boarded out, not by the workhouse, but by the parents, that parent being almost always the mother. It is from that class of workhouse mothers—mostly young servant girls—which thoughtless people say all working girls ought to be; it is from that class more than from any other that cases of illegitimacy come. Those poor little servant girls, who can get out perhaps only in the evening, whose minds are not very cultivated, and who find all the sentiment of their lives in cheap novelettes, fall an easy prey to those who have designs against them. These are the people by whom the babies are mostly put out to nurse, and the mothers have to pay for their keep. Of course the babies are very badly protected.

The Poor Law Guardians are supposed to protect them by appointing inspectors to visit the homes where the babies are boarded.

But, under the law, if a man who ruins a girl pays down a lump sum of twenty pounds, less than a hundred dollars, the boarding home is immune from inspection. As long as a baby-farmer takes only one child at a time, the twenty pounds being paid, the inspectors cannot inspect the house. Of course the babies die with hideous promptness, often long before the twenty pounds have been spent, and then the baby-farmers are free to solicit another victim. For years, as I have said, women have tried in vain to get that one small reform of the Poor Law, to reach and protect all illegitimate children, and to make it impossible for any rich scoundrel to escape future liability for his child because of the lump sum he has paid down. Over and over again it has been tried, but it has always failed, because the ones who really care about the thing are mere women.

I thought I had been a suffragist before I became a Poor Law Guardian, but now I began to think about the vote in women's hands not only as a right but as a desperate necessity. These poor, unprotected mothers and their babies I am sure were potent factors in my education as a militant. In fact, all the women I came in contact with in the workhouse contributed to that education. Very soon after I went on the board I saw that the class of old women who came into the workhouse were in many ways superior to the kind of old men who came into the workhouse. One could not help noticing it. They were, to begin with, more industrious. In fact, it was quite touching to see their industry and patience. Old women, over sixty and seventy years of age, did most of the work of that place, most of the sewing, most of the things that kept the house clean and which supplied the inmates with clothing. I found that the old men were different. One could not get very much work out of them. They liked to stop in the oakum picking-room, where they were allowed to smoke; but as to real work, very little was done by our old men.

I began to make inquiries about these old women. I found that the majority of them were not women who had been dissolute, who had been criminal, but women who had lead perfectly respectable lives, either as wives and mothers, or as single women earning their own living. A great many were of the domestic-servant class, who had not married, who had lost their employment, and had reached a time of life when it was impossible to get more employment. It was through no fault of their own, but simply because they had never earned enough to save. The average wage of working women in England is less than two dollars a week. On this pittance it is difficult enough to keep alive, and of course it is impossible to save. Every one who knows anything about conditions under which our working women live knows that few of them can ever hope to put by enough to keep them in old age. Besides, the average working woman has to support others than herself. How can she save?

Some of our old women were married. Many of them, I found, were widows of skilled artisans who had had pensions from their unions, but the pensions had died with the men. These women, who had given up the power to work for themselves, and had devoted themselves to working for their husbands and children, were left penniless. There was nothing for them to do but to go into the workhouse. Many of them were widows of men who had served their country in the army or the navy. The men had had pensions from the government, but the pensions had died with them, and so the women were in the workhouse.

We shall not in future, I hope, find so many respectable old women in English workhouses. We have an old-age pension law now, which allows old women as well as old men the sum of five shillings—$1.20—a week; hardly enough to live on, but enough to enable the poor to keep their old fathers and mothers out of the workhouse without starving themselves or their children. But when I was a Poor Law Guardian there was simply nothing to do with a woman when her life of toil ceased except make a pauper of her.

I wish I had space to tell you of other tragedies of women I witnessed while I was on that board. In our out-relief department, which exists chiefly for able-bodied poor and dependent persons, I was brought into contact with widows who were struggling desperately to keep their homes and families together. The law allowed these women relief of a certain very inadequate kind, but for herself and one child it offered no relief except the workhouse. Even if the woman had a baby at her breast she was regarded, under the law, as an able-bodied man. Women, we are told, should stay at home and take care of their children. I used to astound my men colleagues by saying to them: "When women have the vote they will see that mothers *can* stay at home and care for their children. You men have made it impossible for these mothers to do that."

I am convinced that the enfranchised woman will find many ways in which to lessen, at least, the curse of poverty. Women have more practical ideas about relief, and especially of prevention of dire poverty, than men display. I was struck with this whenever I attended the District Conferences and the annual Poor Law Union Meetings. In our discussions the women showed themselves much more capable, much more resourceful, than the men. I remember two papers which I prepared and which caused considerable discussion. One of these was on the Duties of Guardians in Times of Unemployment, in which I pointed out that the government had one reserve of employment for men which could always be used. We have, on our northwest coast, a constant washing away of the fore shore. Every once in a while the question of coast reclamation comes up for discussion, but I had never heard any man suggest coast reclamation as a means of giving the unemployed relief.

In 1898 I suffered an irreparable loss in the death of my husband. His death occurred suddenly and left me with the heavy responsibility of caring for a family of children, the eldest only seventeen years of age. I resigned my place on the Board of Guardians, and was almost immediately appointed to the salaried office of Registrar of Births and Deaths in Manchester. We have registrars of births, deaths and marriages in England, but since the act establishing the last named contains the words "male person," a woman may not be appointed a registrar of marriages. The head of this department of the government is the registrar-general, with offices at Somerset House, London, where all vital statistics are returned and all records filed.

It was my duty as registrar of births and deaths to act as chief census officer of my district; I was obliged to receive all returns of births and deaths, record them, and send my books quarterly to the office of the registrar-general. My district was in a working-class quarter, and on this account I instituted evening office hours twice a week. It was touching to observe how glad the women were to have a woman registrar to go to. They used to tell me their stories, dreadful stories some of them, and all of them pathetic with that patient and uncomplaining pathos of poverty. Even after my experience on the Board of Guardians, I was shocked to be reminded over and over again of the little respect there was in the world for women and children. I have had little girls of thirteen come to my office to register the births of their babies, illegitimate, of course. In many of these cases I found that the child's own father or some near male relative was responsible for her state.

There was nothing that could be done in most cases. The age of consent in England is sixteen years, but a man can always claim that he thought the girl was over sixteen. During my term of office a very young mother of an illegitimate child exposed her baby, and it died. The girl was tried for murder and was sentenced to death. This was afterwards commuted, it is true, but the unhappy child had the horrible experience of the trial and the sentence "to be hanged by the neck, until you are dead." The wretch who was, from the point of view of justice, the real murderer of the baby, received no punishment at all.

I needed only one more experience after this one, only one more contact with the life of my time and the position of women, to convince me that if civilisation is to advance at all in the future, it must be through the help of women, women freed of their political shackles, women with full power to work their will in society. In 1900 I was asked to stand as a candidate for the Manchester School Board. The schools were then under the old law, and the school boards were very active bodies. They administered the Elementary Education Act, bought school sites, erected buildings, employed and paid teachers. The school code and the curriculum were framed by the Board of Education, which is part of the central government. Of course this was absurd. A body of men in London could not possibly realise all the needs of boys and girls in remote parts of England. But so it was.

As a member of the school board I very soon found that the teachers, working people of the higher grade, were in exactly the same position as the working people of the lower grades. That is, the men had all the advantage. Teachers had a representative in the school board councils. Of course that representative was a man teacher, and equally of course, he gave preference to the interests of the men teachers. Men teachers received much higher salaries than the women, although many of the women, in addition to their regular class work, had to teach sewing and domestic science into the bargain. They received no extra pay for their extra work.

In spite of this added burden, and in spite of the lower salaries received, I found that the women cared a great deal more about their work, and a great deal more about the children than the men. It was a winter when there was a great deal of poverty and unemployment in Manchester. I found that the women teachers were spending their slender salaries to provide regular dinners for destitute children, and were giving up their time to waiting on them and seeing that they were nourished. They said to me, quite simply:

"You see, the little things are too badly off to study their lessons. We have to feed them before we can teach them."

Well, instead of seeing that women care more for schools and school children than men do and should therefore have more power in education, the Parliament of 1900 actually passed a law which took education in England entirely out of the hands of women. This law abolished the school board altogether and placed the administration of schools in the hands of the municipalities. Certain corporations had formerly made certain grants to technical education—Manchester had built a magnificent technical college—and now the corporations had full control of both elementary and secondary education.

The law did indeed provide that the corporations should co-opt at least one woman on their education boards. Manchester co-opted four women, and at the strong recommendation of the Labour Party, I was one of the women chosen. At their urgent solicitation I was appointed to the Committee on Technical Instruction, the one woman admitted to this committee. I learned that the Manchester Technical College, called the second best in Europe, spending thousands of pounds annually for technical training, had practically no provision for training women. Even in classes where they might easily have been admitted, bakery and confectionery classes and the like, the girls were kept out because the men's trades unions objected to their being educated for such skilled work. It was rapidly becoming clear to my mind that men regarded women as a servant class in the community, and that women were going to remain in the servant class until they lifted themselves out of it. I asked myself many times in those days what was to be done. I had joined the Labour Party, thinking that through its councils something vital might come, some such demand for the women's enfranchisement that the politicians could not possibly ignore. Nothing came.

All these years my daughters had been growing up. All their lives they had been interested in women's suffrage. Christabel and Sylvia, as little girls, had cried to be taken to meetings. They had helped in our drawing-room meetings in every way that children can help. As they grew older we used to talk together about the suffrage, and I was sometimes rather frightened by their youthful confidence in the prospect, which they considered certain, of the success of the movement. One day Christabel startled me with the remark: "How long you women have been trying for the vote. For my part, I mean to get it."

Was there, I reflected, any difference between trying for the vote and getting it? There is an old French proverb, "*If youth could know; if age could do.*" It occurred to me that if the older suffrage workers could in some way join hands with the young, unwearied and resourceful suffragists, the movement might wake up to new life and new possibilities. After that I and my daughters together sought a way to bring about that union of young and old which would find new methods, blaze new trails. At length we thought we had found a way.

Chapter 3

In the summer of 1902—I think it was 1902—Susan B. Anthony paid a visit to Manchester, and that visit was one of the contributory causes that led to the founding of our militant suffrage organisation, the Women's Social and Political Union. During Miss Anthony's visit my daughter Christabel, who was very deeply impressed, wrote an article for the Manchester papers on the life and works of the venerable reformer. After her departure Christabel spoke often of her, and always with sorrow and indignation that such a splendid worker for humanity was destined to die without seeing the hopes of her lifetime realised. My daughter declared:

> It is unendurable to think of another generation of women wasting their lives begging for the vote. We must not lose any more time. We must act.

By this time the Labour Party, of which I was still a member, had returned Mr. Keir Hardie to Parliament, and we decided that the first step in a campaign of action was to make the Labour Party responsible for a new suffrage bill. At a recent annual conference of the party I had moved a resolution calling upon the members to instruct their own member of Parliament to introduce a bill for the enfranchisement of women. The resolution was passed, and we determined to organise a society of women to demand immediate enfranchisement, not by means of any outworn missionary methods, but through political action.

It was in October, 1903, that I invited a number of women to my house in Nelson street, Manchester, for purposes of organisation. We voted to call our new society the Women's Social and Political Union, partly to emphasise its democracy, and partly to define its object as political rather than propagandist. We resolved to limit our membership exclusively to women, to keep ourselves absolutely free from any party affiliation, and to be satisfied with nothing but action on our question. *Deeds, not words*, was to be our permanent motto.

To such a pass had the women's suffrage cause come in my country that the old leaders, who had done such fine educational work in the past, were now seemingly content with expressions of sympathy and regret on the part of hypocritical politicians. This fact was thrust upon me anew by an incident that occurred almost at the moment of the founding of the Women's Social and Political Union. In our Parliament no bill has a chance of becoming a law unless it is made a government measure. Private members are at liberty to introduce measures of their own, but these rarely reach the second reading, or debatable stage. So much time is given to discussion of government measures that very little time can be given to any private bills. About one day in a week is given over to consideration of private measures, to which, as we say, the government give facilities; and since there are a limited number of weeks in a session, the members, on the opening days of Parliament, meet and draw lots to determine who shall have a place in the debates. Only these successful men have a chance to speak to their bills, and only those who have drawn early chances have any prospect of getting much discussion on their measures.

Now, the old suffragists had long since given up hope of obtaining a government suffrage bill, but they clung to a hope that a private member's bill would some time obtain consideration. Every year, on the opening day of Parliament, the association sent a deputation of women to the House of Commons, to meet so-called friendly members and consider the position of the women's suffrage cause. The ceremony was of a most conventional, not to say farcical character. The ladies made their speeches and the members made theirs. The ladies thanked the friendly members for their sympathy, and the members renewed their assurances that they believed in women's suffrage and would vote for it when they had an opportunity to do so. Then the deputation, a trifle sad but entirely tranquil, took its departure, and the members resumed the real business of life, which was support of their party's policies.

Such a ceremony as this I attended soon after the founding of the W. S. P. U. Sir Charles M'Laren was the friendly member who presided over the gathering, and he did his full duty in the matter of formally endorsing the cause of women's suffrage. He assured the delegation of his deep regret, as well as the regret of numbers of his colleagues, that women so intelligent, so devoted, etc., should remain unenfranchised. Other members did likewise. The ceremonies drew to a close, but I, who had not been asked to speak, determined to add something to the occasion.

I began abruptly:

Sir Charles M'Laren has told us that numbers of his colleagues desire the success of the women's suffrage cause. Now every one of us knows that at this moment the members of the House of Commons are balloting for a place in the debates. Will Sir Charles M'Laren tell us if any member is preparing to introduce a bill for women's suffrage? Will he tell us what he and the other members will pledge themselves to *do* for the reform they so warmly endorse?

Of course, the embarrassed Sir Charles was not prepared to tell us anything of the kind, and the deputation departed in confusion and wrath. I was told that I was an interloper, an impertinent intruder. Who asked me to say anything? And what right had I to step in and ruin the good impression they had made? No one could tell how many friendly members I had alienated by my unfortunate remarks.

I went back to Manchester and with renewed energy continued the work of organising for the W. S. P. U.

In the spring of 1904 I went to the annual conference of the Independent Labour Party, determined if possible to induce the members to prepare a suffrage bill to be laid before Parliament in the approaching session. Although I was a member of the National Administrative Council and presumably a person holding some influence in the party, I knew that my plan would be bitterly opposed by a strong minority, who held that the Labour Party should direct all its efforts toward securing universal adult suffrage for both men and women. Theoretically, of course, a Labour party could not be satisfied with anything less than universal adult suffrage, but it was clear that no such sweeping reform could be effected at that time, unless indeed the government made it one of their measures. Besides, while a large majority of members of the House of Commons were pledged to support a bill giving women equal franchise rights with men, it was doubtful whether a majority could be relied upon to support a bill giving adult suffrage, even to men. Such a bill, even if it were a government measure, would probably be difficult of passage.

After considerable discussion, the National Council decided to adopt the original Women's Enfranchisement Bill, drafted by Dr. Pankhurst, and advanced in 1870 to its second reading in the House of Commons. The Council's decision was approved by an overwhelming majority of the conference.

The new session of Parliament, so eagerly looked forward to, met on February 13, 1905. I went down from Manchester, and with my daughter Sylvia, then a student at the Royal College of Art, South Kensington, spent eight days in the Strangers' Lobby of the House of Commons, working for the suffrage bill. We interviewed every one of the members who had pledged themselves to support a suffrage bill when it should be introduced, but we found not one single member who would agree that his chance in the ballot, if he drew such a chance, should be given to introducing the bill. Every man had some other measure he was anxious to further. Mr. Keir Hardie had previously given us his pledge, but his name, as we had feared, was not drawn in the ballot. We next set out to interview all the men whose names had been drawn, and we finally induced Mr. Bamford Slack, who held the fourteenth place, to introduce our bill. The fourteenth place was not a good one, but it served, and the second reading of our bill was set down for Friday, May 12th, the second order of the day.

This being the first suffrage bill in eight years, a thrill of excitement animated not only our ranks but all the old suffrage societies. Meetings were held, and a large number of petitions circulated. When the day came for consideration on our bill, the Strangers' Lobby could not hold the enormous gathering of women of all classes, rich and poor, who flocked to the House of Commons. It was pitiful to see the look of hope and joy that shone on the faces of many of these women. We knew that our poor little measure had the very slightest chance of being passed.

The bill that occupied the first order of the day was one providing that carts travelling along public roads at night should carry a light behind as well as before. We had tried to induce the promoters of this unimportant little measure to withdraw it in the interests of our bill, but they refused. We had tried also to persuade the Conservative Government to give our bill facilities for full discussion, but they also refused. So, as we fully anticipated, the promoters of the Roadway Lighting Bill were allowed to "talk out" our bill. They did this by spinning out the debate with silly stories and foolish jokes. The members listened to the insulting performance with laughter and applause.

When news of what was happening reached the women who waited in the Strangers' Lobby, a feeling of wild excitement and indignation took possession of the throng. Seeing their temper, I felt that the moment had come for a demonstration such as no old-fashioned suffragist had ever attempted. I called upon the women to follow me outside for a meeting of protest against the government. We swarmed out into the open, and Mrs. Wolstenholm-Elmy, one of the oldest suffrage workers in England, began to speak. Instantly the police rushed into the crowd of women, pushing them about and ordering them to disperse. We moved on as far as the great statue of Richard Cœur de Lion that guards the entrance to the House of Lords, but again the police intervened. Finally the police agreed to let us hold a meeting in Broad Sanctuary, very near the gates of Westminster Abbey. Here we made speeches and adopted a resolution condemning the government's action in allowing a small minority to talk out our bill. This was the first militant act of the W. S. P. U. It caused comment and even some alarm, but the police contented themselves with taking our names.

The ensuing summer was spent in outdoor work. By this time the Women's Social and Political Union had acquired some valuable accessions, and money began to come to us. Among our new members was one who was destined to play an important *rôle* in the unfolding drama of the militant movement. At the close of one of our meetings at Oldham a young girl introduced herself to me as Annie Kenney, a mill-worker, and a strong suffrage sympathiser. She wanted to know more of our society and its objects, and I invited her and her sister Jenny, a Board School teacher, to tea the next day. They came and joined our Union, a step that definitely changed the whole course of Miss Kenney's life, and gave us one of our most distinguished leaders and organisers. With her help we began to carry our propaganda to an entirely new public.

In Lancashire there is an institution known as the Wakes, a sort of travelling fair where they have merry-go-rounds, Aunt-Sallies, and other festive games, side-shows of various kinds, and booths where all kinds of things are sold. Every little village has its Wakes-week during the summer and autumn, and it is the custom for the inhabitants of the villages to spend the Sunday before the opening of the Wakes walking among the booths in anticipation of tomorrow's joys. On these occasions the Salvation Army, temperance orators, venders of quack medicines, pedlars, and others, take advantage of the ready-made audience to advance their propaganda. At Annie Kenney's suggestion we went from one village to the other, following the Wakes and making suffrage speeches. We soon rivalled in popularity the Salvation Army, and even the tooth-drawers and patent-medicine pedlars.

The Women's Social and Political Union had been in existence two years before any opportunity was presented for work on a national scale. The autumn of 1905 brought a political situation which seemed to us to promise bright hopes for women's enfranchisement. The life of the old Parliament, dominated for nearly twenty years by the Conservative Party, was drawing to an end, and the country was on the eve of a general election in which the Liberals hoped to be returned to power. Quite naturally the Liberal candidates went to the country with perfervid promises of reform in every possible direction. They appealed to the voters to return them, as advocates and upholders of true democracy, and they promised that there should be a government united in favour of people's rights against the powers of a privileged aristocracy.

Now repeated experiences had taught us that the only way to attain women's suffrage was to commit a government to it. In other words, pledges of support from candidates were plainly useless. They were not worth having. The only object worth trying for was pledges from responsible leaders that the new government would make women's suffrage a part of the official programme. We determined to address ourselves to those men who were likely to be in the Liberal Cabinet, demanding to know whether their reforms were going to include justice to women.

We laid our plans to begin this work at a great meeting to be held in Free Trade Hall, Manchester, with Sir Edward Grey as the principal speaker. We intended to get seats in the gallery, directly facing the platform and we made for the occasion a large banner with the words: "Will the Liberal Party Give Votes for Women?" We were to let this banner down over the gallery rails at the moment when our speaker rose to put the question to Sir Edward Grey. At the last moment, however, we had to alter the plan because it was impossible to get the gallery seats we wanted. There was no way in which we could use our large banner, so, late in the afternoon on the day of the meeting, we cut out and made a small banner with the three-word inscription: "Votes for Women." Thus, quite accidentally, there came into existence the present slogan of the suffrage movement around the world.

Annie Kenney and my daughter Christabel were charged with the mission of questioning Sir Edward Grey. They sat quietly through the meeting, at the close of which questions were invited. Several questions were asked by men and were courteously answered. Then Annie Kenney arose and asked: "If the Liberal party is returned to power, will they take steps to give votes for women?" At the same time Christabel held aloft the little banner that every one in the hall might understand the nature of the question. Sir Edward Grey returned no answer to Annie's question, and the men sitting near her forced her rudely into her seat, while a steward of the meeting pressed his hat over her face. A babel of shouts, cries and catcalls sounded from all over the hall.

As soon as order was restored Christabel stood up and repeated the question: "Will the Liberal Government, if returned, give votes to women?" Again Sir Edward Grey ignored the question, and again a perfect tumult of shouts and angry cries arose. Mr. William Peacock, chief constable of Manchester, left the platform and came down to the women, asking them to write their question, which he promised to hand to the speaker. They wrote:

> Will the Liberal Government give votes to working-women? Signed, on behalf of the Women's Social and Political Union, Annie Kenney, member of the Oldham committee of the card- and blowing-room operatives.

They added a line to say that, as one of 96,000 organised women textile-workers, Annie Kenney earnestly desired an answer to the question.

Mr. Peacock kept his word and handed the question to Sir Edward Grey, who read it, smiled, and passed it to the others on the platform. They also read it with smiles, but no answer to the question was made. Only one lady who was sitting on the platform tried to say something, but the chairman interrupted by asking Lord Durham to move a vote of thanks to the speaker. Mr. Winston Churchill seconded the motion, Sir Edward Grey replied briefly, and the meeting began to break up. Annie Kenney stood up in her chair and cried out over the noise of shuffling feet and murmurs of conversation: "Will the Liberal Government give votes to women?"

Then the audience became a mob. They howled, they shouted and roared, shaking their fists fiercely at the woman who dared to intrude her question into a man's meeting. Hands were lifted to drag her out of her chair, but Christabel threw one arm about her as she stood, and with the other arm warded off the mob, who struck and scratched at her until her sleeve was red with blood. Still the girls held together and shouted over and over: "The question! The question! Answer the question!"

Six men, stewards of the meeting, seized Christabel and dragged her down the aisle, past the platform, other men following with Annie Kenney, both girls still calling for an answer to their question. On the platform the Liberal leaders sat silent and unmoved while this disgraceful scene was taking place, and the mob were shouting and shrieking from the floor.

Flung into the streets, the two girls staggered to their feet and began to address the crowds, and to tell them what had taken place in a Liberal meeting. Within five minutes they were arrested on a charge of obstruction and, in Christabel's case, of assaulting the police. Both were summonsed to appear next morning in a police court, where, after a trial which was a mere farce, Annie Kenney was sentenced to pay a fine of five shillings, with an alternative of three days in prison, and Christabel Pankhurst was given a fine of ten shillings or a jail sentence of one week.

Both girls promptly chose the prison sentence. As soon as they left the court-room I hurried around to the room where they were waiting, and I said to my daughter:

"You have done everything you could be expected to do in this matter. I think you should let me pay your fines and take you home."

Without waiting for Annie Kenney to speak, my daughter exclaimed:

"Mother, if you pay my fine I will never go home."

Before going to the meeting she had said, "We will get our question answered or sleep in prison tonight." I now knew her courage remained unshaken.

Of course the affair created a tremendous sensation, not only in Manchester, where my husband had been so well known and where I had so long held public office, but all over England. The comments of the press were almost unanimously bitter. Ignoring the perfectly well-established fact that men in every political meeting ask questions and demand answers of the speakers, the newspapers treated the action of the two girls as something quite unprecedented and outrageous. They generally agreed that great leniency had been shown them. Fines and jail-sentences were too good for such unsexed creatures. "The discipline of the nursery" would have been far more appropriate. One Birmingham paper declared that "if any argument were required against giving ladies political status and power it had been furnished in Manchester." Newspapers which had heretofore ignored the whole subject now hinted that while they had formerly been in favour of women's suffrage, they could no longer countenance it. The Manchester incident, it was said, had set the cause back, perhaps irrevocably.

This is how it set the cause back. Scores of people wrote to the newspapers expressing sympathy with the women. The wife of Sir Edward Grey told her friends that she considered them quite justified in the means they had taken. It was stated that Winston Churchill, nervous about his own candidacy in Manchester, visited Strangeways Gaol, where the two girls were imprisoned, and vainly begged the governor to allow him to pay their fines. On October 20, when the prisoners were released, they were given an immense demonstration in Free-Trade Hall, the very hall from which they had been ejected the week before. The Women's Social and Political Union received a large number of new members. Above all, the question of women's suffrage became at once a live topic of comment from one end of Great Britain to the other.

We determined that from that time on the little "Votes For Women" banners should appear wherever a prospective member of the Liberal Government rose to speak, and that there should be no more peace until the women's question was answered. We clearly perceived that the new government, calling themselves Liberal, were reactionary so far as women were concerned, that they were hostile to women's suffrage, and would have to be fought until they were conquered, or else driven from office.

We did not begin to fight, however, until we had given the new government every chance to give us the pledge we wanted. Early in December the Conservative Government had gone out, and Sir Henry Campbell-Bannerman, the Liberal leader, had formed a new Cabinet. On December 21 a great meeting was held in Royal Albert Hall, London, where Sir Henry, surrounded by his cabinet, made his first utterance as prime minister. Previous to the meeting we wrote to Sir Henry and asked him, in the name of the Women's Social and Political Union, whether the Liberal Government would give women the vote. We added that our representatives would be present at the meeting, and we hoped that the prime minister would publicly answer the question. Otherwise we should be obliged publicly to protest against his silence.

Of course Sir Henry Campbell-Bannerman returned no reply, nor did his speech contain any allusion to women's suffrage. So, at the conclusion, Annie Kenney, whom we had smuggled into the hall in disguise, whipped out her little white calico banner, and called out in her clear, sweet voice: "Will the Liberal Government give women the vote?"

At the same moment Theresa Billington let drop from a seat directly above the platform a huge banner with the words: "Will the Liberal Government give justice to working-women?" Just for a moment there was a gasping silence, the people waiting to see what the Cabinet Ministers would do. They did nothing. Then, in the midst of uproar and conflicting shouts, the women were seized and flung out of the hall.

This was the beginning of a campaign the like of which was never known in England, or, for that matter, in any other country. If we had been strong enough we should have opposed the election of every Liberal candidate, but being limited both in funds and in members we concentrated on one member of the government, Mr. Winston Churchill. Not that we had any animus against Mr. Churchill. We chose him simply because he was the only important candidate standing for constituencies within reach of our headquarters. We attended every meeting addressed by Mr. Churchill. We heckled him unmercifully; we spoiled his best points by flinging back such obvious retorts that the crowds roared with laughter. We lifted out little white banners from unexpected corners of the hall, exactly at the moment when an interruption was least desired. Sometimes our banners were torn from our hands and trodden under foot. Sometimes, again, the crowds were with us, and we actually broke up the meeting. We did not succeed in defeating Mr. Churchill, but he was returned by a very small majority, the smallest of any of the Manchester Liberal candidates.

We did not confine our efforts to heckling Mr. Churchill. Throughout the campaign we kept up the work of questioning Cabinet Ministers at meetings all over England and Scotland. At Sun Hall, Liverpool, addressed by the Prime Minister, nine women in succession asked the important question, and were thrown out of the hall; this in the face of the fact that Sir Campbell-Bannerman was an avowed suffragist. But we were not questioning him as to his private opinions on the suffrage; we were asking him what his government were willing to do about suffrage. We questioned Mr. Asquith in Sheffield, Mr. Lloyd-George in Altrincham, Cheshire, the prime minister again in Glasgow, and we interrupted a great many other meetings as well. Always we were violently thrown out and insulted. Often we were painfully bruised and hurt.

What good did it do? We have often been asked that question, even by the women our actions spurred into an activity they had never before thought themselves capable of. For one thing, our heckling campaign made women's suffrage a matter of news—it had never been that before. Now the newspapers were full of us. For another thing, we woke up the old suffrage associations. During the general election various groups of non-militant suffragists came back to life and organised a gigantic manifesto in favour of action from the Liberal Government. Among others, the manifesto was signed by the Women's Co-operative Guild with nearly 21,000 members; the Women's Liberal Federation, with 76,000 members; the Scottish Women's Liberal Federation, with 15,000 members; the North-of-England Weavers' Association, with 100,000 members; the British Women's Temperance Association, with nearly 110,000 members; and the Independent Labour Party with 20,000 members. Surely it was something to have inspired all this activity.

We decided that the next step must be to carry the fight to London, and Annie Kenney was chosen to be organiser there. With only two pounds, less than ten dollars, in her pocket the intrepid girl set forth on her mission. In about a fortnight I left my official work as registrar in the hands of a deputy and went down to London to see what had been accomplished. To my astonishment I found that Annie, working with my daughter Sylvia, had organised a procession of women and a demonstration to be held on the opening day of Parliament. The confident young things had actually engaged Caxton Hall, Westminster; they had had printed a large number of handbills to announce the meeting, and they were busily engaged in working up the demonstration. Mrs. Drummond, who had joined the Union shortly after the imprisonment of Annie Kenney and Christabel, sent word from Manchester that she was coming to help us. She had to borrow the money for her railroad-fare, but she came, and, as ever before and since, her help was invaluable.

How we worked, distributing handbills, chalking announcements of the meeting on pavements, calling on every person we knew and on a great many more we knew only by name, canvassing from door to door!

At length the opening day of Parliament arrived. On February 19, 1906, occurred the first suffrage procession in London. I think there were between three and four hundred women in that procession, poor working-women from the East End, for the most part, leading the way in which numberless women of every rank were afterward to follow. My eyes were misty with tears as I saw them, standing in line, holding the simple banners which my daughter Sylvia had decorated, waiting for the word of command. Of course our procession attracted a large crowd of intensely amused spectators. The police, however, made no attempt to disperse our ranks, but merely ordered us to furl our banners. There was no reason why we should not have carried banners but the fact that we were women, and therefore could be bullied. So, bannerless, the procession entered Caxton Hall. To my amazement it was filled with women, most of whom I had never seen at any suffrage gathering before.

Our meeting was most enthusiastic, and while Annie Kenney was speaking, to frequent applause, the news came to me that the King's speech (which is not the king's at all, but the formally announced government programme for the session) had been read, and that there was in it no mention of the women's suffrage question. As Annie took her seat I arose and made this announcement, and I moved a resolution that the meeting should at once proceed to the House of Commons to urge the members to introduce a suffrage measure.

The resolution was carried, and we rushed out in a body and hurried toward the Strangers' Entrance. It was pouring rain and bitterly cold, yet no one turned back, even when we learned at the entrance that for the first time in memory the doors of the House of Commons were barred to women. We sent in our cards to members who were personal friends, and some of them came out and urged our admittance. The police, however, were obdurate. They had their orders. The Liberal government, advocates of the people's rights, had given orders that women should no longer set foot in their stronghold.

Pressure from members proved too great, and the government relented to the extent of allowing twenty women at a time to enter the lobby. Through all the rain and cold those hundreds of women waited for hours their turn to enter. Some never got in, and for those of us who did there was small satisfaction. Not a member could be persuaded to take up our cause.

Out of the disappointment and dejection of that experience I yet reaped a richer harvest of happiness than I had ever known before. Those women had followed me to the House of Commons. They had defied the police. They were awake at last. They were prepared to do something that women had never done before—fight for themselves. Women had always fought for men, and for their children. Now they were ready to fight for their own human rights. Our militant movement was established.

Chapter 4

To account for the phenomenal growth of the Women's Social

and Political Union after it was established in London, to explain why it made such an instant appeal to women hitherto indifferent, I shall have to point out exactly wherein our society differs from all other suffrage associations. In the first place, our members are absolutely single minded; they concentrate all their forces on one object, political equality with men. No member of the W. S. P. U. divides her attention between suffrage and other social reforms. We hold that both reason and justice dictate that women shall have a share in reforming the evils that afflict society, especially those evils bearing directly on women themselves. Therefore, we demand, before any other legislation whatever, the elementary justice of votes for women.

There is not the slightest doubt that the women of Great Britain would have been enfranchised years ago had all the suffragists adopted this simple principle. They never did, and even today, (1914), many English women refuse to adopt it. They are party members first and suffragists afterward; or they are suffragists part of the time and social theorists the rest of the time. We further differ from other suffrage associations, or from others existing in 1906, in that we clearly perceived the political situation that solidly interposed between us and our enfranchisement.

For seven years we had had a majority in the House of Commons pledged to vote favourably on a suffrage bill. The year before, they had voted favourably on one, yet that bill did not become law. Why? Because even an overwhelming majority of private members are powerless to enact law in the face of a hostile government of eleven Cabinet Ministers. The private member of Parliament was once possessed of individual power and responsibility, but Parliamentary usage and a changed conception of statesmanship have gradually lessened the functions of members. At the present time their powers, for all practical purposes, are limited to helping to enact such measures as the government introduces or, in rare instances, private measures approved by the government. It is true that the House can revolt, can, by voting a lack of confidence in the government, force them to resign. But that almost never happens, and it is less likely now than formerly to happen. Figureheads don't revolt.

This, then, was our situation: the government all-powerful and consistently hostile; the rank and file of legislators impotent; the country apathetic; the women divided in their interests. The Women's Social and Political Union was established to meet this situation, and to overcome it. Moreover we had a policy which, if persisted in long enough, could not possibly fail to overcome it. Do you wonder that we gained new members at every meeting we held?

There was little formality about joining the Union. Any woman could become a member by paying a shilling, but at the same time she was required to sign a declaration of loyal adherence to our policy and a pledge not to work for any political party until the women's vote was won. This is still our inflexible custom. Moreover, if at any time a member, or a group of members, loses faith in our policy; if anyone begins to suggest, that some other policy ought to be substituted, or if she tries to confuse the issue by adding other policies, she ceases at once to be a member. Autocratic? Quite so. But, you may object, a suffrage organisation ought to be democratic.

Well the members of the W. S. P. U. do not agree with you. We do not believe in the effectiveness of the ordinary suffrage organisation. The W. S. P. U. is not hampered by a complexity of rules. We have no constitution and by-laws; nothing to be amended or tinkered with or quarrelled over at an annual meeting. In fact, we have no annual meeting, no business sessions, no elections of officers. The W. S. P. U. is simply a suffrage army in the field. It is purely a volunteer army, and no one is obliged to remain in it. Indeed we don't want anybody to remain in it who does not ardently believe in the policy of the army.

The foundation of our policy is opposition to a government who refuse votes to women. To support by word or deed a government hostile to woman suffrage is simply to invite them to go on being hostile. We oppose the Liberal party because it is in power. We would oppose a Unionist government if it were in power and were opposed to woman suffrage. We say to women that as long as they remain in the ranks of the Liberal party they give their tacit approval to the government's anti-suffrage policy. We say to members of Parliament that as long as they support any of the government's policies they give their tacit approval to the anti-suffrage policy. We call upon all sincere suffragists to leave the Liberal party until women are given votes on equal terms with men. We call upon all voters to vote against Liberal candidates until the Liberal Government does justice to women.

We did not invent this policy. It was most successfully pursued by Mr. Parnell in his Home Rule struggle more than thirty-five years ago. Anyone who is old enough to remember the stirring days of Parnell may recall how, in 1885, the Home Rulers, by persistently voting against the government in the House of Commons, forced the resignation of Mr. Gladstone and his Cabinet. In the general election which followed, the Liberal party was again returned to power, but by the slender majority of eighty-four, the Home Rulers having fought every Liberal candidate, even those, who, like my husband, were enthusiastic believers in Home Rule. In order to control the House and keep his leadership, Mr. Gladstone was obliged to bring in a Government Home Rule Bill. The downfall, through private intrigue, and the subsequent death of Parnell prevented the bill from becoming law. For many years afterward the Irish Nationalists had no leader strong enough to carry on Parnell's anti-government policy, but within late years it was resumed by Mr. James Redmond, with the result that the Commons passed a Home Rule Bill.

The contention of the old-fashioned suffragists, and of the politicians as well, has always been that an educated public opinion will ultimately give votes to women without any great force being exerted in behalf of the reform. We agree that public opinion must be educated, but we contend that even an educated public opinion is useless unless it is vigorously utilised. The keenest weapon is powerless unless it is courageously wielded. In the year 1906 there was an immensely large public opinion in favour of woman suffrage. But what good did that do the cause? We called upon the public for a great deal more than sympathy. We called upon it to demand of the government to yield to public opinion and give women votes. And we declared that we would wage war, not only on all anti-suffrage forces, but on all neutral and non-active forces. Every man with a vote was considered a foe to woman suffrage unless he was prepared to be actively a friend.

Not that we believed that the campaign of education ought to be given up. On the contrary, we knew that education must go on, and in much more vigorous fashion than ever before. The first thing we did was to enter upon a sensational campaign to arouse the public to the importance of woman suffrage, and to interest it in our plans for forcing the government's hands. I think we can claim that our success in this regard was instant, and that it has proved permanent. From the very first, in those early London days, when we were few in numbers and very poor in purse, we made the public aware of the woman suffrage movement as it had never been before. We adopted Salvation Army methods and went out into the highways and the byways after converts. We threw away all our conventional notions of what was "ladylike" and "good form," and we applied to our methods the one test question, Will it help? Just as the Booths and their followers took religion to the street crowds in such fashion that the church people were horrified, so we took suffrage to the general public in a manner that amazed and scandalised the other suffragists.

We had a lot of suffrage literature printed, and day by day our members went forth and held street meetings. Selecting a favourable spot, with a chair for a rostrum, one of us would ring a bell until people began to stop to see what was going to happen. What happened, of course, was a lively suffrage speech, and the distribution of literature. Soon after our campaign had started, the sound of the bell was a signal for a crowd to spring up as if by magic. All over the neighbourhood you heard the cry: "Here are the Suffragettes! Come on!" We covered London in this way; we never lacked an audience, and best of all, an audience to which the woman-suffrage doctrine was new. We were increasing our favourable public as well as waking it up. Besides these street meetings, we held many hall and drawing-room meetings, and we got a great deal of press publicity, which was something never accorded the older suffrage methods.

Our plans included the introduction of a government suffrage bill at the earliest possible moment, and in the spring of 1906 we sent a deputation of about thirty of our members to interview the prime minister, Sir Henry Campbell-Bannerman. The prime minister, it was stated, was not at home; so in a few days we sent another deputation. This time the servant agreed to carry our request to the prime minister. The women waited patiently on the doorstep of the official residence, No. 10 Downing Street, for nearly an hour. Then the door opened and two men appeared. One of the men addressed the leader of the deputation, roughly ordering her and the others to leave. "We have sent a message to the prime minister," she replied, "and we are waiting for the answer."

"There will be no answer," was the stern rejoinder, and the door closed.

"Yes, there will be an answer," exclaimed the leader, and she seized the door-knocker and banged it sharply.

Instantly the men reappeared, and one of them called to a policeman standing near, "Take this woman in charge." The order was obeyed, and the peaceful deputation saw its leader taken off to Canon Row Station.

Instantly the women protested vigorously. Annie Kenney began to address the crowd that had gathered, and Mrs. Drummond actually forced her way past the doorkeeper into the sacred residence of the prime minister of the British Empire! Her arrest and Annie's followed.

The three women were detained at the police station for about an hour, long enough, the prime minister probably thought, to frighten them thoroughly and teach them not to do such dreadful things again. Then he sent them word that he had decided not to prosecute them, but would, on the contrary, receive a deputation from the W. S. P. U., and, if they cared to attend, from other suffrage societies as well.

All the suffrage organisations at once began making preparations for the great event. At the same time two hundred members of Parliament sent a petition to the prime minister, asking him to receive their committee that they might urge upon him the necessity of a government measure for woman suffrage. Sir Henry fixed May 19th as the day on which he would receive a joint deputation from Parliament and from the women's suffrage organisations.

The W. S. P. U. determined to make the occasion as public as possible, and began preparations for a procession and a demonstration. When the day came we assembled at the foot of the beautiful monument to the warrior-queen, Boadicea, that guards the entrance to Westminster Bridge, and from there we marched to the Foreign Office. At the meeting eight women spoke in behalf of an immediate suffrage measure, and Mr. Keir Hardie presented the argument for the suffrage members of Parliament. I spoke for the W. S. P. U., and I tried to make the prime minister see that no business could be more pressing than ours. I told him that the group of women organised in our Union felt so strongly the necessity for women enfranchisement that they were prepared to sacrifice for it everything they possessed, their means of livelihood, their very lives, if necessary. I begged him to make such a sacrifice needless by doing us justice now.

What answer do you think Sir Henry Campbell-Bannerman made us? He assured us of his sympathy with our cause, his belief in its justice, and his confidence in our fitness to vote. And then he told us to have patience and wait; he could do nothing for us because some of his Cabinet were opposed to us. After a few more words the usual vote of thanks was moved, and the deputation was dismissed. I had not expected anything better, but it wrung my heart to see the bitter disappointment of the W. S. P. U. women who had waited in the street to hear from the leaders the result of the deputation. We held a great meeting of protest that afternoon, and determined to carry on our agitation with increased vigour.

Now that it had been made plain that the government were resolved not to bring in a suffrage bill, there was nothing to do but to continue our policy of waking up the country, not only by public speeches and demonstrations, but by a constant heckling of Cabinet Ministers. Since the memorable occasion when Christabel Pankhurst and Annie Kenney were thrown out of Sir Edward Grey's meeting in Manchester, and afterward imprisoned for the crime of asking a courteous question, we had not lost an opportunity of addressing the same question to every Cabinet Minister we could manage to encounter. For this we have been unmercifully criticised, and in a large number of cases most brutally handled.

In almost every one of my American meetings I was asked the question, "What good do you expect to accomplish by interrupting meetings?" Is it possible that the time-honoured, almost sacred English privilege of interrupting is unknown in America? I cannot imagine a political meeting from which "the Voice" was entirely absent. In England it is invariably present. It is considered the inalienable right of the opposition to heckle the speaker and to hurl questions at him which are calculated to spoil his arguments. For instance, when Liberals attend a Conservative gathering they go prepared to shatter by witticisms and pointed questions all the best effects of the Conservative orators. The next day you will read in Liberal newspapers headlines like these: "The Voice in Fine Form," "Short Shrift for Tory Twaddle," "Awkward Answers from the Enemy's Platform." In the body of the article you will learn that "Lord X found that the Liberals at his meeting were more than a match for him," that "there was continued interruption during Sir So-and-so's speech," that "Lord M fared badly last night in his encounter with the Voice," or that "Captain Z had the greatest difficulty in making himself heard."

In accordance with this custom we heckle Cabinet Ministers. Mr. Winston Churchill, for example, is speaking. "One great question," he exclaims, "remains to be settled."

"And that is woman suffrage," shouts a voice from the gallery.

Mr. Churchill struggles on with his speech: "The men have been complaining of me——"

"The women have been complaining of you, too, Mr. Churchill," comes back promptly from the back of the hall.

"In the circumstances what can we do but——"

"Give votes to women."

Our object, of course, is to keep woman suffrage in the foreground of interest and to insist on every possible occasion that no other reform advocated is of such immediate importance.

From the first the women's interruptions have been resented with unreasoning anger. I remember hearing Mr. Lloyd-George saying once of a man who interrupted him:

"Let him remain. I like interruptions. They show that people holding different opinions to mine are present, giving me a chance to convert them." But when suffragists interrupt Mr. Lloyd-George he says something polite like this: "Pay no attention to those cats mewing."

Some of the ministers are more well bred in their expressions, but all are disdainful and resentful. All see with approval the brutal ejection of the women by the Liberal stewards.

At one meeting where Mr. Lloyd-George was speaking, we interrupted with a question, and he claimed the sympathy of the audience on the score that he was a friend to woman suffrage. "Then why don't you do something to give votes to women?" was the obvious retort. But Mr. Lloyd-George evaded this by the counter query: "Why don't they go for their enemies? Why don't they go for their greatest enemy?" Instantly, all over the hall, voices shouted, "Asquith! Asquith!" For even at that early day it was known that the then Chancellor of the Exchequer was a stern foe of women's independence.

In the summer of 1906, together with other members of the W. S. P. U., I went to Northampton, where Mr. Asquith was holding a large meeting in behalf of the Government's education bills. We organised a number of outdoor meetings, and of course prepared to attend Mr. Asquith's meeting. In conversation with the president of the local Women's Liberal Association, I mentioned the fact that we expected to be put out, and she indignantly declared that such a thing could not happen in Northampton, where the women had done so much for the Liberal party. I told her that I hoped she would be at the meeting.

I had not intended to go myself, my plans being to hold a meeting of my own outside the door. But our members, before Mr. Asquith began to speak, attempted to question him, and were thrown out with violence. So then, turning my meeting over to them, I slipped quietly into the hall and sat down in the front row of a division set apart for wives and women friends of the Liberal leaders. I sat there in silence, hearing men interrupt the speaker and get answers to their questions. At the close of the speech I stood up and, addressing the chairman, said: "I should like to ask Mr. Asquith a question about education." The chairman turned inquiringly to Mr. Asquith, who frowningly shook his head. But without waiting for the chairman to say a word, I continued:

Mr. Asquith has said that the parents of children have a right to be consulted in the matter of their children's education, especially upon such questions as the kind of religious instruction they should receive. Women are parents. Does not Mr. Asquith think that women should have the right to control their children's education, as men do, through the vote?

At this point the stewards seized me by the arms and shoulders and rushed me, or rather dragged me, for I soon lost my footing, to the door and threw me out of the building.

The effect on the president of the Northampton Women's Liberal Association was most salutary. She resigned her office and became a member of the W. S. P. U. Perhaps her action was influenced further by the press reports of the incident. Mr. Asquith was reported as saying, after my ejection, that it was difficult to enter into the minds of people who thought they could serve a cause which professed to appeal to the reason of the electors of the country by disturbing public meetings. Apparently he could enter into the minds of the men who disturbed public meetings.

To our custom of public heckling of the responsible members of the hostile government we added the practice of sending deputations to them for the purpose of presenting orderly arguments in favour of our cause. After Mr. Asquith had shown himself so uninformed as to the objects of the suffragists, we decided to ask him to receive a deputation from the W. S. P. U. To our polite letter Mr. Asquith returned a cold refusal to be interviewed on any subject not connected with his particular office. Whereupon we wrote again, reminding Mr. Asquith that as a member of the government he was concerned with all questions likely to be dealt with by Parliament. We said that we urgently desired to put our question before him, and that we would send a deputation to his house hoping that he would feel it his duty to receive us.

Our first deputation was told that Mr. Asquith was not at home. He had, in fact, escaped from the house through the back door, and had sped away in a fast motor-car. Two days later we sent a larger deputation, of about thirty women, to his house in Cavendish Square. To be accurate, the deputation got as near the house as the entrance to Cavendish Square; there the women met a strong force of police, who told them that they would not be permitted to go farther.

Many of the women were carrying little "Votes for Women" banners, and these the police tore from them, in some cases with blows and insults. Seeing this, the leader of the deputation cried out: "We will go forward. You have no right to strike women like that." The reply, from a policeman near her, was a blow in the face. She screamed with pain and indignation, whereupon the man grasped her by the throat and choked her against the park railings until she was blue in the face. The young woman struggled and fought back, and for this she was arrested on a charge of assaulting the police. Three other women were arrested, one because, in spite of the police, she succeeded in ringing Mr. Asquith's door-bell and another because she protested against the laughter of some ladies who watched the affair from a drawing-room window. She was a poor working-woman, and it seemed to her a terrible thing that rich and protected women should ridicule a cause that to her was so profoundly serious.

The fourth woman was taken in charge, because after she had been pushed off the pavement, she dared to step back. Charged with disorderly conduct, these women were sentenced to six weeks in the Second Division. They were given the option of a fine, it is true, but the payment of a fine would have been an acknowledgment of guilt, which made such a course impossible. The leader of the deputation was given a two months' sentence, with the option of a fine of ten pounds. She, too, refused to pay, and was sent to prison; but some unknown friend paid the fine secretly, and she was released before the expiration of her sentence.

About the time these things were happening in London, similar violence was offered our women in Manchester, where John Burns, Lloyd-George, and Winston Churchill, all three Cabinet Ministers, were addressing a great Liberal demonstration. The women were there, as usual, to ask government support for our measure. There, too, they were thrown out of the meeting, and three of them were sent to prison.

There are people in England, plenty of them, who will tell you that the Suffragettes were sent to prison for destroying property. The fact is that hundreds of women were arrested for exactly such offences as I have described before it ever occurred to any of us to destroy property. We were determined, at the beginning of our movement, that we would make ourselves heard, that we would force the government to take up our question and answer it by action in Parliament. Perhaps you will see some parallel to our case in the stand taken in Massachusetts by the early Abolitionists, Wendell Phillips and William

Lloyd Garrison. They, too, had to fight bitterly, to face insult and arrest, because they insisted on being heard. And they were heard; and so, in time, were we.

I think we began to be noticed in earnest after our first success in opposing a Liberal candidate. This was in a by-election held at Cockermouth in August, 1906. I shall have to explain that a by-election is a local election to fill a vacancy in Parliament caused by a death or a resignation. The verdict of a by-election is considered as either an endorsement or a censure of the manner in which the government have fulfilled their pre-election pledges. So we went to Cockermouth and told the voters how the Liberal party had fulfilled its pledges of democracy and lived up to its avowed belief in the rights of all the people. We told them of the arrests in London and Manchester, of the shameful treatment of women in Liberal meetings, and we asked them to censure the government who had answered so brutally our demand for a vote. We told them that the only rebuke that the politicians would notice was a lost seat in Parliament, and that on that ground we asked them to defeat the Liberal candidate.

How we were ridiculed! With what scorn the newspapers declared that "those wild women" could never turn a single vote. Yet when the election was over it was found that the Liberal candidate had lost the seat, which, at the general election a little more than a year before, had been won by a majority of 655. This time the Unionist candidate was returned by a majority of 609. Tremendously elated, we hurried our forces off to another by-election.

Now the ridicule was turned to stormy abuse. Mind you, the Liberal Government still refused to notice the women's question; they declared through the Liberal press that the defeat at Cockermouth was insignificant, and that anyhow it wasn't caused by the Suffragettes; yet the Liberal leaders were furiously angry with the W. S. P. U. Many of our members had been Liberals, and it was considered by the men that these women were little better than traitors. They were very foolish and ill-advised, into the bargain, the Liberals said, because the vote, if won at all, must be gained from the Liberal party; and how did the women suppose the Liberal party would ever give the vote to open and avowed enemies? This sage argument was used also by the women Liberals and the constitutional suffragists. They advised us that the proper way was to work for the party. We retorted that we had done that unsuccessfully for too many years already, and persisted with the opposite method of persuasion.

Throughout the summer and autumn we devoted ourselves to the by-election work, sometimes actually defeating the Liberal candidate, sometimes reducing the Liberal majority, and always raising a tremendous sensation and gaining hundreds of new members to the union. In almost every neighbourhood we visited we left the nucleus of a local union, so that before the year was out we had branches all over England and many in Scotland and Wales. I especially remember a by-election in Wales at which Mr. Samuel Evans, who had accepted an officership under the Crown, had to stand for re-election. Unfortunately no candidate had been brought out against him. So there was nothing for my companions and me to do but make his campaign as lively as possible. Mr.—now, (1914), Sir Samuel—Evans was the man who had incensed women by talking out a suffrage resolution introduced into the House by Keir Hardie. So we went to two of his meetings and literally talked him out, breaking up the gatherings amid the laughter and cheers of delighted crowds.

On October 23rd Parliament met for its autumn session, and we led a deputation to the House of Commons in another effort to induce the government to take action on woman suffrage. In accordance with orders given the police, only twenty of us were admitted to the Strangers' Lobby. We sent in for the chief Liberal whip, and asked him to take a message to the prime minister, the message being the usual request to grant women the vote that session. We also asked the prime minister if he intended to include the registration of qualified women voters in the provisions of the plural voting bill, then under consideration. The Liberal whip came back with the reply that nothing could be done for women that session.

"Does the prime minister," I asked, "hold out any hope for the women for any session during this Parliament, or at any future time?" The prime minister, you will remember, called himself a suffragist.

The Liberal whip replied, "No, Mrs. Pankhurst, the prime minister does not."

What would a deputation of unenfranchised men have done in these circumstances—men who knew themselves to be qualified to exercise the franchise, who desperately needed the protection of the franchise, and who had a majority of legislators in favour of giving them the franchise? I hope they would have done at least as much as we did, which was to start a meeting of protest on the spot. The newspapers described our action as creating a disgraceful scene in the lobby of the House of Commons, but I think that history will

Mrs. Pankhurst addressing a By-Election Crowd

otherwise describe it. One of the women sprang up on a settee and began to address the crowd. In less than a minute she was pulled down, but instantly another woman took her place; and after she had been dragged down, still another sprang to her place, and following her another and another, until the order came to clear the lobby, and we were all forced outside.

In the *mêlée* I was thrown to the floor and painfully hurt. The women, thinking me seriously injured, crowded around me and refused to move until I was able to regain myself. This angered the police, who were still more incensed when they found that the demonstration was continued outside. Eleven women were arrested, including Mrs. Pethick Lawrence, our treasurer, Mrs. Cobden Sanderson, Annie Kenney and three more of our organisers; and they were all sent to Holloway for two months. But the strength of our movement was proved by the number of volunteers who immediately came forward to carry on the work. Mrs. Tuke, now, (1914), Hon. Secretary of the W. S. P. U., joined the union at this time. It had not occurred to the authorities that their action would have this effect. They thought to crush the union at a blow, but they gave it the greatest impetus it had yet received. The leaders of the older suffrage organisations for the time forgot their disapproval of our methods, and joined with women writers, physicians, actresses, artists, and other prominent women in denouncing the affair as barbarous.

One more thing the authorities failed to take into account. The condition of English prisons was known to be very bad, but when two of our women were made so ill in Holloway that they had to be released within a few days, the politicians began to tremble for their prestige. Questions were asked in Parliament concerning the advisability of treating the Suffragettes not as common criminals but as political offenders with the right to confinement in the First Division. Mr. Herbert Gladstone, the Home Secretary, replied to these questions that he had no power to interfere with the magistrates' decisions, and could do nothing in the matter of the suffragettes' punishment. I shall ask you to remember this statement of Mr. Herbert Gladstone's, as later we were able to prove it a deliberate falsehood—although really the falsehood proved itself when the women, by government order, were released from prison when they had served just half their sentences. The reason for this was that an important by-election was being held in the north of England, and we had distributed broadcast throughout the constituency hand bills telling the electors that nine women, including the daughter of Richard Cobden, were being held as common criminals by the Liberal Government who were asking for their votes.

I took a group of the released prisoners to Huddersfield, and they told prison stories to such effect that the Liberal majority was reduced by 540 votes. As usual the Liberal leaders denied that our work had anything to do with the slender majority by which the party retained the seat, but among our souvenirs is a handbill, one of thousands given out from Liberal headquarters:

> MEN OF HUDDERSFIELD
> DON'T BE MISLED
> BY SOCIALISTS, SUFFRAGETTES
> OR TORIES
> VOTE FOR SHERWELL

Meanwhile, other demonstrations had taken place before the House of Commons, and at Christmas time twenty-one suffragettes were in Holloway Prison, though they had committed no crime. The government professed themselves unmoved, and members of Parliament spoke with sneers of the "self-made martyrs." However, a considerable group of members, strongly moved by the passion and unquenchable ardour of this new order of suffragists, met during the last week of the year and formed a committee whose object it was to press upon the government the necessity of giving the franchise to women during that Parliament. The committee resolved that its members would work to educate a wider public opinion on the question, and especially to advocate suffrage when addressing meetings in their constituencies, to take Parliamentary action on every possible occasion, and to induce as many members of Parliament as possible to ballot for the introduction of a suffrage bill or motion next session.

Our first year in London had borne wonderful fruits. We had grown from a mere handful of women, a "family party" the newspapers had derisively called us, to a strong organisation with branches all over the country, permanent headquarters in Clements Inn, Strand; we had found good financial backing, and above all, we had created a suffrage committee in the House of Commons.

Book 2: Four Years of Peaceful Militancy

CHAPTER 1

The campaign of 1907 began with a Women's Parliament, called together on February 13th in Caxton Hall, to consider the provisions of the King's speech, which had been read in the national Parliament on the opening day of the session, February 12th. The King's speech, as I have explained, is the official announcement of the government's programme for the session. When our Women's Parliament met at three o'clock on the afternoon of the thirteenth we knew that the government meant to do nothing for women during the session ahead.

I presided over the women's meeting, which was marked with a fervency and a determination of spirit at that time altogether unprecedented. A resolution expressing indignation that woman suffrage should have been omitted from the King's speech, and calling upon the House of Commons to give immediate facilities to such a measure, was moved and carried. A motion to send the resolution from the hall to the prime minister was also carried. The slogan, "Rise up, women," was cried from the platform, the answering shout coming back as from one woman, "Now!" With copies of the resolution in their hands, the chosen deputation hurried forth into the February dusk, ready for Parliament or prison, as the fates decreed.

Fate did not leave them very long in doubt. The government, it appeared, had decided that not again should their sacred halls of Parliament be desecrated by women asking for the vote, and orders had been given that would henceforth prevent women from reaching even the outer precincts of the House of Commons. So when our deputation of women arrived in the neighbourhood of Westminster Abbey they found themselves opposed by a solid line of police, who, at a sharp order from their chief, began to stride through and through the ranks of the procession, trying to turn the women back. Bravely the women rallied and pressed forward a little farther. Suddenly a body of mounted police came riding up at a smart trot, and for the next five hours or more, a struggle, quite indescribable for brutality and ruthlessness, went on.

The horsemen rode directly into the procession, scattering the women right and left. But still the women would not turn back. Again and again they returned, only to fly again and again from the merciless hoofs. Some of the women left the streets for the pavements, but even there the horsemen pursued them, pressing them so close to walls and railings that they were obliged to retreat temporarily to avoid being crushed. Other strategists took refuge in doorways, but they were dragged out by the foot police and were thrown directly in front of the horses.

Still the women fought to reach the House of Commons with their resolution. They fought until their clothes were torn, their bodies bruised, and the last ounce of their strength exhausted. Fifteen of them did actually fight their way through those hundreds on hundreds of police, foot and mounted, as far as the Strangers' Lobby of the House. Here they attempted to hold a meeting, and were arrested. Outside, many more women were taken into custody. It was ten o'clock before the last arrest was made, and the square cleared of the crowds. After that the mounted men continued to guard the approaches to the House of Commons until the House rose at midnight.

The next morning fifty-seven women and two men were arraigned, two and three at a time, in Westminster police court. Christabel Pankhurst was the first to be placed in the dock. She tried to explain to the magistrate that the deputation of the day before was a perfectly peaceful attempt to present a resolution, which, sooner or later, would be presented and acted upon. She assured him that the deputation was but the beginning of a campaign that would not cease until the government yielded to the women's demand. "There can be no going back for us," she declared, "and more will happen if we do not get justice."

The magistrate, Mr. Curtis Bennett, who was destined later to try women for that "more," rebuked my daughter sternly, telling her that the government had nothing to do with causing the disorders of the day before, that the women were entirely responsible for what had occurred, and finally, that these disgraceful scenes in the street must cease—just as King Canute told the ocean that it must roll out instead of in. "The scenes can be stopped in only one way," replied the prisoner. His sole reply to that was, "Twenty shillings or fourteen days." Christabel chose the prison sentence, and so did all the other prisoners. Mrs. Despard, who headed the deputation, and Sylvia Pankhurst, who was with her, were given three weeks in prison.

Of course the raid, as it was called, gave the Women's Social and Political Union an enormous amount of publicity, on the whole, favourable publicity. The newspapers were almost unanimous in condemning the government for sending mounted troops out against unarmed women. Angry questions were asked in Parliament, and our ranks once more increased in size and ardour. The old-fashioned suffragists, men as well as women, cried out that we had alienated all our friends in Parliament; but this proved to be untrue. Indeed, it was found that a Liberal member, Mr. Dickinson, had won the first place in the ballot, and had announced that he intended to use it to introduce a women's suffrage bill. More than this, the prime minister, Sir Henry Campbell-Bannerman, promised to give the bill his support. For a time, a very short time, it is true, we felt that the hour of our freedom might be at hand, that our prisoners had perhaps already won us our precious symbol—the vote.

Soon, however, a number of professed suffragists in the House began to complain that Mr. Dickinson's bill, practically the original bill, was not "democratic" enough, that it would enfranchise only the women of the upper classes—to which, by the way, most of them belonged. That this was not true had been proved again and again from the municipal registers, which showed a majority of working women's names as qualified householders. The contention was but a shallow excuse, and we knew it. Therefore we were not surprised when Sir Henry Campbell-Bannerman departed from his pledge of support, and allowed the bill to be talked out.

Following this event, the second Women's Parliament assembled, on the afternoon of March 20, 1907. As before, we adopted a resolution calling upon the government to introduce an official suffrage measure, and again we voted to send the resolution from the hall to the prime minister. Lady Harberton was chosen to lead the deputation, and instantly hundreds of women sprang up and volunteered to accompany her. This time the police met the women at the door of the hall, and another useless, disgraceful scene of barbarous, brute-force opposition took place. Something like one thousand police had been sent out to guard the House of Commons from the peaceful invasion of a few hundred women. All afternoon and evening we kept

Caxton Hall open, the women returning every now and again, singly and in small groups, to have their bruises bathed, or their torn clothing repaired.

As night fell the crowds in the street grew denser, and the struggle between the women and the police became more desperate. Lady Harberton, we heard, had succeeded in reaching the entrance to the House of Commons, nay, had actually managed to press past the sentries into the lobby, but her resolution had not been presented to the prime minister. She and many others were arrested before the police at last succeeded in clearing the streets, and the dreadful affair was over.

The next day, in Westminster police court, the magistrate meted out sentences varying from twenty shillings or fourteen days to forty shillings or one month's imprisonment. Two of the women, Miss Woodlock and Mrs. Chatterton, who had left Holloway only a week before, were, as "old offenders," given thirty days without the option of a fine. Another woman, Mary Leigh, was given thirty days because she offended the magistrate's dignity by hanging a "Votes for Women" banner over the edge of the dock. Those of my readers who are unable to connect the word "militancy" with anything milder than arson are invited to reflect that within the first two months of the year 1907 the English Government sent to prison one hundred and thirty women whose "militancy" consisted merely of trying to carry a resolution from a hall to the Prime Minister in the House of Commons. Our crime was called obstructing the police. It will be seen that it was the police who did the obstructing.

It may be asked why neither of these deputations was led by me personally. The reason was that I was needed in another capacity, that of leader and supervisor of the suffrage forces in the field to defeat government candidates at by-elections. On the night of the second "riot," while our women were still struggling in the streets, I left London for Hexham in Northumberland, where by our work the majority of the Liberal candidate was reduced by a thousand votes. Seven more by-elections followed in rapid succession.

Our by-election work was such a new thing in English politics that we attracted an enormous amount of attention wherever we went. It was our custom to begin work the very hour we entered a town. If, on our way from the station to the hotel, we encountered a group of men, say, in the market-place, we either stopped and held a meeting on the spot, or else we stayed long enough to tell them when and where our meetings were to be held, and to urge them to attend. The usual first step, after securing lodgings, was to hire a vacant shop, fill the windows with suffrage literature, and fling out our purple, green, and white flag.

Meanwhile, some of us were busy hiring the best available hall. If we got possession of the battle-ground before the men, we sometimes "cornered" all the good halls and left the candidate nothing but schoolhouses for his indoor meetings. Truth to tell, our meetings were so much more popular than theirs that we really needed the larger halls. Often, a candidate with the Suffragettes for rivals spoke to almost empty benches. The crowds were away listening to the women.

Naturally, this greatly displeased the politicians, and it scandalised many of the old-fashioned Liberal partisans. In one place, I think it was Colne Valley in Yorkshire, an amusing instance of masculine hostility occurred. We had arrived on a day when both Conservative and Liberal committees were choosing their candidates, and we thought it a good opportunity to hold a series of outdoor meetings. We tried to get a lorry for a rostrum, but the only man in town who had these big vans to let disapproved of Suffragettes so violently that he wouldn't let us have one. So we borrowed a chair from a woman shopkeeper, and went at it. Soon we had a large crowd and an interested audience. We also got the attention of a number of small boys with pea-shooters, and had to make our speeches under a blistering fire of dried peas.

While I was speaking the fire ceased, to my relief—for dried peas sting. I continued my speech with renewed vigour, only to have one of my best points spoiled by roars of laughter from the crowd. I finished somehow, and sat down; and then it was explained to me that the pea-shooters had been financed by one of the prominent Liberals of the town, another man who disapproved of our policy of opposing the government. As soon as the ammunition gave out this man furnished the boys with a choice supply of rotten oranges. These were not so easily handled, it appeared, for the very first one went wild, and struck the chivalrous gentleman violently in the neck. This it was that had caused the laughter, and stopped the attack on the women.

We met with some pretty rough horse-play, and even with some brutality, in several by-elections, but on the whole we found the men ready, and the women more than ready, to listen to us. We tamed and educated a public that had always been used to violence at elections. We even tamed the boys, who came to the meetings on purpose to skylark. When we were in Rutlandshire that spring three schoolboys came to see me and told me, shyly, that they were interested in suffrage. They had had a debate on the subject at their school, and although the decision had been for the other side, all the boys wanted to know more about it. Wouldn't I please have a meeting especially for them? Of course I consented, and I found my boy audience quite delightful. Indeed, I hope they liked me half as well as I did them.

All through the spring our by-election work continued with amazing success, although our part in the government losses was rarely admitted by the politicians. The voters knew, however. At an election in Suffolk, where we helped to double the Unionist vote, the successful candidate, speaking to the crowd from his hotel window, said, "What has been the cause of the great and glorious victory?" Instantly the crowd roared, "Votes for Women!"—"Three cheers for the Suffragettes!" This was not at all what the successful candidate had intended, but he waved his hand graciously and said, "No doubt the ladies had something to do with it."

The newspaper correspondents were not so reluctant to acknowledge our influence. Even when they condemned our policy, they were unsparing in their admiration for our energy, and the courage and ardour of our workers. Said the correspondent of the London *Tribune*, a Liberal paper hostile to our tactics:

> Their staying power, judging them by the standards of men, is extraordinary. By taking afternoon as well as evening meetings, they have worked twice as hard as the men. They are up earlier, they retire just as late. Women against men, they are better speakers, more logical, better informed, better phrased, with a surer insight for the telling argument.

After a summer spent in strengthening our forces, organising new branches, holding meetings—something like three thousand of these between May and October—invading meetings of Cabinet Ministers—we managed to do that about once every day—electioneering, and getting up huge demonstrations in various cities, we arrived at the end of the year. In the last months of the year, I directed several hotly contested by-elections, at one of which I met with one of the most serious misadventures of my life.

This by-election was held in the division of Mid-Devon, a stronghold of Liberalism. In fact, since its creation in 1885, the seat has never been held by any except a Liberal member. The constituency is a large one, divided into eight districts. The population of the towns is a rough and boisterous one, and its devotion, blind and unreasoning, to the Liberal party has always reflected the rude spirit of the voters. A Unionist woman told me, shortly after my arrival, that my life would be unsafe if I dared openly to oppose the Liberal candidate. She had never dared, she assured me, to wear her party colours in public. However, I did speak—in our headquarters at Newton Abbott, the principal town of the division, at Hull, and at Bovey Tracey. We held meetings twice a day, calling upon the voters to "beat the government in Mid-Devon, as a message that women must have votes next year."

Although some of the meetings were turbulent, we were treated with much more consideration than either of the candidates, who, not infrequently, were howled down and put to flight. Often the air of their meetings was thick with decayed vegetables and dirty snowballs. We had some rather lively sessions, too. Once, at an outdoor meeting, some young roughs dragged our lorry round and round until it seemed that we must be upset, and several times the language hurled at us from the crowd was quite unfit for me to repeat. Still, we escaped actual violence until the day of the election, when it was announced that the Unionist candidate had won the seat by a majority of twelve hundred and eighty. We knew instantly that the deepest resentment of the Liberals would be aroused, but it did not occur to us that the resentment would be directed actively against us.

After the declaration at the polls, my companion, Mrs. Martel, and I started to walk to our lodgings. Some of our friends stopped us, and drew our attention to the newly elected Unionist member of Parliament, who was being escorted from the polling place by a strong guard of police. We were warned that our safety demanded an immediate flight from the town. I laughingly assured our friends that I was never afraid to trust myself in a crowd, and we walked on. Suddenly we were confronted by a crowd of young men and boys, clay-cutters from the pits on the edge of town. These young men, who wore the red rosettes of the Liberal party, had just heard of their candidate's defeat, and they were mad with rage and humiliation.

One of them pointed to us, crying: "They did it! Those women did it!" A yell went up from the crowd, and we were deluged with a shower of clay and rotten eggs. We were not especially frightened, but the eggs were unbearable, and to escape them we rushed into a little grocer's shop close at hand. The grocer's wife closed and bolted the door, but the poor grocer cried out that his place would be wrecked. I did not want that to happen, of course, so I asked them to let us out by the back door. They led us out the door, into a small back yard which led into a little lane, whence we expected to make our escape. But when we reached the yard we found that the rowdies, anticipating our move, had surged round the corner, and were waiting for us.

They seized Mrs. Martel first, and began beating her over the head with their fists, but the brave wife of the shopkeeper, hearing the shouts and the oaths of the men, flung open the door and rushed to our rescue. Between us we managed to tear Mrs. Martel from her captors and get her into the house. I expected to get into the house, too, but as I reached the threshold a staggering blow fell on the back of my head, rough hands grasped the collar of my coat, and I was flung violently to the ground. Stunned, I must have lost consciousness for a moment, for my next sensation was of cold, wet mud seeping through my clothing. Sight returning to me, I perceived the men, silent now, but with a dreadful, lowering silence, closing in a ring around me. In the centre of the ring was an empty barrel, and the horrid thought occurred to me that they might intend putting me in it.

A long time seemed to pass, while the ring of men slowly drew closer. I looked at them, in their drab clothes smeared with yellow pit-clay, and they appeared so underfed, so puny and sodden, that a poignant pity for them swept over me. "Poor souls," I thought, and then I said suddenly, "Are none of you *men?*" Then one of the youths darted toward me, and I knew that whatever was going to happen to me was about to begin.

At that very moment came shouts, and a rush of police who had fought their way through hostile crowds to rescue us. Of course the mob turned tail and fled, and I was carried gently into the shop, which the police guarded for two hours, before it was deemed safe for us to leave in a closed motorcar. It was many months before either Mrs. Martel or I recovered from our injuries.

The rowdies, foiled of their woman prey, went to the Conservative Club, smashed all the windows in the house, and kept the members besieged there through the night. The next morning the body of a man, frightfully bruised about the head, was found in the mill-race. Throughout all this disorder and probable crime, not a man was arrested. Contrast this, if you like, with the treatment given our women in London.

The king opened Parliament in great state on January 29, 1908. Again his speech omitted all mention of woman suffrage, and again the W. S. P. U. issued a call for a Women's Parliament, for February 11th, 12th and 13th. Before it was convened we heard that an excellent place in the ballot had been won by a friend of the movement, Mr. Stanger, who promised to introduce a suffrage bill, February 28th was the day fixed for the second reading, and we realised that strong pressure would have to be brought to bear to prevent the bill being wrecked, as the Dickinson bill had been the previous year. Therefore, on the first day of the Women's Parliament, almost every woman present volunteered for the deputation, which was to try to carry the resolution to the prime minister. Led by two well-known portrait painters, the deputation left Caxton Hall and proceeded in orderly ranks, four abreast, toward the House of Commons. The crowds in the streets were enormous, thousands of sympathisers coming out to help the women, thousands of police determined that the women should not be helped, and thousands of curious spectators. When the struggle was over, fifty women were locked up in police-court cells.

The next morning, when the cases were tried, Mr. Muskett, who prosecuted for the Crown, and who was perhaps a little tired of telling the Suffragettes that these scenes in the streets must cease, and then seeing them go on exactly as if he had not spoken, made a very severe and terrifying address. He told the women that this time they would be subject to the usual maximum of two months' imprisonment, with the option of a fine of five pounds, but that, in case they ever offended again, the law had worse terrors in store for them. It was proposed to revive, for the benefit of the Suffragettes, an Act passed in the reign of Charles II, which dealt with "Tumultuous Petitions, either to the Crown or Parliament."

This act provided that no person should dare to go to the king or to Parliament "with any petition, complaint, remonstrance, declaration or other address" accompanied with a number of persons above twelve. A fine of one hundred pounds, or three months' imprisonment, might be imposed under this law. The magistrate then sentenced all but two of the women to be bound over for twelve months, or to serve six weeks in the second division. Two other women, "old offenders," were given one month in the third division, or lowest class. All the prisoners, except two who had very ill relatives at home, chose the prison sentence.

The next day's session of the Women's Parliament was one of intense excitement, as the women reviewed the events of the previous day, the trials, and especially the threat to revive the obsolete Act of Charles II, an act *which was passed to obstruct the progress of the Liberal party, which came into existence under the Stuarts, and under the second Charles was fighting for its life*. It was an amazing thing that the political descendants of these men were proposing to revive the Act to obstruct the advance of the women's cause, fighting for its life under George V and his Liberal government. At least, it was evidence that the government were baffled in their attempt to crush our movement. Christabel Pankhurst, presiding over the second session of the Women's Parliament, said:

> At last it is realised that women are fighting for freedom, as their fathers fought. If they want twelve women, aye, and more than twelve, if a hundred women are wanted to be tried under that act and sent to prison for three months, they can be found.

I was not present at this session, nor had I been present at the first one. I was working in a by-election at South Leeds, the last of several important by-elections in great industrial centres, where our success was unquestioned, except by the Liberal press. The elections had wound up with a great procession, and a meeting of 100,000 people on Hounslet Moor. The most wonderful enthusiasm marked that meeting. I shall never forget what splendid order the people kept, in spite of the fact that no police protection was given us; how the vast crowd parted to let our procession through; how the throngs of mill women kept up a chorus in broad Yorkshire: "Shall us win? Shall us have the vote? We shall!" No wonder the old people shook their heads, and declared that "there had never been owt like it."

Chapter 2

With those brave shouts in my ears, I hurried down to London for the concluding session of the parliament, for I had determined that I must be the first person to challenge the government to carry out their threat to revive the old Act of Charles II. I made a long speech to the women that day, telling them something of my experiences of the past months, and how all that I had seen and heard throughout the country had only deepened my conviction of the necessity for women's votes. I concluded:

> I feel that the time has come when I must act, and I wish to be one of those to carry our resolution to Parliament this afternoon. My experience in the country, and especially in South Leeds, has taught me things that Cabinet Ministers, who have not had that experience, do not know, and has made me feel that I must make one final attempt to see them, and to urge them to reconsider their position before some terrible disaster

has occurred.

Amid a good deal of excitement and emotion, we chose the requisite thirteen women, who were prepared to be arrested and tried under the Charles II "Tumultuous Petitions" Act. I had not entirely recovered from the attack made upon me at Mid-Devon, and my wrenched ankle was still too sensitive to make walking anything but a painful process. Seeing me begin almost at once to limp badly, Mrs. Drummond, with characteristic, blunt kindness, called to a man driving a dog-cart and asked him if he would drive me to the House of Commons. He readily agreed, and I mounted to the seat behind him, the other women forming in line behind the cart.

We had not gone far when the police, who already surrounded us in great force, ordered me to dismount. Of course I obeyed and walked, or rather limped along with my companions. They would have supported me, but the police insisted that we should walk single-file. Presently I grew so faint from the pain of the ankle that I called to two of the women, who took hold of my arms and helped me on my way. This was our one act of disobedience to police orders. We moved with difficulty, for the crowd was of incredible size. All around, as far as eye could see, was the great moving, swaying, excited multitude, and surrounding us on all sides were regiments of uniformed police, foot and mounted. You might have supposed that instead of thirteen women, one of them lame, walking quietly along, the town was in the hands of an armed mob.

We had progressed as far as the entrance to Parliament Square, when two stalwart policemen suddenly grasped my arms on either side and told me that I was under arrest. My two companions, because they refused to leave me, were also arrested, and a few minutes later Annie Kenney and five other women suffered arrest. That night we were released on bail, and the next morning we were arraigned in Westminster police court for trial under the Charles II Act. But, as it turned out, the authorities, embarrassed by our readiness to test the act, announced that they had changed their minds, and would continue, for the present, to treat us as common street brawlers.

This was my first trial, and I listened, with a suspicion that my ears were playing tricks with my reason, to the most astonishing perjuries put forth by the prosecution. I heard that we had set forth from Caxton Hall with noisy shouts and songs, that we had resorted to the most riotous and vulgar behaviour, knocking off policemen's helmets, assaulting the officers right and left as we marched. Our testimony, and that of our witnesses, was ignored. When I tried to speak in my own defence, I was cut short rudely, and was told briefly that I and the others must choose between being bound over or going to prison, in the second division, for six weeks.

I remember only vaguely the long, jolting ride across London to Holloway Prison. We stopped at Pentonville, the men's prison, to discharge several men prisoners, and I remember shuddering at the thought of our women, many of them little past girlhood, being haled to prison in the same van with criminal men. Arriving at the prison, we groped our way through dim corridors into the reception-ward, where we were lined up against the wall for a superficial medical examination. After that we were locked up in separate cells, unfurnished, except for low, wooden stools.

It seemed an endless time before my cell door was opened by a wardress, who ordered me to follow her. I entered a room where another wardress sat at a table, ready to take an inventory of my effects. Obeying an order to undress, I took off my gown, then paused. "Take off everything," was the next order. "Everything?" I faltered. It seemed impossible that they expected me to strip. In fact, they did allow me to take off my last garments in the shelter of a bathroom. I shivered myself into some frightful underclothing, old and patched and stained, some coarse, brown woollen stockings with red stripes, and the hideous prison dress stamped all over with the broad arrow of disgrace. I fished a pair of shoes out of a big basket of shoes, old and mostly mismates. A pair of coarse but clean sheets, a towel, a mug of cold cocoa, and a thick slice of brown bread were given me, and I was conducted to my cell.

My first sensations when the door was locked upon me were not altogether disagreeable. I was desperately weary, for I had been working hard, perhaps a little too hard, for several strenuous months. The excitement and fatigue of the previous day, and the indignation I had suffered throughout the trial, had combined to bring me to the point of exhaustion, and I was glad to throw myself on my hard prison bed and close my eyes. But soon the relief of being alone, and with nothing to do, passed from me. Holloway Prison is a very old place, and it has the disadvantages of old places which have never known enough air and sunshine. It reeks with the odours of generations of bad ventilation, and it contrives to be at once the stuffiest and the draughtiest building I have ever been in. Soon I found myself sickening for fresh air. My head began to ache. Sleep fled. I lay all night suffering with cold, gasping for air, aching with fatigue, and painfully wide awake.

The next day I was fairly ill, but I said nothing about it. One does not expect to be comfortable in prison. As a matter of fact, one's mental suffering is so much greater than any common physical distress that the latter is almost forgotten. The English prison system is altogether medieval and outworn. In some of its details the system has improved since they began to send the Suffragettes to Holloway. I may say that we, by our public denunciation of the system, have forced these slight improvements. In 1907 the rules were excessively cruel. The poor prisoner, when she entered Holloway, dropped, as it were, into a tomb. No letters and no visitors were allowed for the first month of the sentence. Think of it—a whole month, more than four weeks, without sending or receiving a single word. One's nearest and dearest may have gone through dreadful suffering, may have been ill, may have died, meantime. One was given plenty of time to imagine all these things, for the prisoner was kept in solitary confinement in a narrow, dimly-lit cell, twenty-three hours out of the twenty-four.

Solitary confinement is too terrible a punishment to inflict on any human being, no matter what his crime. Hardened criminals in the men's prisons, it is said, often beg for the lash instead. Picture what it must be to a woman who has committed some small offence, for most of the women who go to Holloway are small offenders, sitting alone, day after day, in the heavy silence of a cell—thinking of her children at home—thinking, thinking. Some women go mad. Many suffer from shattered nerves for a long period after release. It is impossible to believe that any woman ever emerged from such a horror less criminal than when she entered it.

Two days of solitary confinement, broken each day by an hour of silent exercise in a bitterly cold courtyard, and I was ordered to the hospital. There I thought I should be a little more comfortable. The bed was better, the food a little better, and small comforts, such as warm water for washing, were allowed. I slept a little the first night. About midnight I awoke, and sat up in bed, listening. A woman in the cell next mine was moaning in long, sobbing breaths of mortal pain. She ceased for a few minutes, then moaned again, horribly. The truth flashed over me, turning me sick, as I realised that a life was coming into being, there in that frightful prison. A woman, imprisoned by men's laws, was giving a child to the world. A child born in a cell! I shall never forget that night, nor what I suffered with the birth-pangs of that woman, who, I found later, was simply waiting trial on a charge which was found to be baseless.

The days passed very slowly, the nights more slowly still. Being in hospital, I was deprived of chapel, and also of work. Desperate, at last I begged the wardress for some sewing, and she kindly gave me a skirt of her own to hem, and later some coarse knitting to do. Prisoners were allowed a few books, mostly of the "Sunday-school" kind. One day I asked the chaplain if there were not some French or German books in the library, and he brought me a treasure, *Autour de mon Jardin*, by Jules Janin. For a few days I was quite happy, reading my book and translating it on the absurd little slate they gave us in lieu of paper and pencil. That slate was, after all, a great comfort. I did all kinds of things with it. I kept a calendar, I wrote all the French poetry I could remember on it, I even recorded old school chorals and old English exercises. It helped wonderfully to pass the endless hours until my release. I even forgot the cold, which was the harder to bear because of the fur coat, which I knew was put away, ticketed with my name. I begged them for the coat, but they wouldn't let me have it.

At last the time came when they gave me back all my things, and let me go free. At the door the governor spoke to me, and asked me if I had any complaints to make. "Not of you," I replied, "nor of any of the wardresses. Only of this prison, and all of men's prisons. We shall raze them to the ground."

Back in my comfortable home, surrounded by loving friends, I would have rested quietly for a few days, but there was a great meeting that night at Albert Hall, to mark the close of a week of self-denial to raise money for the year's campaign. Women had sold papers, flowers, toys, swept crossings, and sung in the streets for the cause. Many women, well known in the world of art and letters, did these things. I felt that I should be doing little if I merely attended the meeting. So I went. My release was not expected until the following morning, and no one thought of my appearing at the meeting. My chairman's seat was decorated with a large placard with the inscription, "Mrs. Pankhurst's Chair." After all the others were seated, the speakers, and hundreds of ex-prisoners. I walked quietly onto the stage, took the placard out of the chair and sat down. A great cry went up from the women as they sprang from their seats and stretched their hands toward me. It was some time before I could see them for my tears, or speak to them for the emotion that shook me like a storm.

The next morning I, with the other released prisoners, drove off to Peckham, a constituency of London, where the W. S. P. U. members were fighting a vigorous by-election. In open brakes we paraded the streets, dressed in our prison clothes, or exact reproductions of them. Naturally, we attracted a great deal of attention and sympathy, and our daily meetings on Peckham Rye, as their common is known, drew enormous crowds. When polling day came our members were stationed at every polling booth, and many men as they came to the booths told us that they were, for the first time, voting "for the women," by which they meant against the government.

That night, amid great excitement, it was made known that the Liberal majority of 2,339 at the last general election had been turned into a Conservative majority of 2,494. Letters poured into the newspapers, declaring that the loss of this important Liberal seat was due almost entirely to the work of the Suffragettes, and many prominent Liberals called upon party leaders to start doing something for women before the next general election. The Liberal leaders, with the usual perspicacity of politicians, responded not at all. Instead they beheld with approval the rise to highest power the arch-enemy of the suffragists, Mr. Asquith.

Mr. Asquith became prime minister about Easter time, 1908, on the resignation, on account of ill health, of Sir Henry Campbell-Bannerman. Mr. Asquith was chosen, not because of any remarkable record of statesmanship, nor yet because of great personal popularity—for he possessed neither—but simply because no better man seemed available just then. He was known as a clever, astute, and somewhat unscrupulous lawyer. He had filled several high offices to the satisfaction of his party, and under Sir Henry Campbell-Bannerman had been Chancellor of the Exchequer, a post which is generally regarded as a stepping-stone to the premiership. The best thing the Liberal press found to say of the new premier was that he was a "strong" man.

Generally in politics this term is used to describe an obstinate man, and this we already knew Mr. Asquith to be. He was a bluntly outspoken opponent of woman suffrage, and it was sufficiently plain to us that no methods of education or persuasion would ever prove successful where he was concerned. Therefore the necessity of action on our part was greater than ever.

Such an opportunity presented itself at once through changes that took place in the new Cabinet. According to English law, all new comers into the Cabinet are obliged to resign their seats in Parliament and offer themselves to their constituencies for re-election. Besides these vacancies there were several others, on account of death or elevations to the peerage. This made necessary a number of by-elections, and the Women's Social and Political Union once more went into the field against the Liberal candidates. I shall deal no further with these by-elections than is necessary to show the effect of our work on the government, and its subsequent effect on our movement—which was to force us into more and more militancy. I shall leave it to the honest judgment of my readers to place where it ought rightly to be placed the responsibility for those first broken windows.

We selected as our first candidate for defeat Mr. Winston Churchill, who was about to appeal to his constituency of North West Manchester to sanction his appointment as president of the Board of Trade. My daughter Christabel took charge of this election, and the work of herself and her forces was so successful that Mr. Churchill lost his seat by 420 votes. All the newspapers acknowledged that it was the Suffragettes who had defeated Mr. Churchill, and one Liberal newspaper, the London *Daily News*, called upon the party to put a stop to an intolerable state of affairs by granting the women's demand for votes.

Another seat was immediately secured for Mr. Churchill, that of Dundee, then strongly—in the merely party sense—Liberal, and therefore safe. Nevertheless, we determined to fight Mr. Churchill there, to defeat him if possible, and to bring down the Liberal majority in any case. I took personal charge of the campaign, holding a very large meeting in Kinnaird Hall on the evening before Mr. Churchill's arrival. Although he felt absolutely sure of election in this Scottish constituency, Mr. Churchill dreaded the effect of our presence on the Liberal women. The second meeting he addressed in Dundee was held for women only, and instead of asking for support of the various measures actually on the government's programme, the politician's usual method, he talked about the certainty of securing, within a short time, the Parliamentary franchise for women, he declared:

> No one can be blind to the fact that at the next general election woman suffrage will be a real, practical issue; and the next Parliament, I think, ought to see the gratification of the women's claims. I do not exclude the possibility of the suffrage being dealt with in this Parliament.

Mr. Churchill earnestly reiterated his claim to be considered a true friend of the women's cause; but when pressed for a pledge that his government would take action, he urged his inability to speak for his colleagues.

This specious promise, or rather, prophecy of woman suffrage at some indefinite time, won over a great many of the Liberal women, who forthwith went staunchly to work for Mr. Churchill's election. Dundee has a large population of extremely poor people, workers in the jute mills and the marmalade factories. Some concessions in the matter of the sugar tax, timely made, and the announcement that the new government meant to establish old age pensions, created an immense wave of Liberal enthusiasm that swept Mr. Churchill into office in spite of our work, which was untiring. We held something like two hundred meetings, and on election eve, five huge demonstrations—four of them in the open air and one which filled a large drill hall. Polling day, May 9th, was very exciting. For every Suffragette at the polling-booths there were half a dozen Liberal men and women, handing out bills with such legends as "Vote for Churchill, and never mind the women," and "Put Churchill in and keep the women out." Yet for all their efforts, Mr. Churchill polled 2200 votes less than his Liberal predecessor had polled at the general election.

In the first seven by-elections following Mr. Asquith's elevation to the premiership, we succeeded in pulling down the Liberal vote by 6663. Then something happened to check our progress. Mr. Asquith received a deputation of Liberal members of Parliament, who urged him to allow the Stanger suffrage bill, which had passed its second reading by a large majority, to be carried into law. Mr. Asquith replied that he himself did not wish to see women enfranchised, and that it would not be possible for the government to give the required facilities to Mr. Stanger's bill. He added that he was fully alive to the many defects of the electoral system, and that the government intended, "barring accidents," to bring in a reform bill before the close of that Parliament. Woman suffrage would have no place in it, but it would be so worded that a woman-suffrage amendment might be added if any member chose to move one. In that case, said Mr. Asquith, he should not consider it the duty of the government to oppose the amendment if it were approved by a majority of the House of Commons—*provided* that the amendment was on democratic lines, and that it had back of it the support, the strong and undoubted support, of the women of the country as well as the present electorate.

One would not suppose that such an evasive utterance as this would be regarded in any quarter as a promise that woman suffrage would be given any real chances of success under the Asquith Government. That it was, by many, taken quite seriously is but another proof of the gullibility of the party-blinded public. The Liberal press lauded Mr. Asquith's "promise," and called for a truce of militancy in order that the government might have every opportunity to act. Said the *Star*, in a leader typical of many others:

> The meaning of Mr. Asquith's pledge is plain. Woman's suffrage will be passed through the House of Commons before the present government goes to the country.

As for the women's Liberal Associations, they were quite delirious with joy. In a conference called for the purpose of passing resolutions of gratitude, Lady Carlisle said:

> This is a glorious day of rejoicing. Our great prime minister, all honour to him, has opened a way to us by which we can enter into that inheritance from which we have been too long debarred.

At the two following by-elections, the last of the series, enormous posters were exhibited, "Premier's Great Reform Bill: Votes for Women." We tried to tell the electors that the pledge was false on the face of it; that the specious proviso that the amendment be "democratic" left no doubt that the government would cause the rejection of any practical amendment that might be moved. Our words fell on deaf ears, and the Liberal majorities soared.

Just a week later Mr. Asquith was questioned in the House of Commons by a slightly alarmed anti-suffragist member. The member asked Mr. Asquith whether he considered himself pledged to introduce the reform hill during that Parliament, whether he meant to allow such a bill to carry a woman-suffrage amendment, if such were moved, and whether, in that case, the suffrage amendment would become part of the government policy. Evasive as ever, the prime minister, after some sparring, replied, "My honourable friend has asked me a question with regard to a remote and speculative future." Thus was our interpretation of Mr. Asquith's "promise" justified from his own lips. Yet the Liberal women still clung to the hope of government action, and the Liberal press pretended to cling to it. As for the Women's Social and Political Union, we prepared for more work. We had to strike out along a new line, since it was evident that the government could, for a time at least, neutralise our by-election work by more false promises. Consistent with our policy, of never going further than the

Government compelled us to go, we made our first action a perfectly peaceable one.

On the day when the Stanger bill had reached its second reading in the House, and several days after I had gone to Holloway for the first time, Mr. Herbert Gladstone, the Home Secretary, made a speech which greatly interested the Suffragettes. He professed himself a suffragist, and declared that he intended to vote for the bill. Nevertheless, he was confident that it could not pass, because of the division in the Cabinet, and because it had no political party united either for or against it. Woman suffrage, said Mr. Gladstone, must advance to victory through all the stages that are required for great reforms to mature. First academic discussion, then effective action, was the history of men's suffrage; it must be the same with women's suffrage. Mr. Gladstone declared:

> Men have learned this lesson and know the necessity for demonstrating the greatness of their movement, and for establishing that *force majeure* which actuates and arms a government for effective work. That is the task before the supporters of this great movement. Looking back at the great political crises in the thirties, the sixties and the eighties, it will be found that the people did not go about in small crowds, nor were they content with enthusiastic meetings in large halls; they assembled in their tens of thousands all over the country.
>
> Of course, it is not to be expected that women can assemble in such masses, but power belongs to masses, and through this power a government can be influenced into more effective action than a government will be likely to take under present conditions.

The Women's Social and Political Union determined to answer this challenge. If assembling in great masses was all that was necessary to convince the government that woman suffrage had passed the academic stage and now demanded political action, we thought we could undertake to satisfy the most sceptical member of the Cabinet. We knew that we could organise a demonstration that would outrival any of the great franchise demonstrations held by men in the thirties, sixties, and eighties. The largest number of people ever gathered in Hyde Park was said to have approximated 72,000. We determined to organise a Hyde Park demonstration of at least 250,000 people. Sunday, June 21, 1908, was fixed for the date of this demonstration, and for many months we worked to make it a day notable in the history of the movement. Our example was emulated by the non-militant suffragists, who organised a fine procession of their own, about a week before our demonstration. Thirteen thousand women, it was said, marched in that procession.

On our demonstration we spent, for advertising alone, over a thousand pounds, or five thousand dollars. We covered the hoardings of London and of all the principal provincial cities with great posters bearing portraits of the women who were to preside at the twenty platforms from which speeches were to be made; a map of London, showing the routes by which the seven processions were to advance, and a plan of the Hyde Park meeting-place were also shown. London, of course, was thoroughly organised. For weeks a small army of women was busy chalking announcements on sidewalks, distributing handbills, canvassing from house to house, advertising the demonstration by posters and sandwich boards carried through the streets. We invited everybody to be present, including both Houses of Parliament.

A few days before the demonstration Mrs. Drummond and a number of other women hired and decorated a launch and sailed up the Thames to the Houses of Parliament, arriving at the hour when members entertain their women friends at tea on the terrace. Everyone left the tables and crowded to the water's edge as the boat stopped, and Mrs. Drummond's strong, clear voice pealed out her invitation to the Cabinet and the members of Parliament to join the women's demonstration in Hyde Park. "Come to the park on Sunday," she cried. "You shall have police protection, and there will be no arrests, we promise you." An alarmed someone telephoned for the police boats, but as they appeared, the women's boat steamed away.

What a day was Sunday, June 21st—clear, radiant, filled with golden sunshine! As I advanced, leading, with the venerable Mrs. Wolstenholm-Elmy, the first of the seven processions, it seemed to me that all London had turned out to witness our demonstration. And a goodly part of London followed the processions. When I mounted my platform in Hyde Park, and surveyed the mighty throngs that waited there and the endless crowds that were still pouring into the park from all directions, I was filled with amazement not unmixed with awe. Never had I imagined that so many people could be gathered together to share in a political demonstration. It was a gay and beautiful as well as an awe-inspiring spectacle, for the white gowns and flower-trimmed hats of the women, against the background of ancient trees, gave the park the appearance of a vast garden in full bloom.

The bugles sounded, and the speakers at each of the twenty platforms began their addresses, which could not have been heard by more than half or a third of the vast audience. Notwithstanding this, they remained to the end. At five o'clock the bugles sounded again, the speaking ceased, and the resolution calling upon the government to bring in an official woman-suffrage bill without delay was carried at every platform, often without a dissenting vote. Then, with a three-times-repeated cry of "Votes for Women!" from the assembled multitude, the great meeting dispersed.

The London *Times* said next day:

> Its organisers had counted on an audience of 250,000. That expectation was certainly fulfilled, and probably it was doubled, and it would be difficult to contradict anyone who asserted that it was trebled. Like the distances and the number of the stars, the facts were beyond the threshold of perception.

The *Daily Express* said:

> It is probable that so many people never before stood in one square mass anywhere in England. Men who saw the great Gladstone meeting years ago said that compared with yesterday's multitude it was as nothing.

We felt that we had answered the challenge in Mr. Gladstone's declaration that "power belongs to the masses," and that through this power the government could be influenced; so it was with real hope that we despatched a copy of the resolution to the prime minister, asking him what answer the government would make to that unparalleled gathering of men and women. Mr. Asquith replied formally that he had nothing to add to his previous statement—that the government intended, at some indefinite time, to bring in a general reform bill which *might* be amended to include woman suffrage. Our wonderful demonstration, it appeared, had made no impression whatever upon him.

Chapter 3

Now we had reached a point where we had to choose between two alternatives. We had exhausted argument. Therefore either we had to give up our agitation altogether, as the suffragists of the eighties virtually had done, or else we must act, and go on acting, until the selfishness and the obstinacy of the government was broken down, or the government themselves destroyed. Until forced to do so, the government, we perceived, would never give women the vote.

We realised the truth of John Bright's words, spoken while the reform bill of 1867 was being agitated. Parliament, John Bright then declared, had never been hearty for any reform. The Reform Act of 1832 had been wrested by force from the government of that day, and now before another, he said, could be carried, the agitators would have to fill the streets with people from Charing Cross to Westminster Abbey. Acting on John Bright's advice, we issued a call to the public to join us in holding a huge demonstration, on June 30th outside the House of Commons. We wanted to be sure that the government saw as well as read of our immense following. A public proclamation from the Commissioner of Police, warning the public not to assemble in Parliament Square and declaring that the approaches to the Houses of Parliament must be kept open, was at once issued.

We persisted in announcing that the demonstration would take place, and I wrote a letter to Mr. Asquith telling him that a deputation would wait upon him at half-past four on the afternoon of June 30th. We held the usual Women's Parliament in Caxton Hall, after which Mrs. Pethick Lawrence, eleven other women, and myself, set forth. We met with no opposition from the police, but marched through cheering crowds of spectators to the Strangers' Entrance to the House of Commons. Here we were met by a large group of uniformed men commanded by Inspector Scantlebury, of the police. The inspector, whom I knew personally, stepped forward and demanded officially, "Are you Mrs. Pankhurst, and is this your deputation?"

"Yes," I replied.

"My orders are to exclude you from the House of Commons."

"Has Mr. Asquith received my letter?" I asked.

For answer the inspector drew my letter from his pocket and handed it to me.

"Did Mr. Asquith return no message, no kind of reply?" I inquired.

"No," replied the inspector.

We turned and walked back to Caxton Hall, to tell the waiting audience what had occurred. We resolved that there was nothing to do but wait patiently until evening, and see how well the public would respond to our call to meet in Parliament Square. Already we knew that the streets were filled with people, and early as it was the crowds were increasing rapidly. At eight we went out in groups from Caxton Hall, to find Parliament Square packed with a throng, estimated next day at least 100,000. From the steps of public buildings, from stone copings, from the iron railings of the Palace Yard, to which they clung precariously, our women made speeches until the police pulled them down and flung them into the moving, swaying, excited crowds. Some of the women were arrested, others were merely ordered to move on. Mingled cheers and jeers rose from the spectators.

Some of the men were roughs who had come out to amuse themselves. Others were genuinely sympathetic, and tried valiantly to help us to reach the House of Commons. Again and again the police lines were broken, and it was only as the result of repeated charges by mounted police that the people's attacks were repelled. Many members of Parliament, including Mr. Lloyd-George, Mr. Winston Churchill, and Mr. Herbert Gladstone, came out to witness the struggle, which lasted until midnight and resulted in the arrest of twenty-nine women. Two of these women were arrested after they had each thrown a stone through a window of Mr. Asquith's official residence in Downing Street, the value of the windows being about $2.40.

This was the first window-breaking in our history. Mrs. Mary Leigh and Miss Edith New, who had thrown the stones, sent word to me from the police court that, having acted without orders, they would not resent repudiation from headquarters. Far from repudiating them, I went at once to see them in their cells, and assured them of my approval of their act. The smashing of windows is a time-honoured method of showing displeasure in a political situation. As one of the newspapers, commenting on the affair, truly said:

> When the king and queen dine at Apsley on the 13th inst. they will be entertained in rooms the windows of which the Duke of Wellington was obliged to protect with iron shutters from the fury of his political opponents.

In Winchester a few years ago, to give but one instance, a great riot took place as a protest against the removal of a historic gun from one part of the town to another. In the course of this riot windows were broken and other property of various kinds was destroyed, very serious damage being done. No punishment was administered in respect of this riot and the authorities, bowing to public opinion thus riotously expressed, restored the gun to its original situation.

Window-breaking, when Englishmen do it, is regarded as honest expression of political opinion. Window-breaking, when Englishwomen do it, is treated as a crime. In sentencing Mrs. Leigh and Miss

New to two months in the first division, the magistrate used very severe language, and declared that such a thing must never happen again. Of course the women assured him that it would happen again. Said Mrs. Leigh:

> We have no other course but to rebel against oppression, and if necessary to resort to stronger measures. This fight is going on.

The summer of 1908 is remembered as one of the most oppressively hot seasons the country had known for years. Our prisoners in Holloway suffered intensely, some being made desperately ill from the heat, the bad air, and the miserable food. We who spent the summer campaigning suffered also, but in less degree. It was a tremendous relief when the cool days of autumn set in, and it was with renewed vigour that we prepared for the opening day of Parliament, which was October 12th. Again we resolved to send a deputation to the prime minister, and again we invited the general public to take part in the demonstration. We had printed thousands of little handbills bearing this inscription:

> Men and Women, Help the Suffragettes to Rush the House of Commons, on Tuesday Evening, October 13th, at 7:30.

On Sunday, October 11th, we held a large meeting in Trafalgar Square, my daughter Christabel, Mrs. Drummond and I speaking from the plinth of the Nelson monument. Mr. Lloyd-George, as we afterward learned, was a member of the audience. The police were there, taking ample notes of our speeches. We had not failed to notice that they were watching us daily, dogging our footsteps, and showing in numerous ways that they were under orders to keep track of all our movements. The climax came at noon on October 12th, when Christabel, Mrs. Drummond and I were each served with an imposing legal document which read:

> Information has been laid this day by the Commissioner of Police that you, in the month of October, in the year 1908, were guilty of conduct likely to provoke a breach of the peace by initiating and causing to be initiated, by publishing and causing to be published, a certain handbill, calling upon and inciting the public to do a certain wrongful and illegal act, *viz.*, to rush the House of Commons at 7:30 p.m. on October 13th inst.

The last paragraph was a summons to appear at Bow Street police

Mrs. Pankhurst and Christabel hiding from the police on the Roof Garden at Clements Inn, October, 1908

station that same afternoon at three o'clock. We did not go to Bow Street police station. We went instead to a crowded "At Home" at Queen's Hall, where it can be imagined that our news created great excitement. The place was surrounded by constables, and the police reporters were on hand to take stenographic reports of everything that was said from the platform. Once an excited cry was raised that a police inspector was coming in to arrest us. But the officer merely brought a message that the summons had been adjourned until the following morning.

It did not suit our convenience to obey the adjourned summons quite so early, so I wrote a polite note to the police, saying that we would be in our headquarters, No. 4 Clements Inn, the next evening at six o'clock, and would then be at his disposal. Warrants for our arrests were quickly issued, and Inspector Jarvis was instructed to execute them at once. This he found impossible to do, for Mrs. Drummond was spending her last day of liberty on private business, while my daughter and I had retreated to another part of Clements Inn, which is a big, rambling building. There, in the roof-garden of the Pethick Lawrence's private flat, we remained all day, busy, under the soft blue of the autumn sky, with our work and our preparations for a long absence. At six we walked downstairs, dressed for the street. Mrs. Drummond arrived promptly, the waiting officers read the warrants, and we all proceeded to Bow Street in cabs. It was too late for the trial to be held. We asked for bail, but the authorities had no mind to allow us to take part in the "rush" which we had incited, so we were obliged to spend the night in the police station. All night I lay awake, thinking of the scenes which were going on in the streets.

The next morning, in a courtroom crowded to its utmost capacity, my daughter rose to conduct her first case at law. She had earned the right to an LL.B. after her name, but as women are not permitted to practise law in England, she had never appeared at the bar in any capacity except that of defendant. Now she proposed to combine the two *rôles* of defendant and lawyer, and conduct the case for the three of us. She began by asking the magistrate not to try the case in that court, but to send it for trial before a judge and jury. We had long desired to take the Suffragettes' cases before bodies of private citizens, because we had every reason to suspect that the police-court officials acted under the direct commands of the very persons against whom our agitation was directed. Jury trial was denied us; but after the preliminary examination was over the magistrate, Mr. Curtis Bennett, allowed a week's adjournment for preparation of the case.

On October 21st the trial was resumed, with the courtroom as full as before and the press table even more crowded, for it had been widely published that we had actually subpoenaed two members of the government, who had witnessed the scenes on the night of October 13th. The first witness to enter the box was Mr. Lloyd-George. Christabel examined him at some length as to the meaning and merits of the word rush, and succeeded in making him very uncomfortable—and the charge against ourselves look very flimsy. She then questioned him about the speeches he had heard at Trafalgar Square, and as to whether there had been any suggestion that property be destroyed or personal violence used. He admitted that the speeches were temperate and the crowds orderly.

Then Christabel suddenly asked, "There were no words used so likely to incite to violence as the advice you gave at Swansea, that the women should be ruthlessly flung out of your meeting?"

Mr. Lloyd-George looked black, and answered nothing. The magistrate hastened to the protection of Mr. Lloyd-George. "This is quite irrelevant," he said. "That was a private meeting." It was a public meeting, and Christabel said so. "It was a private meeting *in a sense*," insisted the magistrate.

Mr. Lloyd-George assumed an air of pompous indignation when Christabel asked him, "Have we not received encouragement from you, and if not from you from your colleagues, to take action of this kind?" Mr. Lloyd-George rolled his eyes upward as he replied, "I should be very much surprised to hear that, Miss Pankhurst."

"Is it not a fact," asked Christabel, "that you yourself have set us an example of revolt?"

"I never incited a crowd to violence," exclaimed the witness.

"Not in the Welsh graveyard case?" she asked.

"No!" he cried angrily.

"You did not tell them to break down a wall and disinter a body?" pursued Christabel.

He could not deny this but, "I gave advice which was found by the Court of Appeal to be sound legal advice," he snapped, and turned his back as far as he could in the narrow witness-box.

Mr. Herbert Gladstone had asked to be allowed to testify early, as he was being detained from important public duties. Christabel asked to question one witness before Mr. Gladstone entered the box. The witness was Miss Georgiana Brackenbury, who had recently suffered six weeks' imprisonment for the cause, and had since met and had a talk with Mr. Horace Smith, the magistrate, who had made to her a most important and damaging admission of the government's interference in suffragists' trials. Christabel asked her one question. "Did Mr. Horace Smith tell you in sentencing you that he was doing what he had been told to do?"

"You must not put that question!" exclaimed the magistrate.

But the witness had already answered "Yes." There was an excited stir in the courtroom. It had been recorded under oath that a magistrate had admitted that Suffragettes were being sentenced not by himself, according to the evidence and according to law, but by the government, for no one could possibly doubt where Mr. Horace Smith's orders came from.

Mr. Gladstone, plump, bald, and ruddy, in no way resembles his illustrious father. He entered the witness-box smiling and confident, but his complacence vanished when Christabel asked him outright if the government had not ordered the Commissioner of Police to take this action against us. Of course the magistrate intervened, and Mr. Gladstone did not answer the question. Christabel tried again. "Did you instruct Mr. Horace Smith to decide against Miss Brackenbury, and to send her to prison for six weeks?" That too was objected to, as were all questions on the subject.

All through the examination the magistrate constantly intervened to save the Cabinet Minister from embarrassment, but Christabel finally succeeded in making Mr. Gladstone admit, point by point, that he had said that women could never get the vote because they could not fight for it as men had fought.

A large number of witnesses testified to the orderly nature of the demonstration on the 13th, and then Christabel rose to plead. She began by declaring that these proceedings had been taken, as the legal saying is, "in malice and vexation," in order to lame a political enemy. She declared that, under the law, the charge which might properly be brought against us was that of illegal assembly, but the government had not charged us with this offence, because the government desired to keep the case in a police court. She declared:

> The authorities dare not see this case come before a jury because they know perfectly well that if it were heard before a jury of our countrymen we should be acquitted, just as John Burns was acquitted years ago for taking action far more dan-

Christabel, Mrs. Drummond and Mrs. Pankhurst in the dock, first conspiracy trial October, 1908

gerous to the public peace than we have taken. We are deprived of trial by jury. We are also deprived of the right to appeal against the magistrate's decision. Very carefully has this procedure been thought out.

Of the handbill she said:

We do not deny that we issued this bill; none of us three has wished to deny responsibility. We did issue the bill; we did cause it to be circulated; we did put upon it the words 'Come and help the suffragettes rush the House of Commons.' For these words we do not apologise. It is very well known that we took this action in order to press forward a claim, which, according to the British constitution, we are well entitled to make.

In all that the Suffragettes had done, in all that they might ever do, declared my daughter, they would only be following in the footsteps of men now in Parliament.

Mr. Herbert Gladstone has told us in the speech I read to him that the victory of argument alone is not enough. As we cannot hope to win by force of argument alone, it is necessary to overcome by other means the savage resistance of the government to our claim for citizenship. He says, 'Go on, fight as the men did.' And then, when we show our power and get the people to help us, he takes proceedings against us in a manner that would have been disgraceful even in the old days of coercion. Then there is Mr. Lloyd-George, who, if any man has done so, has set us an example. His whole career has been a series of revolts. He has said that if we do not get the vote—mark these words—we should be justified in adopting the methods the men had to adopt, namely, pulling down the Hyde Park railings.

She quoted Lord Morley as saying of the Indian unrest:

'We are in India in the presence of a living movement, and a movement for what? For objects which we ourselves have taught them to think are desirable objects; and unless we can somehow reconcile order with satisfaction of those ideals and aspirations, the fault will not be theirs, it will be ours—it will mark the breakdown of British statesmanship.'—Apply those words to our case.

Remember that we are demanding of Liberal statesmen that

which is for us the greatest boon and the most essential right—and if the present government cannot reconcile order with our demand for the vote without delay, it will mark the breakdown of their statesmanship. Yes, their statesmanship has broken down already. They are disgraced. It is only in this court that they have the smallest hope of being supported.

My daughter had spoken with passion and fervour, and her righteous indignation had moved her to words that caused the magistrate's face to turn an angry crimson. When I rose to address the court I began by assuming an appearance of calmness which I did not altogether feel. I endorsed all that Christabel had said of the unfairness of our trial and the malice of the government; I protested against the trial of political offenders in a common police court, and I said that we were not women who would come into the court as ordinary lawbreakers. I described Mrs. Drummond's worthy career as a wife, a mother, and a self-sustaining business woman. I said,

> Before you decide what is to be done with us, I should like you to hear from me a statement of what has brought me into the dock this morning.

And then I told of my life and experiences, many of which I have related in these pages of what I had seen and known as a Poor Law Guardian and a registrar of births and deaths; of how I had learned the burning necessity of changing the status of women, of altering the laws under which they and their children live, and of the essential justice of making women self-governing citizens.

> I have seen that men are encouraged by law to take advantage of the helplessness of women. Many women have thought as I have, and for many, many years have tried, by that influence of which we have been so often reminded, to alter these laws, but we find that influence counts for nothing. When we went to the House of Commons we used to be told, when we were persistent, that members of Parliament were not responsible to women, they were responsible only to voters, and that their time was too fully occupied to reform those laws, although they agreed that they needed reforming.
> We women have presented larger petitions in support of our enfranchisement than were ever presented for any other reform; we have succeeded in holding greater public meetings

than men have ever held for any reform, in spite of the difficulty which women have in throwing off their natural diffidence, that desire to escape publicity which we have inherited from generations of our foremothers. We have broken through that. We have faced hostile mobs at street corners, because we were told that we could not have that representation for our taxes that men have won unless we converted the whole of the country to our side. Because we have done this, we have been misrepresented, we have been ridiculed, we have had contempt poured upon us, and the ignorant mob have been incited to offer us violence, which we have faced unarmed and unprotected by the safeguards which Cabinet Ministers enjoy. We have been driven to do this; we are determined to go on with this agitation because we feel in honour bound. Just as it was the duty of your forefathers, it is our duty to make the world a better place for women than it is today, (1914).

Lastly, I want to call attention to the self-restraint which was shown by our followers on the night of the 13th, after we had been arrested. Our rule has always been to be patient, exercise self-restraint, show our so-called superiors that we are not hysterical; to use no violence, but rather to offer ourselves to the violence of others.

That is all I have to say to you, sir. We are here, not because we are lawbreakers; we are here in our efforts to become lawmakers.

The burly policemen, the reporters, and most of the spectators were in tears as I finished. But the magistrate, who had listened part of the time with his hand concealing his face, still held that we were properly charged in a common police court as inciters to riot. Since we refused to be bound over to keep the peace, he sentenced Mrs. Drummond and myself to three months' imprisonment, and Christabel to ten weeks' imprisonment. It was destined to be a kind of imprisonment the authorities had never yet been called upon to deal with.

Chapter 4

My first act on reaching Holloway was to demand that the governor be sent for. When he came I told him that the Suffragettes had resolved that they would no longer submit to being treated as ordinary law-breakers. In the course of our trial two Cabinet Ministers had admitted that we were political offenders, and therefore we should henceforth refuse to be searched or to undress in the presence of the wardresses. For myself I claimed the right, and I hoped the others would do likewise, to speak to my friends during exercise, or whenever I came in contact with them. The governor, after reflection, yielded to the first two demands, but said that he would have to consult the Home Office before permitting us to break the rule of silence.

We were accordingly allowed to change our clothing privately, and, as a further concession, were placed in adjoining cells. This was little advantage to me, however, since within a few days I was removed to a hospital cell, suffering from the illness which prison life always inflicts on me. Here the governor visited me with the unwelcome news that the Home Secretary had refused to allow me the privilege of speech with my fellow prisoners. I asked him if I might, when I was strong enough to walk, take exercise with my friends. To this he assented, and I soon had the joy of seeing my daughter and the other brave comrades, and walking with them in the dismal courtyard of the prison.

Single file we walked, at a distance of three or four feet from one another, back and forth under the stony eyes of the wardresses. The rough flags of the pavement hurt our feet, shod in heavy, shapeless prison boots. The autumn days were cold and cheerless, and we shivered violently under our scanty cloaks. But of all our hardships the ceaseless silence of our lives was worst.

At the end of the second week I decided I would no longer endure it. That afternoon at exercise I suddenly called my daughter by name and bade her stand still until I came up to her. Of course she stopped, and when I reached her side we linked arms and began to talk in low tones. A wardress ran up to us, saying: "I shall listen to everything you say."

I replied: "You are welcome to do that, but I shall insist on my right to speak to my daughter."

Another wardress had hastily left the yard, and now she returned with a large number of wardresses. They seized me and quickly removed me to my cell, while the other suffrage prisoners cheered my action at the top of their voices. For their "mutiny" they got three days' solitary confinement, and I, for mine, a much more severe punishment. Unrepentant, I told the governor that, in spite of any punishment he might impose on me, I would never again submit to the silence rule. To forbid a mother to speak to her daughter was infamous. For this I was characterised as a "dangerous criminal" and was sent into solitary confinement, without exercise or chapel, while a wardress

MRS. PANKHURST AND MISS CHRISTABEL PANKHURST
IN PRISON DRESS

was stationed constantly at my cell door to see that I communicated with no one.

It was two weeks before I saw any of my friends again, and meantime the health of Mrs. Drummond had been so seriously impaired that she was released for hospital treatment. My daughter also, I learned, was ill, and in desperation I made application to the Board of Visiting Magistrates to be allowed to see her. After a long conference, during which I was made to wait outside in the corridor, the magistrates returned a refusal, saying that I might renew my application in a month. The answer then, they said, would depend on my conduct. A month! My girl might be dead by that time. My anxiety sent me to bed ill again, but, although I did not know it, relief was already on its way. I had told the visiting magistrates that I would wait until public opinion got within those walls, and this happened sooner than I had dared to hope.

Mrs. Drummond, as soon as she was able to appear in public, and the other suffrage prisoners, as they were released, spread broadcast the story of our mutiny, and of a subsequent one led by Miss Wallace Dunlop, which sent a large number of women into solitary confinement. The Suffragettes marched by thousands to Holloway, thronging the approaches to the prison street. Round and round the prison they marched, singing the Women's *Marseillaise* and cheering. Faintly the sound came to our ears, infinitely lightening our burden of pain and loneliness. The following week they came again, so we afterwards learned, but this time the police turned them back long before they reached the confines of the prison.

The demonstrations, together with a volley of questions asked in the House of Commons, told at last. Orders came from the Home Office that I was to see my daughter, and that we were to be allowed to exercise and to talk together for one hour each day. In addition, we were to be permitted the rare privilege of reading a daily newspaper. Then, on December 8th, the day of Christabel's release, orders came that I, too, should be discharged, two weeks before the expiration of my sentence.

At the welcome breakfast given us, as released prisoners, at Lincoln's Inn Hotel, I told our members that henceforth we should all insist on refusing to abide by ordinary prison rules. We did not propose to break laws and then shirk punishment. We simply meant to assert our right to be recognised as political prisoners. We reached this point after due reflection. We first set ourselves not to complain of prison, not to say anything about it, to avoid it, to keep away from all side issues, to keep along the straight path of political reform, to get the vote; because we knew that when we had won it we could reform prisons and a great many other abuses as well. But now that we had had in the witness box the admission of Cabinet Ministers that we are political offenders, we should in future demand the treatment given to men political offenders in all civilised countries. I said:

> If nations are still so governed that they make political offenders, then Great Britain is going to treat her political offenders as well as political offenders are treated by other nations. If it were the custom to treat political offenders as ordinary offenders against the well-being of society are treated, we should not have complained if we were treated like that; but it is not the international custom to do it, and so, for the dignity of the women of the country, and for the sake of the consciences of the men of the country, and for the sake of our nation amongst the nations of the earth, we are not going to allow the Liberal government to treat us like ordinary lawbreakers in future.

I said the same thing that night in a great meeting held in Queen's Hall to welcome the released prisoners, and, although we all knew that our determination involved a bitter struggle, our women endorsed it without a moment's hesitation. Had they been able to look forward to the events which were even then overshadowing us, could they have foreseen the new forms of suffering and danger that lay in waiting, I am certain that they would still have done the same thing, for our experiences had taught us to dispense with fear. Whatever of timidity, of shrinking from pain or hardship any of us had originally possessed, it had all vanished. There were no terrors that we were not now ready to face.

The year 1909 marks an important point in our struggle, partly because of this decision of ours, never again to submit to be classed with criminals; and partly because in this year we forced the Liberal Government to go on record, publicly, in regard to the oldest of popular rights, the right of petition. We had long contemplated this step, and now the time seemed ripe for taking it.

In the closing days of 1908 Mr. Asquith, speaking on the policy to be carried out in 1909, commented on the various deputations he was obliged at that time to receive. They called on him, he said, "from all quarters and in all causes, on an average of something like two hours on three days in every week." The deputations all asked for different things, and, although all of the things could not possibly be included in the King's speech, Mr. Asquith was inclined to agree that many of them ought to be included. This declaration from the prime minister that he was constantly receiving deputations of men, and listening favourably to their suggestions of what policies to pursue, aroused in the Suffragettes feelings of deep indignation. This in part they expressed on January 25th, when the first meeting of the Cabinet Council took place. A small deputation from the W. S. P. U. proceeded to Downing Street to claim the right to be heard, as men were heard. For knocking at the door of the official residence four of the women, including my sister, Mrs. Clark, were arrested and sent to prison for one month.

A month later the seventh of our Women's Parliaments was called against this and against the fact that no mention of women had been included in the King's speech. Led by Mrs. Pethick Lawrence, Lady Constance Lytton and Miss Daisy Solomon, a deputation of women endeavoured to carry the resolution to the House of Commons. They were promptly arrested and, next day, were sent to prison on sentences of from one to two months. The time was rapidly approaching when the legality of these arrests would have to be tested. In June of the year 1909 the test was made.

It will be remembered that we had endeavoured to force the authorities to make good their threat to charge us under the obsolete Charles II "Tumultuous Petitions Act," which prescribes severe penalties for persons proceeding to Parliament in groups of more than twelve for the purpose of presenting petitions. It had been stated that if we were charged under that act our case would be given a hearing before a judge and jury instead of a police magistrate. Since this was exactly what we desired to have happen we had sent deputation after deputation of more than twelve persons, but always they were tried in police courts, and were sent to prison often for periods as long as that prescribed in the Charles II Act. Now we determined to do something still more ambitious; we resolved to test, not the Charles II Act, but the constitutional right of the subject to petition the prime minister as the seat of power.

The right of petition, which has existed in England since the earliest known period, was written into the Bill of Rights which became law in 1689 on the accession of William and Mary. It was, in fact, one of the conditions attaching to the accession of the joint monarchs. According to the Bill of Rights, "It is the right of subjects to petition the king and all commitments, and prosecutions for such petitionings are illegal." The power of the king having passed almost completely into the hands of Parliament, the prime minister now stands where the king's majesty stood in former times. Clearly, then, the right of the subject to petition the prime minister cannot be legally denied. Thus were we advised, and in order to keep within the strict letter of the law, we accepted the limitations of the right of petition laid down in the Charles II Act, and decided that our petition should be carried to the House of Commons by small groups of women.

Again I called together, on the evening of June 29th, a Parliament of women. Previously I had written to Mr. Asquith stating that a deputation of women would wait on him at the House of Commons at eight o'clock in the evening. I wrote him further that we were not to be refused, as we insisted upon our constitutional right to be received. To my note the prime minister returned a formal note declining to receive us. Nevertheless we continued our preparations, because we knew that the prime minister would continue to decline, but that in the end he would be forced to receive us.

An incident which occurred a week before the date of the deputation was destined to have important consequences. Miss Wallace Dunlop went to St. Stephen's Hall in the House of Commons, and marked with printer's ink on the stone work of the hall an extract from the Bill of Rights. The first time she made the attempt she was interrupted by a policeman, but two days later she succeeded in stamping on the ancient walls the reminder to Parliament that women as well as men possess constitutional rights, and that they were proposing to exercise those rights. She was arrested and sentenced to prison for one month, in the third division. The option of a heavy fine was given her, which of course she refused.

Miss Wallace Dunlop's prison term began on June 22nd. Perhaps her deed had something to do with the unusual interest taken in the approaching deputation, an interest which was shown not only by the public but by many members of Parliament. In the House of Commons a strong feeling that the women ought this time to be received manifested itself in many questions put to the government. One member even asked leave to move the adjournment of the House on a matter of urgent public importance, namely the danger to the public peace, owing to the refusal of the prime minister to receive the deputation. This was denied, however, and the government mendaciously disclaimed all responsibility for what action the police might take toward the deputation.

The Home Secretary, Mr. Gladstone, when asked by Mr. Kier Hardie to give instructions that the deputation, if orderly, should be admitted to St. Stephen's, replied: "I cannot say what action the police ought to take in the matter." Our Women's Parliament met at half past seven on the evening of June 29th, and the petition to the prime minister was read and adopted. Then our deputation set forth. Accompanying me as leader were two highly respectable women of advanced years, Mrs. Saul Solomon, whose husband had been prime minister at the Cape, and Miss Neligan, one of the foremost of the pioneer educators of England. We three and five other women were preceded by Miss Elsie Howey, who, riding fast, went on horse-back to announce our coming to the enormous crowds that filled the streets. She, we afterward learned, progressed as far as the approaches to the House of Commons before being turned back by the police. As for the deputation, it pressed on through the crowd as far as St. Margaret's Church, Westminster, where we found a long line of police blocking the road. We paused for a moment, gathering strength for the ordeal of trying to push through the lines, when an unexpected thing happened.

An order was given from someone, and instantly the police lines parted, leaving a clear space through which we walked towards the House. We were escorted on our way by Inspector Wells, and as we passed the crowd broke into vociferous cheering, firmly believing that we were after all to be received. As for myself I did little speculating as to what was about to happen. I simply led my deputation on as far as the entrance to St. Stephen's Hall. There we encountered another strong force of police commanded by our old acquaintance, Inspector Scantlebury, who stepped forward and handed me a letter. I opened it and read in aloud to the women.

> The prime minister, for the reasons which he has already given in a written reply to their request, regrets that he is unable to receive the proposed deputation.

I dropped the note to the ground and said:

> I stand upon my rights, as a subject of the king, to petition the prime minister, and I am firmly resolved to stand here until I am received.

Inspector Scantlebury turned away and walked rapidly towards the door of the Strangers' Entrance. I turned to Inspector Jarvis, who re-

Inspector Wells conducting Mrs. Pankhurst to the House of Commons, June, 1908

mained, to several members of Parliament and some newspaper men who stood looking on, and begged them to take my message to the prime minister, but no one responded, and the inspector, seizing my arm, began to push me away. I now knew that the deputation would not be received and that the old miserable business of refusing to leave, of being forced backward, and returning again and again until arrested, would have to be re-enacted. I had to take into account that I was accompanied by two fragile old ladies, who, brave as they were to be there at all, could not possibly endure what I knew must follow. I quickly decided that I should have to force an immediate arrest, so I committed an act of technical assault on the person of Inspector Jarvis, striking him very lightly on the cheek. He said instantly, "I understand why you did that," and I supposed then that we would instantly be taken. But the other police apparently did not grasp the situation, for they began pushing and jostling our women. I said to the inspector: "Shall I have to do it again?" and he said "Yes." So I struck him lightly a second time, and then he ordered the police to make the arrests.

The matter did not end with the arrest of our deputation of eight women. In recurring deputations of twelve the Suffragettes again and again pressed forward in vain endeavour to reach the House of Commons. In spite of the fact that the crowds were friendly and did everything they could to aid the women, their deputations were broken up by the police and many of the women arrested. By nine o'clock Parliament Square was empty, an enormous force of mounted police having beaten the people back into Victoria Street and across Westminster Bridge. For a short time all looked tranquil, but soon little groups of women, seven or eight at a time, kept appearing mysteriously and making spirited dashes toward the House. This extraordinary procedure greatly exasperated the police, who could not unravel the mystery of where the women came from.

As a matter of bygone history the explanation is that the W. S. P. U. had hired thirty offices in the neighbourhood, in the shelter of which the women waited until it was time for them to sally forth. It was a striking demonstration of the ingenuity of women opposing the physical force of men, but it served still another purpose. It diverted the attention of the police from another demonstration which was going on. Other Suffragettes had gone to the official residence of the First Lord of the Admiralty, to the Home Office, the Treasury and Privy Council Offices, and had registered their contempt for the government's refusal to receive the deputation by the time-honoured method of breaking a window in each place.

One hundred and eight women were arrested that night, but instead of submitting to arrests and trial, the Women's Social and Political Union announced that they were prepared to prove that the government and not the women had broken the law in refusing to receive the petition. My case, coupled with that of the Hon. Mrs. Haverfield, was selected as a test case for all the others, and Lord Robert Cecil was retained for the defence. Mr. Muskett, who conducted the case for the prosecution, tried to prove that our women had not gone to the House of Commons to present a petition, but this was easily demonstrated to be an unwarranted claim.

The speeches of the leader, the official articles published in our newspaper, *Votes for Women*, and the letters sent to Mr. Asquith, not to speak of the indisputable facts that every member of the deputation carried a copy of the petition in her hand, furnished evidence enough of the nature of our errand. The whole case of the subject's right of petition was then brought forward for discussion. Mr. Muskett spoke first, then our council, Mr. Henle, then Lord Robert Cecil. Last of all I spoke, describing the events of June 29th. I told the magistrate that should he decide that we and not the government had been guilty of an infraction of the law, we should refuse to be bound over, but should all choose to go to prison. In that case we should not submit to being treated like criminals I said, pointing to the benches where my fellow-prisoners sat:

> There are one hundred and eight of us here today, and just as we have thought it is our duty to defy the police in the street, so when we get into prison, as we are political prisoners, we shall do our best to bring back into the twentieth century the treatment of political prisoners which was thought right in the case of William Cobbett, and other political offenders of his time.

The magistrate, Sir Albert de Rutzen, an elderly, amiable man, rather bewildered by this unprecedented situation, then gave his decision. He agreed with Mr. Henle and Lord Robert Cecil that the right of petition was clearly guaranteed to every subject, but he thought that when the women were refused permission to enter the House of Commons, and when Mr. Asquith had said that he would not receive them, the women acted wrongly to persist in their demands. He should, therefore, fine them five pounds each, or sentence them to prison for one month in the second division. The sentence would be suspended for the present until learned counsel could obtain a decision from a higher court on the legal point of the right of petition.

I then put in a claim for all the prisoners, and asked that all their cases might be held over until the test case was decided, and this was agreed to, except in regard to fourteen women charged with window-breaking. They were tried separately and sent to prison on sentences varying from six weeks to two months. Of them later.

The appeal against Sir Albert de Rutzen's decision was tried in a Divisional Court early in December of that year. Lord Robert Cecil again appeared for the defence, and in a masterly piece of argumentation, contended that in England there was and always had been the right of petition, and that the right had always been considered a necessary condition of a free country and a civilised government. The right of petition, he pointed out, had three characteristics: In the first place, it was the right to petition the actual repositories of power; in the second place, it was the right to petition in person; and in the third place, the right must be exercised reasonably. A long list of historical precedents were offered in support of the right to petition in person, but Lord Robert argued that even if these did not exist, the right was admitted in the Charles II "Tumultuous Petitions Act," which provides:

> That no person or persons whatsoever shall repair to His Majesty or both or either Houses of Parliament upon pretence of presenting or delivering any petition, complaint, remonstrance, or declaration or other address, accompanied with excessive number of people . . . etc.

The Bill of Rights had specially confirmed the right of petition in so far as the king personally was concerned. Lord Robert pursued:

> The women had gone to Parliament Square on June 29th in the exercise of a plain constitutional right, and that in going there with a petition they had acted according to the only constitutional method they possessed, being voteless, for the redress of their grievances.

If then it were true, as contended, the subject not only possessed the right to petition, but to petition in person, the only point to be considered was whether the right had been exercised reasonably. If persons desired to interview the prime minister, it was surely reasonable to go to the House of Commons, and to present themselves at the Strangers' Entrance. Mrs. Pankhurst, Mrs. Haverfield and the others had, as the evidence showed, proceeded along the public highway and had been escorted to the door of the House of Commons by an officer of the police, and could not therefore, up to that point, have been acting in an unlawful manner. The police had kept clear a large open space opposite the House of Commons, the crowd being kept at a certain distance away. Within the open space there were only persons having business in the House of Commons, members of the police force and the eight women who formed the deputation.

It could not possibly be contended that these eight women had caused an obstruction. It was true that a police officer told them that the prime minister was not in the House of Commons, but when one desired an interview with a Member of Parliament one did not make his request of a casual policeman in the street. Moreover, the police did not possess any authority to stop anyone from going into the House of Commons.

The letter given the women, in which the prime minister said that he could not or would not see them, had been cited. Now, had the prime minister, in his letter, said that he could not or would not see the women at that time, that the time was not convenient; but that he would at some future time, at a more convenient time, receive them, that would have been a sufficient answer. The women would not have been justified in refusing to accept such an answer, because the right to petition must be exercised reasonably. But the letter contained an unqualified refusal, and that, if we allow the right of petition to exist, was no answer at all. Last of all Lord Robert argued that if there is a right to petition a Member of Parliament, then it must be incumbent on the part of a Member of Parliament to receive the petition, and that no one has a right to interfere with the petitioner. If the eight women were legally justified in presenting their petition, then they were also justified in refusing to obey the orders of the police to leave the place.

In an address full of bias, and revealing plainly that he had no accurate knowledge of any of the events that had led up to the case in hand, the Lord Chief Justice delivered judgment. He said that he entirely agreed with Lord Robert Cecil as to the right to present a petition to the prime minister, either as prime minister or as a Member of Parliament; and he agreed also that petitions to the king should be presented to the prime minister. But the claim of the women, he said, was not merely to present a petition, but to be received in a deputation. He did not think it likely that Mr. Asquith would have refused to receive a petition from the women, but his refusal to receive the deputation was not unnatural, "in consequence of what we know did happen on previous occasions." (Mr. Asquith had never, since becoming prime minister, received a deputation of women, nor had he ever received a deputation of the W. S. P. U. So it was absurd of the Lord Chief Justice to speak of "what did happen, on previous occasions.")

Referring to the Metropolitan Police Act of 1839, which provides that it shall be lawful for the Commissioner of Police to make regulations and to give instructions to the constable for keeping order, and for preventing any obstruction of thoroughfares in the immediate neighbourhood of the House of Commons, and the Sessional Order empowering the police to keep clear the approaches to the House of Commons, the Lord Chief Justice decided that I and the other women were guilty of an infraction of the law when we insisted on a right to enter the House of Commons. The Lord Chief Justice therefore ruled that our conviction in the lower court had been proper, and our appeal was dismissed with costs.

Thus was destroyed in England the ancient constitutional right of petition, secured to the people by the Bill of Rights, and cherished by uncounted generations of Englishmen. I say the right was destroyed, for of how much value is a petition which cannot be presented in person? The decision of the high court was appalling to the members of the W. S. P. U., as it closed the last approach, by constitutional means, to our enfranchisement. Far from discouraging or disheartening us, it simply spurred us on to new and more aggressive forms of militancy.

CHAPTER 5

Between the time of the arrest in June and the handing down of the absurd decision of the Lord Chief Justice that although we, as subjects, possessed the right of petition, yet we had committed an offence in exercising that right, nearly six months had passed. In that interval certain grave developments had lifted the militant movement onto a new and more heroic plane. It will be remembered that a week before our deputation to test the Charles II Act, Miss Wallace Dunlop had been sent to prison for one month for stamping an extract from the Bill of Rights on the stone walls of St. Stephen's Hall. On arriving at Holloway on Friday evening, July 2nd, she sent for the governor and demanded of him that she be treated as a political offender. The governor replied that he had no power to alter the sentence of the magistrate, whereupon Miss Wallace Dunlop informed him that it was the unalterable resolution of the Suffragettes never again to submit to the prison treatment given to ordinary offenders against the law.

Therefore she should, if placed in the second division as a common criminal, refuse to touch food until the government yielded her point. It is hardly likely that the government or the prison authorities realised the seriousness of Miss Wallace Dunlop's action, or the heroic mould of the Suffragettes' character. At all events the Home Secretary paid no attention to the letter sent him by the prisoner, in which she explained simply but clearly her motives for her desperate act, and the prison authorities did nothing except seek means of breaking down her resistance.

The ordinary prison diet was replaced by the most tempting food, and this instead of being brought to her cell at intervals, was kept there night and day, but always untouched. Several times daily the doctor came to feel her pulse and observe her growing weakness. The doctor, as well as the governor and the wardresses argued, coaxed and threatened, but without effect. The week passed without any sign of surrender on the part of the prisoner. On Friday the doctor reported that she was rapidly reaching a point at which death might at any time supervene. Hurried conferences were carried on between the prison and the Home Office, and that evening, June 8th, Miss Wallace Dunlop was sent home, having served one-fourth of her sentence, and having ignored completely all the terms of her imprisonment.

On the day of her release the fourteen women who had been convicted of window breaking received their sentences, and learning of Miss Wallace Dunlop's act, they, as they were being taken to Holloway in the prison van, held a consultation and agreed to follow her example. Arrived at Holloway they at once informed the officials that they would not give up any of their belongings, neither would they put on prison clothing, perform prison labour, eat prison food or keep the rule of silence.

The governor agreed for the moment to allow them to retain their property and to wear their own clothing, but he told them that they had committed an act of mutiny and that he would have to so charge them at the next visit of the magistrates. The women then addressed petitions to the Home Secretary, demanding that they be given the prison treatment universally allowed political offenders. They decided to postpone the hunger strike until the Home Secretary had had time to reply. Meanwhile, after a vain appeal for more fresh air, for the weather was stiflingly hot, the women committed one more act of mutiny, they broke the windows of their cells.

We learned this from the prisoners themselves. Several days after they had gone to prison, my daughter Christabel and Mrs. Tuke, filled with anxiety for their fate, gained admission to an upper story room of a house overlooking the prison. Calling at the top of their voices and waving a flag of the Union, they succeeded in attracting the prisoners' attention. The women thrust their arms through the broken panes, waving handkerchiefs, Votes for Women badges, anything they could get hold of, and in a few shouted words told their tale. That same day the visiting magistrates arrived, and the mutineers were sentenced to terms of seven to ten days of solitary confinement in the punishment cells. In these frightful cells, dark, unclean, dripping with moisture, the prisoners resolutely hunger struck. At the end of five days one of the women was reduced to such a condition that the Home Secretary ordered her released. The next day several more were released, and before the end of the week the last of the fourteen had gained their liberty.

The affair excited the greatest sympathy all over England, sympathy which Mr. Gladstone tried to divert by charging two of the prisoners with kicking and biting the wardresses. In spite of their vigorous denials these two women were sentenced, on these charges, one to ten days and the other to a month in prison. Although still very weak from the previous hunger strike, they at once entered upon a second hunger strike, and in three days had to be released.

After this each succeeding batch of Suffragette prisoners, unless otherwise directed, followed the example of these heroic rebels. The prison officials, seeing their authority vanish, were panic stricken. Holloway and other women's prisons throughout the Kingdom became perfect dens of violence and brutality. Hear the account given by Lucy Burns of her experience:

> We remained quite still when ordered to undress, and when they told us to proceed to our cells we linked arms and stood with our backs to the wall. The governor blew his whistle and a great crowd of wardresses appeared, falling upon us, forcing us apart and dragging us towards the cells. I think I had twelve wardresses for my share, and among them they managed to trip me so that I fell helplessly to the floor. One of the wardresses grasped me by my hair, wound the long braid around her wrist

and literally dragged me along the ground. In the cell they fairly ripped the clothing from my back, forcing on me one coarse cotton garment and throwing others on the bed for me to put on myself. Left alone exhausted by the dreadful experience I lay for a time gasping and shivering on the floor.

By and by a wardress came to the door and threw me a blanket. This I wrapped around me, for I was chilled to the bone by this time. The single cotton garment and the rough blanket were all the clothes I wore during my stay in prison. Most of the prisoners refused everything but the blanket. According to agreement we all broke our windows and were immediately dragged off to the punishment cells. There we hunger struck, and after enduring great misery for nearly a week, we were one by one released.

How simply they tell it. "After enduring great misery—" But no one who has not gone through the awful experience of the hunger strike can have any idea of how great that misery is. In an ordinary cell it is great enough. In the unspeakable squalor of the punishment cells it is worse. The actual hunger pangs last only about twenty-four hours with most prisoners. I generally suffer most on the second day. After that there is no very desperate craving for food. Weakness and mental depression take its place. Great disturbances of digestion divert the desire for food to a longing for relief from pain. Often there is intense headache, with fits of dizziness, or slight delirium. Complete exhaustion and a feeling of isolation from earth mark the final stages of the ordeal. Recovery is often protracted, and entire recovery of normal health is sometimes discouragingly slow.

The first hunger strike occurred in early July. In the two months that followed scores of women adopted the same form of protest against a government who would not recognise the political character of their offences. In some cases the hunger strikers were treated with unexampled cruelty. Delicate women were sentenced, not only to solitary confinement, but to wear handcuffs for twenty-four hours at a stretch. One woman on refusing prison clothes was put into a straight-waistcoat.

The irony of all this appears the greater when it is considered that, at this precise time, the leaders of the Liberal Party in the House of Commons were in the midst of their first campaign against the veto power of the Lords.

On September 17th a great meeting was held in Birmingham, on which occasion Mr. Asquith was to throw down his challenge to the Lords, and to announce that their *veto* was to be abolished, leaving the people's will paramount in England. Of course the Suffragettes seized this opportunity for a demonstration. This course was perfectly logical. Denied the right of petition, shut out now from every Cabinet Minister's meeting, the women were forced to take whatever means that remained to urge their cause upon the government. Mrs. Mary Leigh and a group of Birmingham members addressed a warning to the public not to attend Mr. Asquith's meeting as disturbances were likely to happen.

From the time that the prime minister and his Cabinet left the House of Commons until the train drew in to the station at Birmingham they were completely surrounded with detectives and policemen. The precautions taken to guard Mr. Asquith have never been equalled except in the case of the *Tsar* during outbreaks of revolution in Russia. From the station he was taken by an underground passage a quarter of a mile in length to his hotel, where he dined in solitary state, after having been carried upstairs in a luggage lift. Escorted to the Bingley Hall by a strong guard of mounted police, he was so fearful of encountering the Suffragettes that he entered by a side door.

The hall was guarded as for a siege. Over the glass roof a thick tarpaulin had been stretched. Tall ladders were placed on either side of the building, and firemen's hose were laid in readiness—not to extinguish fires, but to play upon the Suffragettes should they appear at an inaccessible spot on the roof. The streets on every hand were barricaded, and police, in regiments, were drawn up to defend the barricades against the onslaughts of the women. Nobody was allowed to pass the barricades without showing his entrance tickets to long files of police, and then the ticket holders were squeezed through the narrow doors one by one.

Their precautions were in vain, for the determined Suffragettes found more than one way in which to turn Mr. Asquith's triumph into a fiasco. Although no women gained access to the hall, there were plenty of men sympathisers present, and before the meeting had proceeded far thirteen men had been violently thrown out for reminding the prime minister that "the people" whose right to govern he was professing to uphold, included women as well as men. Outside, mingling in the vast crowds, bands of women attacked the barricades, the outer barricades being thrown down in spite of the thousands of police. From the roof of a neighbouring house Mrs. Leigh and Charlotte Marsh tore up dozens of slates and threw them on the roof of Bingley Hall and in the streets below, taking care, however, to strike no one. As Mr. Asquith drove away the women hurled slates at the guarded motor car. The fire hose was brought forth and the firemen were ordered to turn the water on the women. They refused, to their credit be it said, but the police, infuriated by their failure to keep the peace, did not scruple to play the cold water on the women as they crouched and clung to the dangerous slope of the roof. Roughs in the streets flung bricks at them, drawing blood. Eventually the women were dragged down by the police and in their dripping garments marched through the streets to the police station.

The Suffragettes who had rushed the barricades and flung stones at Mr. Asquith's departing train received sentences from a fortnight to one month, but Miss Marsh and Mrs. Leigh were sent to prison for three and four months respectively. All of the prisoners adopted the hunger strike, as we knew they would.

Several days later we were horrified to read in the newspapers that these prisoners were being forcibly fed by means of a rubber tube thrust into the stomach. Members of the Union applied at once both at the prison and at the Home Office to learn the truth of the report, but all information was refused. On the following Monday at our request, Mr. Keir Hardie, at question time in the House, insisted on information from the government. Mr. Masterman, speaking for the Home Secretary, reluctantly admitted that, in order to preserve the dignity of the government and at the same time save the lives of the prisoners, "hospital treatment" was being administered.

"Hospital treatment" was the term used to draw attention from one of the most disgusting and brutal expedients ever resorted to by prison authorities. No law allows it except in the case of persons certified to be insane, and even then when the operation is performed by skilled nursing attendants under the direction of skilled medical men, it cannot be called safe. In fact, the asylum cases usually die after a short time. *The Lancet*, perhaps the best known medical journal in the language, published a long list of opinions from distinguished physicians and surgeons who condemned the practice as applied to the suffrage prisoners as unworthy of civilisation.

One physician told of a case which had come under his observation in which death had occurred almost as soon as the tube had been inserted. Another cited a case where the tongue, twisted behind the feeding tube, had, in the struggle, been almost bitten off. Cases where food had been injected into the lungs were not unknown. Mr. C. Mansell-Moullin, M.D., F.R.C.S., wrote to *The Times* that as a hospital surgeon of more than thirty years' experience he desired indignantly to protest against the government's term "Hospital treatment" in connection with the forcible feeding of women. It was a foul libel, he declared, for violence and brutality have no place in hospitals. A memorial signed by 116 well-known physicians was addressed to the prime minister protesting against the practice of forcible feeding, and pointing out to him in detail the grave dangers attaching to it.

So much for medical testimony against a form of brutality which continued and still continues in our English prisons, as a punishment for women who are there for consciences' sake. As for the testimony of the victims, it makes a volume of most revolting sort. Mrs. Leigh, the first victim, is a woman of sturdy constitution, else she could scarcely have survived the experience. Thrown into Birmingham prison after the Asquith demonstration, she had broken the windows of her cell, and as a punishment was sent to a dark and cold punishment cell. Her hands were handcuffed, behind her during the day, and at night in front of her body *with the palms out*. She refused to touch the food that was brought to her, and three days after her arrival she was taken to the doctor's room. What she saw was enough to terrify the bravest. In the centre of the room was a stout chair resting on a cotton sheet. Against the wall, as if ready for action stood four wardresses. The junior doctor was also on hand. The senior doctor spoke, saying:

> Listen carefully to what I have to say. I have orders from my superior officers that you are not to be released even on medical grounds. If you still refrain from food I must take other measures to compel you to take it.

Mrs. Leigh replied that she did still refuse, and she said further that she knew that she could not legally be forcibly fed because an operation could not be performed without the consent of the patient if sane. The doctor repeated that he had his orders and would carry them out. A number of wardresses then fell upon Mrs. Leigh, held her down and tilted her chair backward. She was so taken by surprise that she could not resist successfully that time. They managed to make her swallow a little food from a feeding cup. Later two doctors and the wardresses appeared in her cell, forced Mrs. Leigh down to the bed and held her there. To her horror the doctors produced a rubber tube, two yards in length, and this he began to stuff up her nostril. The pain was so dreadful that she shrieked again and again. Three of the wardresses burst into tears and the junior doctor begged the other to desist. Having had his orders from the government, the doctor persisted and the tube was pushed down into the stomach. One of the doctors, standing on a chair and holding the tube high poured liquid food through a funnel almost suffocating the poor victim. She said afterwards:

> The drums of my ears seemed to be bursting. I could feel the pain to the end of the breast bone. When at last the tube was withdrawn it felt as if the back of my nose and throat were being torn out with it.

In an almost fainting condition Mrs. Leigh was taken back to the punishment cell and laid on her plank bed. The ordeal was renewed day after day. The other prisoners suffered similar experiences.

CHAPTER 6

The militant movement was at this point when, in October, 1909, I made my first visit to the United States. I shall never forget the excitement of my landing, the first meeting with the American "reporter," an experience dreaded by all Europeans. In fact the first few days seemed a bewildering whirl of reporters and receptions, all leading up to my first lecture at Carnegie Hall on October 25th. The huge hall was entirely filled, and an enormous crowd of people thronged the streets outside for blocks. With me on the stage were several women whom I had met in Europe, and in the chair was an old friend, Mrs. Stanton Blatch, whose early married life had been spent in England. The great crowd before me, however, was made up of strangers, and I could not know how they would respond to my story. When I rose to speak a deep hush fell, but at my first words: "I am what you call a hooligan—" a great shout of warm and sympathetic laughter shook the walls.

Then I knew that I had found friends in America. And this all the rest of the tour demonstrated. In Boston the committee met me with a big grey automobile decorated in the colours of our Union, and that night at Tremont Temple I spoke to an audience of 2,500 people all most generous in their responsiveness. In Baltimore professors, and students from Johns Hopkins University acted as stewards of the meeting. I greatly enjoyed my visit to Bryn Mawr College and to

Rosemary Hall, a wonderful school for girls in Connecticut. In Chicago, I met, among other notable people, Miss Jane Addams and Mrs. Ella Flagg Young, superintendent of schools. My visit to Canada will always be remembered, especially Toronto, where the mayor, dressed in the chains of his office, welcomed me. I met too the venerable Goldwin Smith, since dead.

Everywhere I found the Americans kind and keen, and I cannot say too much for the wonderful hospitality they showed me. The women I found were remarkably interested in social welfare. The work of the women's clubs struck me very favourably, and I thought these institutions a perfect basis for a suffrage movement. But at that time, 1909, the suffrage movement in the United States was in a curious state of quiescence. A large number of women with whom I came in contact appeared to think it only just that they should have a vote, but few seemed to realise any actual need of it. Some, it is true, were beginning to connect the vote with the reforms for which they were working so unselfishly and so devotedly. It was when talking with the younger women that I came to feel that under the surface of things in America, a strong suffrage movement was stirring. Those young women, leaving their splendid colleges to begin life were realising in a very intelligent fashion that they needed and would be obliged to secure for themselves a political status.

On December 1st I sailed on the *Mauretania* for England, and on arriving I learned that the prison sentence which hung over me while the petitions case had been argued, was discharged, some unknown friend having paid my fine while I was on the ocean.

The year 1910 began with a general election, precipitated by the House of Lords' rejection of Mr. Lloyd-George's 1909 budget. The Liberal Party went to the country with promises of taxes on land values. They promised also abolition of the veto power of the Lords, Irish Home Rule, disestablishment of the Church of Wales, and other reforms. Woman suffrage was not directly promised, but Mr. Asquith pledged that, if retained in office, he would introduce an electoral reform bill which could be amended to include woman suffrage. The Unionists under the leadership of Mr. Balfour, had tariff reform for their programme, and they offered not even a vague promise of a possible suffrage measure.

Yet we, as usual, went into the constituencies and opposed the Liberal Party. We had no faith in Mr. Asquith's pledge, and besides, if we had failed to oppose the party in power we should but have invited

Mr. Asquith and Mr. Balfour to enter into an agreement not to deal with the suffrage, with the view of keeping the cause permanently outside practical politics. We were in something of the same position as the Irish Nationalists in 1885, when neither the Liberal nor the Conservative leaders would include home rule in their programme. The Irish opposed the Liberal Party, with the result that it was returned by such a narrow majority that the Liberal Government was dependent on the Irish vote in Parliament in order to remain in office. On this account they were obliged to bring in a Home Rule Bill.

The other suffrage societies and many of the Liberal women begged us not to oppose the Liberal party at this election. We were implored to waive our claim "just this once" in view of the importance of the struggle between the Commons and the House of Lords over the budget. We replied that the same plea had been made in 1906 when we were implored to waive our claim "just this once" on account of the fiscal issue. For women there was only one political issue, we said, and that was the issue of their own enfranchisement. The dispute between the Lords and the Commons was far less vital than the claims of the people—represented in this case by women—to be admitted to citizenship. From our point of view both Houses of Parliament were unrepresentative until women had a voice in choosing legislators and influencing law making.

We opposed Liberal candidates in forty constituencies, and in almost everyone of these the Liberal majorities were reduced and no less than eighteen seats were wrested from the Liberal candidates. It really was a terrible election for the government. Mr. Asquith travelled from one constituency to another accompanied by a body guard of detectives, and official "chuckers out," whose sole duty was to eject women, and men as well, who interrupted his meetings on the question of Votes for Women. The halls where he spoke had the windows boarded up or the glass covered with strong wire netting. Every thoroughfare leading to the halls was barricaded, traffic was suspended, and large forces of police were on guard. The most extraordinary precautions were taken to protect the prime minister.

At one place he went to his meeting strongly guarded and by way of a secret pathway that led through gooseberry bushes and a cabbage patch to a back door. After the meeting he escaped through the same door and was solemnly guided along a path heavily laid with sawdust to deaden his footsteps, to a concealed motorcar, where he sat until the crowd had all dispersed.

The other ministers had to resort to similar precautions. They lived under the constant protection of bodyguards. Their meetings were policed in a manner without precedent. Of course no women were admitted to their meetings, but they got in just the same. Two women hid for twenty-five hours in the rafters of a hall in Louth where Mr. Lloyd-George spoke. They were arrested, but not until after they had made their demonstration. Two others hid under a platform for twenty-two hours in order to question the prime minister. I could continue this record almost indefinitely.

We had printed a wonderful poster showing the process of forcible feeding, and we used it on hoardings everywhere. We told the electors that the "Liberal Party," the people's friend, had imprisoned 450 women for the crime of asking for a vote. They were torturing women at that time in Holloway. It was splendid ammunition and it told. The Liberal Party was returned to power, but with their majority over all sections of the House of Commons swept away. The Asquith Government were dependent now for their very existence on the votes of the Labour Party and the Irish Nationalists.

Chapter 7

The first months of 1910 were occupied by the re-elected government in a struggle to keep control of affairs. A coalition with the Irish party, the leaders of which agreed, if the Home Rule bill were advanced, to stand by the budget. No publicly announced coalition with the Labour Party was made at that time, Keir Hardie, at the annual conference of the party, announcing that they would continue to be independent of the government. This was important to us because it meant that the Labour Party, instead of entering into an agreement to give general support to all government measures, would be free to oppose the government in the event of the continued withholding of a franchise bill. Other things combined to make us hopeful that the tide had turned in our favour. It was hinted to us that the government were weary of our opposition and were ready to end the struggle in the only possible way, providing they could do so without appearing to yield to coercion. We therefore, early in February, declared a truce to all militancy.

Parliament met on February 15th and the King's speech was read on February 21st. No mention of women's suffrage was made in the speech nor was any private member successful in winning a place in the ballot for a suffrage bill. However, since the situation, on account of the proposed abolition of the Lord's power of *veto*, was strained and abnormal, we decided to wait patiently for a while. It was confidently expected that another general election would have to be held before the contentions between the two Houses of Parliament were settled, and this event unquestionably would have occurred, not later than June, but for the unexpected death of King Edward VII. This interrupted the strained situation. The passing of the king served as an occasion for the temporary softening of animosities and produced a general disposition to compromise on all troubled issues. The question of women's enfranchisement was taken up again in this spirit, and in a manner altogether creditable to the members with whom the movement originated.

A strictly non-party committee on women's suffrage had been established in the House of Commons in 1887, mainly through the efforts of Miss Lydia Becker, whom I have mentioned before as the Susan B. Anthony of the English suffrage movement. In 1906, for reasons not necessary to enumerate, the original committee had been allowed to lapse, the Liberal supporters of women's suffrage forming a committee of their own. Now, in this period of good feeling, at the suggestion of certain members, led by Mr. H. N. Brailsford, not himself a member of Parliament, formed another non-party body which they called the Conciliation Committee. Its object was declared to be the bringing together of the full strength of suffragists of the House of Commons, regardless of party affiliation, and of framing a suffrage measure that could be passed by their united effort.

The Earl of Lytton accepted the chairmanship of the committee and Mr. Brailsford was made its secretary. The committee consisted of twenty-five Liberals, seventeen Conservatives, six Irish Nationalists, and six members of the Labour Party. Under difficulties which I can hardly hope to make clear to American readers the committee laboured to frame a bill which should win the support of all sections of the House. The Conservatives insisted on a moderate bill, whilst the Liberals were concerned lest the terms of the bill should add to the power of the propertied classes. The original suffrage bill, drafted by my husband, Dr. Pankhurst, giving the vote to women on equal terms with men, was abandoned, and a bill was drawn up along the lines of the existing municipal franchise law.

The basis of the municipal franchise is occupation, and the Conciliation Bill, as first drafted, proposed to extend the Parliamentary vote to women householders, and to women occupiers of business premises paying ten pounds rental and upwards. It was estimated that about ninety-five *per cent.* of the women who would be enfranchised under the bill were householders. This, in England, does not mean a person occupying a whole house. Anyone who inhabits even a single room over which he or she exercises full control is a householder.

The text of the Conciliation Bill was submitted to all the suffrage societies and other women's organisations, and it was accepted by every one of them. Our official newspaper said editorially:

> We of the Women's Social and Political Union are prepared to share in this united and peaceful action. The new bill does not give us all that we want, but we are for it if others are also for it.

It seemed certain that an overwhelming majority of the House of Commons were for the bill, and were prepared to vote it into law. Although we knew that it could not possibly pass unless the government agreed that it should, we hoped that the leaders of all parties and the majority of their followers would unite in an agreement that the bill should pass. This settlement by consent is rare in the English Parliament, but some extremely important and hard fought measures have been carried thus. The extension of the franchise in 1867 is a case in point.

The Conciliation Bill was introduced into the House of Commons on June 14th, 1910, by Mr. D. J. Shackleton, and was received with the most extraordinary enthusiasm. The newspapers remarked on the feeling of reality which marked the attitude of the House towards the bill. It was plain that the members realised that here was no academic question upon which they were merely to debate and to register their opinions, but a measure which was intended to be carried through all its stages and to be written into English law. The enthusiasm of the House swept all over the kingdom. The medical profession sent in a memorial in its favour, signed by more than three hundred of the most distinguished men and women in the profession.

Memorials from writers, clergymen, social workers, artists, actors, musicians, were also sent. The Women's Liberal Federation met and unanimously resolved to ask the prime minister to give full facilities to the bill. Some advanced spirits in the Federation actually proposed to send then and there a deputation to the House of Commons with the resolution, but this proposal was rejected as savouring too much of militancy. A request for an interview was sent to Mr. Asquith, and he replied promising to receive, at an early day, representatives of both the

OVER 1,000 WOMEN HAD BEEN IN PRISON—BROAD ARROWS IN THE 1910 PARADE

Liberal Women's Federation and of the National Union of Women's Suffrage Societies.

The joint deputation was received by Mr. Asquith on June 21st, and Lady M'Laren, as a representative of the Women's Liberal Federation, spoke very directly to her party's leader. She said in part:

> If you refuse our request we shall have to go to the country and say you, who are against the *veto* of the House of Lords, are placing a *veto* on the House of Commons by refusing to allow a second reading of this bill.

Mr. Asquith replied warily that he could not decide alone on such a serious matter, but would have to consult his Cabinet, the majority of whom, he admitted, were suffragists. Their decision, he said, would be given in the House of Commons.

The Women's Social and Political Union arranged a demonstration in support of the Conciliation Bill, the greatest that had, up to that time, been made. It was a national, indeed an inter-national affair in which all the suffrage groups took part, and its massed ranks were so great that the procession required an hour and a half to pass a given point. At the head marched six hundred and seventeen women, white clad and holding long silver staves tipped with the broad arrow. These were the women who had suffered imprisonment for the cause, and all along the line of march they received a tribute of cheers from the public. The immense Albert Hall, the largest hall in England, although it was packed from orchestra to the highest gallery, was not large enough to hold all the marchers. Amid great joy and enthusiasm Lord Lytton delivered a stirring address in which he confidently predicted the speedy advance of the bill. The women, he declared, had every reason to believe that their enfranchisement was actually at hand.

It was true that the time for passing a suffrage bill was ripe. Not in fifty years had the way been so clear, because the momentary absence of ordinary legislation left the field open for an electoral reform bill. Yet when the prime minister was asked in the House of Commons whether he would give the members an early opportunity for discussion, the answer was not encouraging. The government, said Mr. Asquith, were prepared to give time before the close of the session for full debate and division on second reading, but they could not allow any further facilities. He stated frankly that he personally did not want the bill to pass, but the government realised that the House of Commons ought to have an opportunity, if that was their deliberate desire, for effectively dealing with the whole question.

This cryptic utterance was taken by the majority of the suffragists, by the press and by the public generally to mean that the government were preparing gracefully to yield to the undoubted desire of the House of Commons to pass the bill. But the Women's Social and Political Union were doubtful. Mr. Asquith's remark was ambiguous, and was capable of being interpreted in several ways. It could mean that he was prepared to accept the verdict of the majority and let the bill pass through all its stages. That of course would be the only way to allow the House opportunity effectively to deal with the whole question.

On the other hand Mr. Asquith might be intending to let the bill pass through its debating stages and be afterwards smothered in committee. We feared treachery, but in view of the announcement that the government had set apart July 11 and 12 for debate on the second reading, we preserved a spirit of waiting calm. July 26th had been fixed as the day for the adjournment of Parliament, and if the bill was voted on favourably on the 12th there would be ample time to take it through its final stages. When a bill passes its second reading it is normally sent upstairs to a Grand Committee which sits while the House of Commons is transacting other business, and thus the committee stage can proceed without special facilities.

The bill does not go back to the House until the report stage is reached, at which time the third and last reading occurs. After that the bill goes to the House of Lords. A week at most is all that is required for this procedure. A bill may be referred to the Whole House, and in this case it cannot be brought up for its committee stage unless it is given special facilities. In our paper and in many public speeches we urged that the members vote to send the bill to a Grand Committee.

Some days before the bill reached its second reading it was rumoured that Mr. Lloyd-George was going to speak against it, but we refused to credit this. Unfair to women as Mr. Lloyd-George had shown himself in various ways, he had consistently posed as a staunch friend of women's suffrage, and we could not believe that he would turn against us at the eleventh hour. Mr. Winston Churchill, whose speech to the women of Dundee I quoted in a previous chapter, the promoters of the Bill also counted upon, as it was known that he had more than once expressed sympathy with its objects.

But when the debates began we found both of these ardent suffragists arrayed against the bill. Mr. Churchill, after making a conventional anti-suffrage speech, in which he said that women did not need the ballot, and that they really had no grievances, attacked the Conciliation Bill because the class of women who would be enfranchised under it did not suit him. Some women, he conceded, ought to be enfranchised, and he thought the best plan would be to select "some of the best women of all classes" on considerations of property, education and earning capacity. These special franchises would be carefully balanced, "so as not on the whole to give undue advantage to the property vote against the wage earning vote." A more fantastic proposal and one less likely to find favour in the House of Commons could not possibly be imagined. Mr. Churchill's second objection to the bill was that it was anti-democratic! It seemed to us that anything was more democratic than his proposed "fancy" franchises.

Mr. Lloyd-George said that he agreed with everything Mr. Churchill had said "both relevant and irrelevant." He made the amazing assertion that the Conciliation Committee that had drafted the bill was a "committee of women meeting outside the House." And that this committee said to the House of Commons not only that they must vote for a women's suffrage bill but "You must vote for the particular form upon which we agree, and we will not even allow you to deliberate upon any other form."

Of course these statements were wholly false. The Conciliation Bill was drafted by men, and it was introduced because the government had refused to bring in a party measure. The suffragists would have been only too glad to have had the government deliberate on a broader form of suffrage. Because they refused to deliberate on any form, this private bill was introduced.

This fact was brought forward in the course of Mr. Lloyd-George's speech. It had been urged, said he, that this bill was better than none at all, but why should that be the alternative? "What is the other?" called out a member, but Mr. Lloyd-George dodged the question with a careless "Well, I cannot say for the present."

Later on he said:

> If the promoters of this bill say that they regard the second reading merely as an affirmation of the principle of women's suffrage, and if they promise that when they reintroduce the bill it will be in a form which will enable the House of Commons to move any amendment either for restriction or extension I shall be happy to vote for this bill.

Mr. Philip Snowden, replying to this, said:

We will withdraw this bill if the Right Honourable gentleman, on behalf of the government, or the prime minister himself will undertake to give to this House the opportunity of discussing and carrying through its various stages another form of franchise bill. If we cannot get that, then we shall prosecute this bill.

The government made no reply at all to this, and the debate proceeded. Thirty-nine speeches were made, the prime minister showing plainly in his speech that he intended to use all his power to prevent the bill becoming law. He began by saying that a franchise measure ought never to be sent to a Grand Committee, but to one of the Whole House. He said also that his conditions, that the majority of women should show beyond any doubt that they desired the franchise, and that the bill be democratic in its terms, had not been complied with.

When the division was taken it was seen that the Conciliation Bill had passed its second reading by a majority of 109, a larger majority than the government's far famed budget or the House of Lords Resolution had received. In fact no measure during that Parliament had received so great a majority—299 members voted for it as against 190 opposed. Then the question arose as to which committee should deal with the bill. Mr. Asquith had said that all franchise bills should go to a Committee of the Whole House, so that in the division his words moved many sincere friends of the bill to send it there. Others understood that this was a mischievous course, but were afraid of incurring the anger of the prime minister. Of course all the anti-suffragists voted the same way, and thus the bill went to the Whole House.

Even then the bill could have been advanced to its final reading. The House had time on their hands, as virtually all important legislative work was halted because of the deadlock between the Lords and the Commons. Following the death of the king a conference of leaders of the Conservative and the Liberal Parties had been arranged to adjust the matters at issue, and this conference had not yet reported. Hence Parliament had little business on hand. The strongest possible pressure was brought to bear upon the government to give facilities to the Conciliation Bill. A number of meetings were held in support of the bill. The Men's Political Union for Women's Enfranchisement, the Men's League for Women's Suffrage and the Conciliation Committee held a joint meeting in Hyde Park. Some of the old school of suffragists held another large meeting in Trafalgar Square. The Women's

The Head of the Deputation on Black Friday November, 1910

Social and Political Union, on July 23rd, which was the anniversary of the day in 1867 on which working men, agitating for their vote, had pulled down the Hyde Park railings, held another enormous demonstration there. A space of half a square mile was cleared, forty platforms erected, and two great processions marched from east and west to the meeting. Many other suffrage societies co-operated with us on this occasion. On the very day of that meeting Mr. Asquith wrote to Lord Lytton refusing to allow any more time for the bill during that session.

Those who still had faith that the government could be induced to do justice to women set their hopes on the autumn session of Parliament. Resolutions urging the government to give the bill facilities during the autumn were sent, not only by the suffrage associations but from many organisations of men. The Corporations of thirty-eight cities, including Liverpool, Manchester, Glasgow, Dublin and Cork, sent resolutions to this effect. Cabinet Ministers were besieged with requests to receive deputations of women, and since the country was on the verge of a general election, and the Liberal Party wanted the services of women, their requests could not altogether be ignored. Mr. Asquith, early in October, received a deputation of women from his own constituency of East Fife, but all he had to tell them was that the bill could not be advanced that year. "What about next year?" They asked, and he replied shortly: "Wait and see."

It had been exceedingly difficult, during these troublous days, to hold all the members of the W. S. P. U. to the truce, and when it became perfectly apparent that the Conciliation Bill was doomed, war was again declared. At a great meeting held in Albert Hall on November 10th, I myself threw down the gage of battle. I said, because I wanted the whole matter to be clearly understood by the public as well as by our members:

> This is the last constitutional effort of the Women's Social and Political Union to secure the passage of the bill into law. If the bill, in spite of our efforts, is killed by the government, then first of all, I have to say there is an end of the truce. If we are met by the statement that there is no power to secure on the floor of the House of Commons time for our measure, then our first step is to say, 'We take it out of your hands, since you fail to help us, and we resume the direction of the campaign ourselves.'

Another deputation, I declared, must go to the House of Commons to carry a petition to the prime minister. I myself would lead, and if no one cared to follow me I would go alone. Instantly, all over the hall, women sprang to their feet crying out, "Mrs. Pankhurst, I will go with you!" "I will go!" "I will go!" And I knew that our brave women were as ever ready to give themselves, their very lives, if need be, for the cause of freedom.

The autumn session convened on Friday, November 18th, and Mr. Asquith announced that Parliament would be adjourned on November 28th. While his speech was in progress, 450 women, in small groups, to keep within the strict letter of the law, were marching from Caxton Hall and from the headquarters of the Union.

How to tell the story of that dreadful day, Black Friday, as it lives in our memory—how to describe what happened to English women at the behest of an English Government, is a difficult task. I will try to tell it as simply and as accurately as possible. The plain facts, baldly stated, I am aware will strain credulity.

Remember that the country was on the eve of a general election, and that the Liberal Party needed the help of Liberal women. This fact made the wholesale arrest and imprisonment of great numbers of women, who were demanding the passage of the Conciliation Bill, extremely undesirable from the government's point of view. The Women's Liberal Federations also wanted the passage of the Conciliation Bill, although they were not ready to fight for it. What the government feared, was that the Liberal women would be stirred by our sufferings into refraining from doing election work for the party. So the government conceived a plan whereby the Suffragettes were to be punished, were to be turned back and defeated in their purpose of reaching the House, but would not be arrested.

Orders were evidently given that the police were to be present in the streets, and that the women were to be thrown from one uniformed or ununiformed policeman to another, that they were to be so rudely treated that sheer terror would cause them to turn back. I say orders were given and as one proof of this I can first point out that on all previous occasions the police had first tried to turn back the deputations and when the women persisted in going forward, had arrested them. At times individual policemen had behaved with cruelty and malice toward us, but never anything like the unanimous and wholesale brutality that was shown on Black Friday.

The government very likely hoped that the violence of the police towards the women would be emulated by the crowds, but instead the crowds proved remarkably friendly. They pushed and struggled to

For hours scenes like this were enacted on Black Friday November, 1910

make a clear pathway for us, and in spite of the efforts of the police my small deputation actually succeeded in reaching the door of the Strangers' Entrance. We mounted the steps to the enthusiastic cheers of the multitudes that filled the streets, and we stood there for hours gazing down on a scene which I hope never to look upon again.

At intervals of two or three minutes small groups of women appeared in the square, trying to join us at the Strangers' Entrance. They carried little banners inscribed with various mottoes, "Asquith Has Vetoed Our Bill," "Where There's a Bill There's a Way," "Women's Will Beats Asquith's Won't," and the like. These banners the police seized and tore in pieces. Then they laid hands on the women and literally threw them from one man to another. Some of the police used their fists, striking the women in their faces, their breasts, their shoulders. One woman I saw thrown down with violence three or four times in rapid succession, until at last she lay only half conscious against the curb, and in a serious condition was carried away by kindly strangers. Every moment the struggle grew fiercer, as more and more women arrived on the scene. Women, many of them eminent in art, in medicine and science, women of European reputation, subjected to treatment that would not have been meted out to criminals, and all for the offence of insisting upon the right of peaceful petition.

This struggle lasted for about an hour, more and more women successfully pushing their way past the police and gaining the steps of the House. Then the mounted police were summoned to turn the women back. But, desperately determined, the women, fearing not the hoofs of the horses or the crushing violence of the police, did not swerve from their purpose. And now the crowds began to murmur. People began to demand why the women were being knocked about; why, if they were breaking the law, they were not arrested; why, if they were not breaking the law, they were not permitted to go on unmolested. For a long time, nearly five hours, the police continued to hustle and beat the women, the crowds becoming more and more turbulent in their defence. Then, at last the police were obliged to make arrests. One hundred and fifteen women and four men, most of them bruised and choked and otherwise injured, were arrested.

While all this was going on outside the House of Commons, the prime minister was obstinately refusing to listen to the counsels of some of the saner and more justice-loving members of the House. Keir Hardie, Sir Alfred Mondell and others urged Mr. Asquith to receive the deputation, and Lord Castlereagh went so far as to move as an amendment to a government proposal, another proposal which would have compelled the government to provide immediate facilities to the Conciliation Bill. We heard of what was going on, and I sent in for one and another friendly member and made every possible effort to influence them in favour of Lord Castlereagh's amendment. I pointed to the brutal struggle that was going on in the square, and I begged them to go back and tell the others that it must be stopped. But, distressed as some of them undoubtedly were, they assured me that there was not the slightest chance for the amendment.

"Is there not a single *man* in the House of Commons," I cried, "one who will stand up for us, who will make the House see that the amendment must go forward?"

Well, perhaps there were men there, but all save fifty-two put their party loyalty before their manhood, and, because Lord Castlereagh's proposal would have meant censure of the government, they refused to support it. This did not happen, however, until Mr. Asquith had resorted to his usual crafty device of a promise of future action. In this instance he promised to make a statement on behalf of the government on the following Tuesday.

The next morning the suffrage prisoners were arraigned in police court. Or rather, they were kept waiting outside the court room while Mr. Muskett, who prosecuted on behalf of the Chief Commissioner of Police, explained to the astounded magistrate that he had received orders from the Home Secretary that the prisoners should all be discharged. Mr. Churchill it was declared, had had the matter under careful consideration, and had decided that:

> No public advantage would be gained by proceeding with the prosecution, and accordingly no evidence would be given against the prisoners.

Subdued laughter and, according to the newspapers, some contemptuous booing were raised in the court, and when order was restored the prisoners were brought in in batches and told that they were discharged.

On the following Tuesday the W. S. P. U. held another meeting of the Women's Parliament in Caxton Hall to hear the news from the House of Commons. Mr. Asquith said:

> The government will, if they are still in power, give facilities in the next Parliament for effectively proceeding with a franchise bill which is so framed as to admit of free amendment.

He would not promise that this would be done during the first year of Parliament.

We had demanded facilities for the Conciliation Bill, and Mr. Asquith's promise was too vague and too ambiguous to please us. The Parliament now about to be dissolved had lasted a scant ten months. The next one might not last longer. Therefore, Mr. Asquith's promise, as usual, meant nothing at all. I said to the women, "I am going to Downing Street. Come along, all of you." And we went.

We found a small force of police in Downing Street, and we easily broke through their line and would have invaded the prime minister's residence had not reinforcements of police arrived on the scene. Mr. Asquith himself appeared unexpectedly, and as we thought, very opportunely.

Before he could have realised what was happening he found himself surrounded by angry Suffragettes. He was well hooted and, it is said, well shaken, before he was rescued by the police. As his taxicab rushed away some object struck one of the windows, smashing it.

Another Cabinet Minister, Mr. Birrell, unwittingly got into the midst of the *mêlée*, and I am obliged to record that he was pretty thoroughly hustled. But it is not true that his leg was injured by the women. His haste to jump into a taxicab resulted in a slightly sprained ankle.

That night and the following day windows were broken in the houses of Sir Edward Grey, Mr. Winston Churchill, Mr. Lewis Harcourt and Mr. John Burns; and also in the official residences of the Premier and the Chancellor of the Exchequer.

That week 160 Suffragettes were arrested, but all except those charged with window-breaking or assault were discharged. This amazing court action established two things: First, that when the Home Secretary stated that he had no responsibility for the prosecution and sentencing of Suffrage prisoners, he told a colossal falsehood; and second, that the government fully realised that it was bad election tactics to be responsible for the imprisonment of women of good character who were struggling for citizenship.

Chapter 8

Almost immediately after the events chronicled in the preceding chapter I sailed for my second tour through the United States. I was delighted to find a thoroughly alive and progressive suffrage movement, where before had existed with most people only an academic theory in favour of equal political rights between men and women. My first meeting, held in Brooklyn, was advertised by sandwich women walking through the principal streets of the city, quite like our militant suffragists at home. Street meetings, I found, were now daily occurrences in New York. The Women's Political Union had adopted an election policy, and throughout the country as far west as I travelled, I found women awakened to the necessity of political action instead of mere discussion of suffrage.

My second visit to America, like my first one, is clouded in my memory with sorrow. Very soon after my return to England a beloved sister, Mrs. Mary Clarke died. My sister, who was a most ardent suffragist and a valued worker in the Women's Social and Political Union, was one of the women who was shockingly maltreated in Parliament Square on Black Friday. She was also one of the women who, a few days later, registered their protest against the government by throwing a stone through the window of an official residence.

For this act she was sent to Holloway prison for a term of one month. Released on December 21st, it was plain to those who knew her best that her health had suffered seriously from the dreadful experience of Black Friday and the after experience of prison. She died suddenly on Christmas day, to the profound sorrow of all her associates. Hers was not the only life that was sacrificed as a result of that day. Other deaths occurred, mostly from hearts weakened by overstrain. Miss Henria Williams died on January 2nd, 1911, from heart failure. Miss Cecelia Wolseley Haig was another victim. Ill treatment on Black Friday resulted in her case in a painful illness which ended, after a year of intense suffering, in her death on December 21st, 1911.

It is not possible to publish a full list of all the women who have died or have been injured for life in the course of the suffrage agitation in England. In many cases the details have never been made public, and I do not feel at liberty to record them here. A very celebrated case, which is public property, is that of Lady Constance Lytton, sister of the Earl of Lytton, who acted as chairman of the Conciliation Committee. Lady Constance had twice in 1909 gone to prison as a result of suffrage activities, and on both occasions had been given special privileges on account of her rank and family influence. In spite of her protests and her earnest pleadings to be accorded the same treatment as other suffrage prisoners, the snobbish and cowardly authorities insisted in retaining Lady Constance in the hospital cells and discharging her before the expiration of her sentence. This was done

Riot scenes on Black Friday November, 1910

on a plea of her ill health, and it was true that she suffered from a valvular disease of the heart.

Smarting under the sense of the injustice done her comrades in this discrimination, Lady Constance Lytton did one of the most heroic deeds to be recorded in the history of the suffrage movement. She cut off her beautiful hair and otherwise disguised herself, put on cheap and ugly clothing, and as "Jane Warton" took part in a demonstration at Newcastle, again suffering arrest and imprisonment. This time the authorities treated her as an ordinary prisoner. Without testing her heart or otherwise giving her an adequate medical examination, they subjected her to the horrors of forcible feeding. Owing to her fragile constitution she suffered frightful nausea each time, and when on one occasion the doctor's clothing was soiled, he struck her contemptuously on the cheek. This treatment was continued until the identity of the prisoner suddenly became known. She was, of course, immediately released, but she never recovered from the experience, and is now a hopeless invalid. (Lady Constance Lytton's story is told in her book *Prisons and Prisoners*).

I want to say right here, that those well-meaning friends on the outside who say that we have suffered these horrors of prison, of hunger strikes and forcible feeding, because we desired to martyrise ourselves for the cause, are absolutely and entirely mistaken. We never went to prison in order to be martyrs. We went there in order that we might obtain the rights of citizenship. We were willing to break laws that we might force men to give us the right to make laws. That is the way men have earned their citizenship. Truly says Mazzini that the way to reform has always led through prison.

The result of the general election, which took place in January, 1911, was that the Liberal Party was again returned to power. Parliament met on January 31st, but the session formally opened on February 6th with the reading of the King's speech. The programme for the session included the Lords' *veto* measure, Home Rule, payment for members of Parliament, and the abolishment of plural voting. Invalid insurance was also mentioned and certain amendments to the old age pension bill. Women's suffrage was not mentioned. Nevertheless, we were singularly lucky, the first three places in the ballot being secured by members of the Conciliation Committee. Mr. Philips, an Irish member, drew the first place, but as the Irish party had decided not to introduce any bills that session, he yielded to Sir George Kemp, who announced that he would use his place for the purpose of taking a second reading debate on the new Conciliation Bill.

The old bill had been entitled: "A Bill to give the Vote to Women Occupiers," a title that made amendment difficult. The new bill bore the more flexible title, "A Bill to Confer the Parliamentary Franchise on Women," thus doing away with one of Mr. Lloyd-George's most plausible objections to it. The £10 occupation clause was omitted, doing away with another objection, that of the possibility of "faggot voting," that is, of a rich man conferring the vote on a family of daughters by the simple expedient of making them tenants of slices of his own property. The Conciliation Bill now read:

> 1. Every woman possessed of a household qualification within the meaning of the Representation of the People Act (1884) shall be entitled to be registered as a voter, and when registered to vote in the county or borough in which the qualifying premises are situated.
>
> 2. For the purposes of this Act a woman shall not be disqualified by marriage for being registered as a voter, provided that a husband and wife shall not both be registered as voters in the same Parliamentary borough or county division.

This bill met with even warmer approval than the first one, because it was believed that it would win votes from those members who felt that the original measure had fallen short of being truly democratic. Nevertheless, the prime minister showed from the first that he intended to oppose it, as he had all previous suffrage measures. He announced that all Fridays up to Easter and also all time on Tuesdays and Wednesdays usually allowed for private members' bills were to be occupied with consideration of government measures. Hardly a Liberal voice was raised against this arbitrary ruling. The Irish members indeed were delighted with it, since it gave the Home Rule Bill an advantage. The Labour members seemed complacent, and the rest of the coalition were indifferent. One back bench Liberal went so far as to rise and thank the prime minister for the courtesy with which the gagging process was accomplished. There was some show of fight made by the Opposition, but Conservative indignation was tempered by the reflection that the precedent established might be followed to advantage when their party came into power.

Sir George Kemp then announced that he would take May 5th for the second reading of the Conciliation Bill, and the supporters of the bill, according to their various convictions, set to work to further its interests. The conviction of the W. S. P. U. was that Mr. Asquith's Government would never allow the bill to pass until they were actually forced to do so, and we adopted our own methods to secure a definite pledge from the government that they would give facilities to the bill.

In April of that year the census was to be taken, and we organised a census resistance on the part of women. According to our law the census of the entire kingdom must be taken every ten years on a designated day. Our plan was to reduce the value of the census for statistical purposes by refusing to make the required returns. Two ways of resistance presented themselves. The first and most important was direct resistance by occupiers who should refuse to fill in the census papers. This laid the register open to a fine of £5 or a month's imprisonment, and thus required the exercise of considerable courage. The second means of resistance was evasion—staying away from home during the entire time that the enumerators were taking the census. We made the announcement of this plan and instantly there ensued a splendid response from women and a chorus of horrified disapproval from the conservative public. The *Times* voiced this disapproval in a leading article, to which I replied, giving our reasons for the protest. I wrote:

> The Census is a numbering of the people. Until women count as people for the purpose of representation in the councils of the nation as well as for purposes of taxation, we shall refuse to be numbered.

On the subject of laws made by men—without the assistance of women—for the protection of women and children, I have a very special feeling. From my experience as poor law guardian and as Registrar of Births and Deaths, I know how ridiculously, say rather how tragically, these laws fall short of protection. Take for instance the vaunted "Children's Charter" of 1906, the measure which spread Mr. Lloyd-George's fame throughout the world. A volume could be filled with the mistakes and the cruelties of that Act, the object of which is the preservation and improvement of child life. A distinguishing characteristic of the act is that it puts most of the responsibility for neglect of children on the backs of the mothers, who, under the laws of England, have no rights as parents. Two or three especially striking cases of this kind came into notice about this time, and gave the census resistance an additional justification.

The case of Annie Woolmore was a very pitiful one. She was arrested and sentenced to Holloway for six weeks for neglecting her children. The evidence showed that the woman lived with her husband and children in a miserable hovel, which would have been almost impossible to keep clean even if there had been water in the house. As it was the poor soul, who was in ill health and weakened by deprivation, had to carry all the water she used across a great distance. The children as well as the house were very dirty, it was true, but the children were well nourished and kindly treated. The husband, a labourer, out of work much of the time, testified that his wife "starved herself to feed the kids." Yet she had violated the terms of the "Children's Charter" and she went to prison. I am glad to say that owing to the efforts of suffragists she was pardoned and provided with a better home.

Another case was that of Helen Conroy, who was charged with living in one wretched room, with her husband and seven children, the youngest a month old. According to the law the mother was forbidden to have this infant in bed with her overnight, yet part of the charge against her was that the child was found sleeping in a box of damp straw. Doubtless she would have preferred a cradle, or even a box of dry straw. But direst poverty made the cradle impossible and the conditions of the tenement kept the straw damp. Both parents in this instance were sent to prison for three months at hard labour. The magistrate casually remarked that the house in which these poor people lived had been condemned two years before, but some respectable property owner was still collecting rents from it.

Another poor mother, evicted from her home because she could not pay the rent, took her four children out into the open country, and when found was sleeping with them in a gravel pit. She was sent to prison for a month and the children went to the workhouse.

These sorry mothers, logical results of the subjection of women, are enough in themselves to justify almost any defiance of a government who deny the women the right to work out their destinies in freedom. No pledge having been secured from the prime minister by April 1st, we carried out, and most successfully, our census resistance. Many thousands of women all over the country refused or evaded the returns. I returned my census paper with the words "No vote no census" written across it, and other women followed that example with similar messages. One woman filled in the blank with full information about her one man servant, and added that there were many women but no more persons in her household. In Birmingham sixteen women of wealth packed their houses with women resisters. They slept on the floors, on chairs and tables, and even in the baths. The head of a large college threw open the building to 300 women. Many women in other cities held all night parties for friends who wished to remain away from home. In some places unoccupied houses were rented for the night by resisters, who lay on the bare boards. Some groups of women hired gipsy vans and spent the night on the moors.

In London we gave a great concert at Queen's Hall on Census night. Many of us walked about Trafalgar Square until midnight and then repaired to Aldwich skating rink, where we amused ourselves until morning. Some skated while others looked on, and enjoyed the admirable musical and theatrical entertainment that helped to pass the hours. We had with us a number of the brightest stars in the theatrical world, and they were generous in their contributions. It being Sunday night, the chairman had to call on each of the artists for a "speech" instead of a song or other turn. An all-night restaurant near at hand did a big business, and on the whole the resisters had a very good time. The Scala Theatre was the scene of another all-night entertainment.

There was a good deal of curiosity to see what the government would devise in the way of a punishment for the rebellious women, but the government realised the impossibility of taking punitive action, and Mr. John Burns, who, as head of the Local Government Board, was responsible for the census, announced that they had decided to treat the affair with magnanimity. The number of evasions, he declared, was insignificant. But every one knew that this was the exact reverse of the facts.

The Conciliation Bill was debated on May 5th and passed its second reading by the enormous majority of 137. And now the public and a section of the press united in a strong demand that the government yield to the undoubted will of the House and grant facilities to the bill. The Conciliation Committee sent a deputation of members to the prime minister to remind him of his pre-election promise that the House of Commons should have an opportunity of dealing with the whole question of woman suffrage, but they succeeded only in getting his assurance that he had the matter under consideration. Late in the month the announcement was made in the House that the government would not grant facilities during that session, but, since the new bill fulfilled the conditions named by the prime minister, and was now capable of amendment, the government recognised it to be their duty to grant facilities in some session of the present Parliament.

In this manner thousands of women throughout the kingdom slept in unoccupied houses over Census night

They would be prepared next session, when the bill had been again read for the second time, either as a result of obtaining a good place in the ballot, or (if that did not happen) by a grant of a government day for the purpose, to give a week, which they understood to be the time suggested as reasonable by the promoters for its further stages.

This pledge was made in order to deter the W. S. P. U. from making a militant demonstration in connection with the coronation of the king.

Keir Hardie asked if the government would, by means of a closure or otherwise, make certain that the bill would go through in the week, and the prime minister replied, "No, I cannot give an assurance of that kind. After all, it is a problem of the very greatest magnitude."

This reply seemed to make the government's pledge practically worthless. The Conciliation Committee also realised the possibilities of the bill being talked out, and Lord Lytton wrote to Mr. Asquith and asked him for assurances that the facilities offered were intended not for academic discussion but for effective opportunity for carrying the bill. He also asked that the week offered should not be construed rigidly but that, providing the committee stage were got through in the time, additional days for the report and third reading stages might be forthcoming. Reasonable opportunity for making use of the closure was also asked. To Lord Lytton's letter the prime minister replied as follows:

> My dear Lytton—In reply to your letter on the subject of the Women's Enfranchisement Bill, I would refer you to some observations recently made in a speech at the National Liberal Club by Sir Edward Grey, which accurately expresses the intention of the government.
>
> It follows (to answer your specific inquiries), that the "week" offered will be interpreted with reasonable elasticity, that the government will interpose no reasonable obstacle to the proper use of the closure, and that if (as you suggest) the bill gets through committee in the time proposed, the extra days required for report and third reading will not be refused.
>
> The government, though divided in opinion on the merits of the bill, are unanimous in their determination to give effect, not only in the letter but in the spirit, to the promise in regard to facilities which I made on their behalf before the last general election.
>
> Yours etc., H. H. Asquith.

Sceptical up to this point, the W. S. P. U. was now convinced that the government were sincere in their promise to give the bill full facilities in the following year. We held a joyful mass meeting in Queen's Hall and I again declared that warfare against the government was at an end. Our new policy was the inauguration of a great holiday campaign, with the object of making victory in 1912 absolutely certain. Electors must be aroused, members of Parliament held to their allegiance. Women must be organised in order that questions that vitally affect the social welfare of the country might be placed before them. I chose Scotland and Wales as the scenes of my holiday labours.

I may say that our confidence was fully shared by the public at large. The belief in Mr. Asquith's pledge was accurately reflected in a leader published in *The Nation*, which said:

> From the moment the prime minister signed the frank and ungrudging letter to Lord Lytton which appeared in last Saturday's newspapers, women became, in all but the legal formality, voters and citizens. For at least two years, if not for longer, nothing has been lacking save a full and fair opportunity for the House of Commons to translate its convictions into the precise language of a statute. That opportunity has been promised for next session and promised in terms and under conditions which ensure success.

The only thing, as we thought, that we had to fear were wrecking amendments to the bill, and in the new by-election policy which we adopted we worked against all candidates of every party who would refuse to promise, not only to support the Conciliation Committee to carry the bill, but also to vote against any amendment the committee thought dangerous. We believed that we had covered every possibility of disaster. But we had something yet to learn of the treachery of the Asquith Ministry and their capacity for cold-blooded lying.

Mr. Lloyd-George from the first was an open enemy of the bill, but since we had no doubt of the sincerity of the prime minister, we could only conclude that Mr. Lloyd-George had detached himself from the main body of the government and had become the self-constituted leader of the opposition. In an address to a large Liberal group Mr. Lloyd-George advised that Liberal members be asked to ballot for a place for a "democratic measure," in order that such a measure might claim the prime minister's pledge for facilities next session. In one or two other speeches he made vague allusions to the possibilities of introducing another suffrage bill. His own idea was to amend the bill to give a vote to wives of all electors—making married women voters in virtue of their husband's qualification.

The inevitable effect of such an amendment would be to wreck the bill, since it would have enfranchised about 6,000,000 women in addition to the million and a half who would benefit by the original terms of the bill. Such a wholesale addition to the electorate was never known in England; the number enfranchised by the Reform Bill of 1832 being hardly more than half a million. The Reform Bill of 1867 admitted a million new voters, and that of 1884 perhaps two millions. The absurdity of Mr. Lloyd-George's proposition was such that we did not regard it seriously.

We did not allow his opposition to give us serious alarm until a day in August when a Welsh member, Mr. Leif Jones, asked the prime minister from the floor of the House, whether he was aware that his promise for facilities for the Conciliation Bill in the next session was being claimed exclusively for that bill, and asked further for a statement that the promised facilities would be equally granted to any other suffrage bill that might secure a second reading and was capable of amendment. Mr. Lloyd-George, speaking for the government, replied that they could not undertake to give facilities to more than one bill on the same subject, but that any bill which, satisfying these tests, secured a second reading, would be treated by them as falling within their engagements.

Astounded at this plain evasion of a sacred promise, Lord Lytton again wrote to the prime minister, reviewing the entire matter, and asking for another statement of the government's intentions. The following is the text of Mr. Asquith's reply:

> My dear Lytton—I have no hesitation in saying that the promises made by, and on behalf of the government, in regard to giving facilities to the Conciliation Bill, will be strictly adhered to, both in letter and in spirit.
>
> Yours sincerely, H. H. Asquith.
> August 23, 1911.

Again we were reassured, and our confidence in the premier's pledge remained unshaken throughout the campaign, although Mr. Lloyd-George continued to throw out hints that the promises of facilities for the bill were altogether illusory. We could not believe him, and when, two months later, I was asked in America: "When will

English women vote?" I replied with perfect conviction, "Next year."

This was in Louisville, Kentucky, where I attended the 1911 Annual Convention of the National American Woman Suffrage Association.

I remember this third visit to the United States with especial pleasure. I was the guest in New York of Dr. and Mrs. John Winters Brannan, and through the courtesy of Dr. Brannan, who is at the head of all the city hospitals, I saw something of the penal system and the institutional life of America. We visited the workhouse and the penitentiary on Blackwell's Island, and although I am told that these places are not regarded as model institutions, I can assure my readers that they are infinitely superior to the English prisons where women are punished for trying to win their political freedom. In the American prisons, much as they lacked in some essentials, I saw no solitary confinement, no rule of silence, no deadly air of officialdom. The food was good and varied, and above all there was an air of kindness and good feeling between the officials and the prisoners that is almost wholly lacking in England.

But, after all, in the United States as in other countries, the problem of the relations between unfranchised women and the State remains unsolved and unsatisfactory. One night my friends took me to that sombre and terrible institution, the Night Court for Women. We sat on the bench with the magistrate, and he very courteously explained everything to us. The whole business was heart-breaking. All the women, with one exception—an old drunkard—were charged with solicitation. Most of them were of high type by nature. It all seemed so hopeless, and it was clear that they were victims of an evil system. Their conviction was a foregone conclusion.

The magistrate said that in most cases the reason for their coming there was economic. One case of a little cigar maker, who said very simply that she only went on the streets when out of work, and that when in work she earned $8 a week, was very tragic and touching. I could not keep the Night Court out of my speeches after that. The whole dreadful injustice of women's lives seemed mirrored in that place.

I went as far west as the Pacific Coast on this visit, spending Christmas day in Seattle, and for the first time seeing a community where women and men existed on terms of exact equality. It was a delightful experience. As I wrote home to our members, the men of the western States seemed to my eyes eager, earnest, rough men, building a great community in a great hurry, but never have I seen greater respect, courtesy and chivalry shown to women than in that one Suffrage State it has been my privilege to visit.

I am getting a little ahead of my story, however. It was in November, when I was in the city of Minneapolis, that a crushing blow descended on the English suffragists. I learned of this through cabled despatches in the newspapers and from private cables, and was so staggered that I could scarcely command myself sufficiently to fill my immediate engagements. This was the news, that the government had broken their plighted word and had deliberately destroyed the Conciliation Bill. My first wild thought, on hearing of this act of treachery, was to cancel all engagements and return to England, but my final decision to remain afterwards proved the right one, because the women at home, without a moment's loss of time, struck the answering blow, guided by that insight which has been characteristic of every act of the members of our union. I did not return to England until January 11, 1912, and by that time great deeds had been done. Our movement had entered upon a new and more vigorous stage of militancy.

Book 3: The Women's Revolution

CHAPTER 1

Parliament had reassembled on October 25th, 1911, and the first move on the part of the government was, to say the least of it, rather unpropitious. The prime minister submitted two motions, the first one empowering them to take all the time of the House during the remainder of the session, and the second guillotining discussion on the Insurance Bill so as to force the measure through before Christmas. One day only was allotted to the clauses relating to women in that bill. These clauses were notoriously unfair; they provided for sickness insurance of about four million women and unemployment insurance of no women at all. Under the provision of the bill eleven million men were ensured against sickness and about two and a half million against unemployment.

Women were given lower benefits for the same premium as men, and premiums paid out of the family income were credited solely to the men's account. The bill as drafted provided no form of insurance for wives, mothers and daughters who spent their lives at home working for the family. It penalised women for staying in the home, which most men agree is women's only legitimate sphere of action. The amended bill grudgingly allowed aside from maternity benefits, a small insurance, on rather difficult terms, for workingmen's wives.

Thus the re-elected government's first utterance to women was one of contempt; and this was followed, on November 7th, by the almost incredible announcement that the government intended, at the next session, to introduce a manhood suffrage bill. This announcement was not made in the House of Commons, but to a deputation of men from the People's Suffrage Federation, a small group of people who advocated universal adult suffrage. The deputation, which was very privately arranged for, was received by Mr. Asquith, and the then

Master of Elibank (Chief Liberal Whip). The spokesman asked Mr. Asquith to bring in a government measure for universal adult suffrage, including adult women.

The prime minister replied that the government had pledged facilities for the Conciliation Bill, which was as far as they were prepared to go in the matter of women's suffrage. But, he added, the government intended in the next session to introduce and to pass through all its stages a genuine reform bill which would sweep away existing qualifications for the franchise, and substitute a single qualification of residence. The bill would apply to adult males only, but it would be so framed as to be open to a woman suffrage amendment in case the House of Commons desired to make that extension and amendment.

This portentous announcement came like a bolt from the blue, and there was strong condemnation of the government's treachery to women. Said the *Saturday Review*:

> With absolutely no demand, no ghost of a demand, for more votes for men, and with—beyond all cavil—a very strong demand for votes for women, the government announce their Manhood Suffrage Bill and carefully evade the other question! For a naked, avowed plan of gerrymandering no government surely ever did beat this one.

The *Daily Mail* said that:

> The policy which Mr. Asquith proposes is absolutely indefensible.

And the *Evening Standard and Globe* said:

> We are no friends of female suffrage, but anything more contemptible than the attitude assumed by the government it is difficult to imagine.

If the government hoped to deceive any one by their dishonest reference to the possibility of a woman suffrage amendment, they were disappointed. Said the *Evening News*:

Mr. Asquith's bombshell will blow the Conciliation Bill to smithereens, for it is impossible to have a manhood suffrage for men and a property qualification for women. True, the premier consents to leave the question of women's suffrage to the House, but he knows well enough what the decision of the House will be. The Conciliation Bill had a chance, but the larger measure has none at all.

I have quoted these newspaper leaders to show you that our opinion of the government's action was shared even by the press. Universal suffrage in a country where women are in a majority of one million is not likely to happen in the lifetime of any reader of this volume, and the government's generous offer of a possible amendment was nothing more than a gratuitous insult to the suffragists.

The truce, naturally, came to an abrupt end. The W. S. P. U. wrote to the prime minister, saying that consternation had been aroused by the government's announcement, and that it had been decided accordingly to send a deputation representing the Women's Social and Political Union to wait upon himself and the Chancellor of the Exchequer, on the evening of November 21st. The purpose of the deputation was to demand that the proposed manhood suffrage bill be abandoned, and that in its place should be introduced a government measure giving equal franchise rights to men and women. A similar letter was despatched to Mr. Lloyd-George.

Six times before on occasions of crisis had the W. S. P. U. requested an interview with Mr. Asquith, and each time they had been refused. This time the prime minister replied that he had decided to receive a deputation of the various suffrage societies on November 17th, "including your own society, if you desire it." It was proposed that each society appoint four representatives as members of the deputation which would be received by the prime minister and the Chancellor of the Exchequer.

Nine suffrage societies sent representatives to the meeting, our own representatives being Christabel Pankhurst, Mrs. Pethick Lawrence, Miss Annie Kenney, Lady Constance Lytton and Miss Elizabeth Robins. Christabel and Mrs. Lawrence spoke for the union, and they did not hesitate to accuse the two ministers to their faces of having grossly tricked and falsely misled women. Mr. Asquith, in his reply to the deputation, resented these imputations.

He had kept his pledge, he insisted, in regard to the Conciliation Bill. He was perfectly willing to give facilities to the bill, if the women preferred that to an amendment to his reform bill. Moreover, he denied that he had made any new announcement. As far back as 1908 he had distinctly declared that the government regarded it as a sacred duty to bring forward a manhood suffrage bill before that Parliament came to an end. It was true that the government did not carry out that binding obligation, and it was also true that until the present time nothing more was ever said about a manhood suffrage bill, but that was not the government's fault. The crisis of the Lord's *veto*, had momentarily displaced the bill. Now he merely proposed to fulfil his promise made in 1908, and also his promise about giving facilities to the Conciliation Bill. He was ready to keep both promises. Well he knew that those promises were incompatible, that the fulfilment of both was therefore impossible, and Christabel told him so bluntly and fearlessly. "We are not satisfied," she warned him, and the prime minister said acidly: "I did not expect to satisfy *you*."

The reply of the W. S. P. U. was immediate and forceful. Led by Mrs. Pethick Lawrence, our women went out with stones and hammers and broke hundreds of windows in the Home Office, the War and Foreign Offices, the Board of Education, the Privy Council Office, the Board of Trade, the Treasury, Somerset House, the National Liberal Club, several post offices, the Old Banqueting Hall, the London and South Western Bank, and a dozen other buildings, including the residence of Lord Haldane and Mr. John Burns. Two hundred and twenty women were arrested and about 150 of them sent to prison for terms varying from a week to two months.

One individual protest deserves mention because of its prophetic character. In December Miss Emily Wilding Davison was arrested for attempting to set fire to a letter box at Parliament Street Post Office. In court Miss Davison said that she did it as a protest against the government's treachery, and as a demand that women's suffrage be included in the King's speech. She said:

> The protest was meant to be serious, and so I adopted a serious course. In past agitation for reform the next step after window-breaking was incendiarism, in order to draw the attention of the private citizens to the fact that this question of reform was their concern as well as that of women.

Miss Davison received the severe sentence of six months' imprisonment for her deed.

To this state of affairs I returned from my American tour. I had the comfort of reflecting that my imprisoned comrades were being accorded better treatment than the early prisoners had known. Since early in 1910 some concessions had been granted, and some acknowledgment of the political character of our offences had been made. During the brief period when these scant concessions to justice were allowed, the hunger strike was abandoned and prison was robbed of its worst horror, forcible feeding. The situation was bad enough, however, and I could see that it might easily become a great deal worse. We had reached a stage at which the mere sympathy of members of Parliament, however sincerely felt, was no longer of the slightest use. Reminding our members this, in the first speeches made after returning to England I asked them to prepare themselves for more action. If women's suffrage was not included in the next King's speech we should have to make it absolutely impossible for the government to touch the question of the franchise.

The King's speech, when Parliament met in February, 1912, alluded to the franchise question in very general terms. Proposals, it was stated, would be brought forward for the amendment of the law with respect to the franchise and the registration of electors. This might be construed to mean that the government were going to introduce a manhood suffrage bill or a bill for the abolition of plural voting, which had been suggested in some quarters as a substitute for the manhood suffrage bill. No precise statement of the government's intentions was made, and the whole franchise question was left in a cloud of uncertainty. Mr. Agg Gardner, a Unionist member of the Conciliation Committee, drew the third place in the ballot, and he announced that he should reintroduce the Conciliation Bill.

This interested us very slightly, for knowing its prospect of success to have been destroyed, for we were done with the Conciliation Bill forever. Nothing less than a government measure would henceforth satisfy the W. S. P. U., because it had been clearly demonstrated that only a government measure would be allowed to pass the House of Commons. With sublime faith, or rather with a deplorable lack of political insight, the Women's Liberal Federation and the National Union of Women's Suffrage Societies professed full confidence in the proposed amendment to a manhood suffrage bill, but we knew how futile was that hope. We saw that the only course to take was to offer determined opposition to any measure of suffrage that did not include as an integral part, equal suffrage for men and women.

On February 16th we held a large meeting of welcome to a number of released prisoners who had served two and three months for the window breaking demonstration that had taken place in the previous November. At this meeting we candidly surveyed the situation and agreed on a course of action which we believed would be sufficiently strong to prevent the government from advancing their threatened franchise bill. I said on this occasion:

We don't want to use any weapons that are unnecessarily strong. If the argument of the stone, that time-honoured official political argument, is sufficient, then we will never use any stronger argument. And that is the weapon and the argument that we are going to use next time. And so I say to every volunteer on our demonstration, 'Be prepared to use that argument.' I am taking charge of the demonstration, and that is the argument I am going to use. I am not going to use it for any sentimental reason, I am going to use it because it is the easiest and the most readily understood.

Why should women go to Parliament Square and be battered about and insulted, and most important of all, produce less effect than when we throw stones? We tried it long enough. We submitted for years patiently to insult and assault. Women had their health injured. Women lost their lives. We should not have minded if that had succeeded, but that did not succeed, and we have made more progress with less hurt to ourselves by breaking glass than ever we made when we allowed them to break our bodies.

After all, is not a woman's life, is not her health, are not her limbs more valuable than panes of glass? There is no doubt of that, but most important of all, does not the breaking of glass produce more effect upon the government? If you are fighting a battle, that should dictate your choice of weapons. Well, then, we are going to try this time if mere stones will do it. I do not think it will ever be necessary for us to arm ourselves as Chinese women have done, but there are women who are prepared to do that if it should be necessary. In this Union we don't lose our heads. We only go as far as we are obliged to go in order to win, and we are going forward with this next protest demonstration in full faith that this plan of campaign, initiated by our friends whom we honour tonight, will on this next occasion prove effective.

Ever since militancy took on the form of destruction of property the public generally, both at home and abroad, has expressed curiosity as to the logical connection between acts such as breaking windows, firing pillar boxes, *et cetera*, and the vote. Only a complete lack of historical knowledge excuses that curiosity. For every advance of men's political freedom has been marked with violence and the destruction of property. Usually the advance has been marked by war, which is called glorious. Sometimes it has been marked by riotings, which are deemed less glorious but are at least effective. That speech of mine, just quoted, will probably strike the reader as one inciting to violence and illegal action, things as a rule and in ordinary circumstances quite inexcusable. Well, I will call the reader's attention to what was, in this connection, a rather singular coincidence.

At the very hour when I was making that speech, advising my audience of the political necessity of physical revolt, a responsible member of the government, in another hall, in another city, was telling his audience precisely the same thing. This Cabinet Minister, the right Honourable C. E. H. Hobhouse, addressing a large anti-suffrage meeting in his constituency of Bristol, said that the suffrage movement was not a political issue because its adherents had failed to prove that behind this movement existed a large public demand. He declared that:

In the case of the suffrage demand there has not been the kind of popular sentimental uprising which accounted for Nottingham Castle in 1832 or the Hyde Park railings in 1867. There has not been a great ebullition of popular feeling.

The "popular sentimental uprising" to which Mr. Hobhouse alluded was the burning to the ground of the castle of the anti-suffrage Duke of Newcastle, and of Colwick Castle, the country seat of another of the leaders of the opposition against the franchise bill. The militant men of that time did not select uninhabited buildings to be fired. They burned both these historic residences over their owners' heads. Indeed, the wife of the owner of Colwick Castle died as a result of shock and exposure on that occasion. No arrests were made, no men imprisoned. On the contrary the king sent for the premier, and begged the Whig Ministers favourable to the franchise bill not to resign, and intimated that this was also the wish of the Lords who had thrown out the bill. Molesworth's *History of England* says:

These declarations were imperatively called for. The danger was imminent and the ministers knew it and did all that lay in their power to tranquillise the people, and to assure them that the bill was only delayed and not finally defeated.

For a time the people believed this, but soon they lost patience, and seeing signs of a renewed activity on the part of the anti-suffragists, they became aggressive again. Bristol, the very city in which Mr. Hobhouse made his speech, was set on fire. The militant reformers burned the new gaol, the toll houses, the Bishop's Palace, both sides of Queen's Square, including the Mansion House, the custom house, the excise office, many warehouses, and other private property, the whole valued at over £100,000—five hundred thousand dollars. It was as a result of such violence, and in fear of more violence, that the reform bill was hurried through Parliament and became law in June, 1832.

Our demonstration, so mild by comparison with English men's political agitation, was announced for March 4th, and the announcement created much public alarm. Sir William Byles gave notice that he would "ask the Secretary of State for the Home Department whether his attention had been drawn to a speech by Mrs. Pankhurst last Friday night, openly and emphatically inciting her hearers to violent outrage and the destruction of property, and threatening the use of firearms if stones did not prove sufficiently effective; and what steps he proposes to take to protect Society from this outbreak of lawlessness."

The question was duly asked, and the Home Secretary replied that his attention had been called to the speech, but that it would not be desirable in the public interest to say more than this at present.

Whatever preparations the police department were making to prevent the demonstration, they failed because, while as usual, we were able to calculate exactly what the police department were going to do, they were utterly unable to calculate what we were going to do. We had planned a demonstration for March 4th, and this one we announced. We planned another demonstration for March 1st, but this one we did not announce. Late in the afternoon of Friday, March 1st, I drove in a taxicab, accompanied by the Hon. Secretary of the Union, Mrs. Tuke and another of our members, to No. 10 Downing Street, the official residence of the prime minister. It was exactly half past five when we alighted from the cab and threw our stones, four of them, through the window panes. As we expected we were promptly arrested and taken to Cannon Row police station. The hour that followed will long be remembered in London. At intervals of fifteen minutes relays of women who had volunteered for the demonstration did their work.

The first smashing of glass occurred in the Haymarket and Piccadilly, and greatly startled and alarmed both pedestrians and police. A large number of the women were arrested, and everybody thought that this ended the affair. But before the excited populace and the frustrated shop owners' first exclamation had died down, before the police had reached the station with their prisoners, the ominous crashing and splintering of plate glass began again, this time along both sides of Regent Street and the Strand. A furious rush of police and people towards the second scene of action ensued. While their attention was being taken up with occurrences in this quarter, the third relay of women began breaking the windows in Oxford Circus and Bond Street. The demonstration ended for the day at half past six with the breaking of many windows in the Strand. The *Daily Mail* gave this graphic account of the demonstration:

From every part of the crowded and brilliantly lighted streets came the crash of splintered glass. People started as a window shattered at their side; suddenly there was another crash in front of them; on the other side of the street; behind—everywhere. Scared shop assistants came running out to the pavements; traffic stopped; policemen sprang this way and that; five minutes later the streets were a procession of excited groups, each surrounding a woman wrecker being led in custody to the nearest police station. Meanwhile the shopping quarter of London had plunged itself into a sudden twilight. Shutters were hurriedly fitted; the rattle of iron curtains being drawn came from every side. Guards of commissionaires and shopmen were quickly mounted, and any unaccompanied lady in sight, especially if she carried a hand bag, became an object of menacing suspicion.

At the hour when this demonstration was being made a conference was being held at Scotland Yard to determine what should be done to prevent the smashing of windows on the coming Monday night. But we had not announced the hour of our March 4th protest. I had in my speech simply invited women to assemble in Parliament Square on the evening of March 4th, and they accepted the invitation. Said the *Daily Telegraph*:

By six o'clock the neighbourhood Houses of Parliament were in a stage of siege. Shopkeepers in almost every instance barricaded their premises, removed goods from the windows and prepared for the worst. A few minutes before six o'clock a huge force of police, amounting to nearly three thousand constables, was posted in Parliament Square, Whitehall, and streets adjoining, and large reserves were gathered in Westminster Hall and Scotland Yard. By half past eight Whitehall was packed from end to end with police and public. Mounted constables rode up and down Whitehall keeping the people on the move. At no time was there any sign of danger. . . .

The demonstration had taken place in the morning, when a hundred or more women walked quietly into Knightsbridge and walking

THE ARGUMENT OF THE BROKEN WINDOW PANE

singly along the streets demolished nearly every pane of glass they passed. Taken by surprise the police arrested as many as they could reach, but most of the women escaped.

For that two days' work something like two hundred suffragettes were taken to the various police stations, and for days the long procession of women streamed through the courts. The dismayed magistrates found themselves facing, not only former rebels, but many new ones, in some cases, women whose names, like that of Dr. Ethel Smyth, the composer, were famous throughout Europe. These women, when arraigned, made clear and lucid statements of their positions and their motives, but magistrates are not schooled to examine motives. They are trained to think only of laws and mostly of laws protecting property. Their ears are not tuned to listen to words like those spoken by one of the prisoners, who said:

> We have tried every means—processions and meetings—which were of no avail. We have tried demonstrations, and now at last we have to break windows. I wish I had broken more. I am not in the least repentant. Our women are working in far worse condition than the striking miners. I have seen widows struggling to bring up their children. Only two out of every five are fit to be soldiers. What is the good of a country like ours? England is absolutely on the wane. You only have one point of view, and that is the men's, and while men have done the best they could, they cannot go far without the women and the women's views. We believe the whole is in a muddle too horrible to think of.

The coal miners were at that time engaging in a terrible strike, and the government, instead of arresting the leaders, were trying to come to terms of peace with them. I reminded the magistrate of this fact, and I told him that what the women had done was but a fleabite by comparison with the miners' violence. I said further:

> I hope our demonstration will be enough to show the government that the women's agitation is going on. If not, if you send me to prison, I will go further to show that women who have to help pay the salaries of Cabinet Ministers, and your salary too, sir, are going to have some voice in the making of the laws they have to obey.

I was sentenced to two months' imprisonment. Others received sentences ranging from one week to two months, while those who were accused of breaking glass above five pounds in value, were committed for trial in higher courts. They were sent to prison on remand, and when the last of us were behind the grim gates, not only Holloway but three other women's prisons were taxed to provide for so many extra inmates.

It was a stormy imprisonment for most of us. A great many of the women had received, in addition to their sentences, "hard labour," and this meant that the privileges at that time accorded to Suffragettes, as political offenders, were withheld. The women adopted the hunger strike as a protest, but as the hint was conveyed to me that the privileges would be restored, I advised a cessation of the strike. The remand prisoners demanded that I be allowed to exercise with them, and when this was not answered they broke the windows of their cells. The other suffrage prisoners, hearing the sound of shattered glass, and the singing of the *Marseillaise*, immediately broke their windows. The time had long gone by when the Suffragettes submitted meekly to prison discipline. And so passed the first days of my imprisonment.

Chapter 2

The panic stricken government did not rest content with the imprisonment of the window breakers. They sought, in a blind and blundering fashion, to perform the impossible feat of wrecking at a blow the entire militant movement. Governments have always tried to crush reform movements, to destroy ideas, to kill the thing that cannot die. Without regard to history, which shows that no government have ever succeeded in doing this, they go on trying in the old, senseless way.

For days before the two demonstrations described in the last chapter our headquarters in Clement's Inn had been under constant observation by the police, and on the evening of March 5th an inspector of police and a large force of detectives suddenly descended on the place, with warrants for the arrest of Christabel Pankhurst and Mr. and Mrs. Pethick Lawrence, who with Mrs. Tuke and myself were charged with "conspiring to incite certain persons to commit malicious damage to property."

When the officers entered they found Mr. Pethick Lawrence at work in his office, and Mrs. Pethick Lawrence in her flat upstairs. My daughter was not in the building. The Lawrences, after making brief preparations drove in a taxicab to Bow Street Station, where they spent the night. The police remained in possession of the offices, and detectives were despatched to find and arrest Christabel. But that arrest never took place. Christabel Pankhurst eluded the entire force of detectives and uniformed police, trained hunters of human prey.

Christabel had gone home, and at first, on hearing of the arrest of Mr. and Mrs. Pethick Lawrence, had taken her own arrest for granted. A little reflection however showed her the danger in which the Union would stand if completely deprived of its accustomed leadership, and seeing that it was her duty to avoid arrest, she quietly left the house. She spent that night with friends who, next morning, helped her to make the necessary arrangements and saw her safely away from London. The same night she reached Paris, where she has since remained. My relief, when I learned of her flight, was very great, because I knew that whatever happened to the Lawrences and myself, the movement would be wisely directed, this in spite of the fact that the police remained in full possession of headquarters.

The offices in Clement's Inn were thoroughly ransacked by the police, in a determined effort to secure evidence of conspiracy. They went through every desk, file and cabinet, taking away with them two cab loads of books and papers, including all my private papers, photographs of my children in infancy, and letters sent me by my husband long ago. Some of these I never saw again.

The police also terrorised the printer of our weekly newspaper, and although the paper came out as usual, about a third of its columns were left blank. The headlines, however, with the ensuing space mere white paper produced a most dramatic effect. "History Teaches" read one headline to a blank space, plainly indicating that the government were not willing to let the public know some of the things that history teaches. "Women's Moderation" suggested that the destroyed paragraph called for comparison of the women's window breaking with men's greater violence in the past. Most eloquent of all was the editorial page, absolutely blank except for the headline, "A Challenge!" and the name at the foot of the last column, Christabel Pankhurst. What words could have breathed a prouder defiance, a more implacable resolve? Christabel was gone, out of the clutches of the government, yet she remained in complete possession of the field.

For weeks the search for her went relentlessly on. Police searched every railway station, every train, every sea port. The police of every city in the kingdom were furnished with her portrait. Every amateur Sherlock Holmes in England joined with the police in finding her.

She was reported in a dozen cities, including New York. But all the time she was living quietly in Paris, in daily communication with the workers in London, who within a few days were once more at their appointed tasks. My daughter has remained in France ever since.

Meanwhile, I found myself in the anomalous position of a convicted offender serving two months' prison sentence, and of a prisoner on remand waiting to be charged with a more serious offence. I was in very bad health, having been placed in a damp and unwarmed third division cell, the result being an acute attack of bronchitis. I addressed a letter to the Home Secretary, telling him of my condition, and urging the necessity of liberty to recover my health and to prepare my case for trial. I asked for release on bail, the plain right of a remand prisoner, and I offered if bail were granted now to serve the rest of my two months' sentence later on. The sole concessions granted me, however, were removal to a better cell and the right to see my secretary and my solicitor, but only in the presence of a wardress and a member of the prison clerical staff. On March 14th Mr. and Mrs. Pethick Lawrence, Mrs. Tuke and myself were brought up for preliminary hearing on the charge of having, on November 1, 1911, and on various other dates "conspired and combined together unlawfully and maliciously to commit damage, etc."

The case opened on March 14th in a crowded courtroom in which I saw many friends. Mr. Bodkin, who appeared for the prosecution, made a very long address, in which he endeavoured to prove that the Women's Social and Political Union was a highly developed organisation of most sinister character. He produced much documentary evidence, some of it of such amusing character that the court rocked with stifled laughter, and the judge was obliged to conceal his smiles behind his hand. Mr. Bodkin cited our code book with the assistance of which we were able to communicate private messages. His voice sank to a scandalised half whisper as he stated the fact that we had presumed to include the sacred persons of the government in our private code. Mr. Bodkin said portentously:

> We find that public men in the service of His Majesty as members of the Cabinet are tabulated here under code names. We find that the Cabinet collectively has its code word "Trees," and individual members of the Cabinet are designated by the name, sometimes of trees, but I am also bound to say the commonest weeds as well.

Here a ripple of laughter interrupted. Mr. Bodkin frowned heavily, and continued solemnly:

There is one called Pansy; another one—more complimentary—Roses, another, Violets, and so on.

Each of the defendants was designated by a code letter. Thus Mrs. Pankhurst was identified by the letter F; Mrs. Pethick Lawrence, D; Miss Christabel Pankhurst, E. Every public building, including the House of Commons, had its code name. The deadly possibilities of the code were illustrated by a telegram found in one of the files. It read:

Silk, thistle, pansy, duck, wool, E. Q.

Translated by the aid of the code book the telegram read:

Will you protest Asquith's public meeting tomorrow evening but don't get arrested unless success depends on it. Wire back to Christabel Pankhurst, Clements Inn.

More laughter followed these revelations, which after all proved no more than the business-like methods employed by the W. S. P. U. The laughter proved something a great deal more significant, for it was a plain indication that the old respect in which Cabinet Ministers had been held was no more. We had torn the veil from their *sacrosanct* personalities and shown them for what they were, mean and scheming politicians. More serious from the point of view of prosecution was the evidence brought in by members of the police department in regard to the occurrences of March 1st and 4th. The policemen who arrested me and my two companions in Downing Street on March 1st, after we had broken the windows in the Premier's house, testified that following the arrest, we had handed him our reserve stock of stones, and that they were all alike, heavy flints.

Other prisoners were found in possession of similar stones, tending to prove that the stones all came from one source. Other officers testified to the methodical manner in which the window breaking of March 1st and 4th was carried out, how systematically it had been planned and how soldierly had been the behaviour of the women. By twos and threes March 4th they had been seen to go to the headquarters at Clement's Inn, carrying handbags, which they deposited at headquarters, and had then gone on to a meeting at the Pavilion Music Hall. The police attended the meeting, which was the usual rally preceding a demonstration or a deputation. At five o'clock the meeting adjourned and the women went out, as if to go home. The police observed that many of them, still in groups of twos and threes, went to the Gardenia restaurant in Catherine Street, Strand, a place where many Suffragette breakfasts and teas had been held. The police thought that about one hundred and fifty women congregated there on March 4th.

They remained until seven o'clock, and then, under the watching eyes of the police, they sauntered out and dispersed. A few minutes later, when there was no reason to expect such a thing, the noise was heard, in many streets, of wholesale window smashing. The police authorities made much of the fact that the women who had left their bags at headquarters and were afterwards arrested, were bailed out that night by Mr. Pethick Lawrence. The similarity of the stones used; the gathering of so many women in one building, prepared for arrest; the waiting at the Gardenia Restaurant; the apparent dispersal; the simultaneous destruction in many localities of plate glass, and the bailing of prisoners by a person connected with the headquarters mentioned, certainly showed a carefully worked out plan. Only a public trial of the defendants could establish whether or not the plan was a conspiracy.

On the second day of the Ministerial hearing, Mrs. Tuke, who had been in the prison infirmary for twenty days and had to be attended in court by a trained nurse, was admitted to bail. Mr. Pethick Lawrence made a strong plea for bail for himself and his wife, pointing out that they had been in prison on remand for two weeks and were entitled to bail. I also demanded the privileges of a prisoner on remand. Both of these pleas were denied by the court, but a few days later the Home Secretary wrote to my solicitor that the remainder of my sentence of two months would be remitted until after the conspiracy trail at Bow Street. Mr. and Mrs. Pethick Lawrence had already been admitted to bail. Public opinion forced the Home Secretary to make these concessions, as it is well known that it is next to impossible to prepare a defence while confined in prison. Aside from the terrible effect of prison on one's body and nerves, there is the difficulty of consulting documents and securing other necessary data to be considered.

On April 4th the Ministerial hearing ended in the acquittal of Mrs. Tuke, whose activities in the W. S. P. U. were shown to be purely secretarial. Mr. and Mrs. Pethick Lawrence and myself were committed for trial at the next session of the Central Criminal Court, beginning April 23rd. Because of the weak state of my health the judge was with great difficulty prevailed upon to postpone the trial two weeks and it was, therefore, not until May 15th that the case was opened.

The trial at Old Bailey is a thing that I shall never forget. The scene is clear before me as I write, the judge impressively bewigged and scarlet robed, dominating the crowded courtroom, the solicitors at their table, the jury, and looking very far away, the anxious pale faces of our friends who crowded the narrow galleries.

By the veriest irony of fate this judge, Lord Coleridge, was the son of Sir Charles Coleridge who, in the year 1867, appeared with my husband, Dr. Pankhurst, in the famous case of Chorlton v. Lings, and sought to establish that women were persons, and as such were entitled to the Parliamentary vote. To make the irony still deeper the Attorney General, Sir Rufus Isaacs, who appeared as Counsel for the prosecution against women militants, himself had been guilty of remarkable speeches in corroboration of our point of view. In a speech made in 1910, in relation to the abolition of the Lords' *veto*, Sir Rufus made the statement that, although the agitation against privilege was being peacefully conducted, the indignation behind it was very intense. Said Sir Rufus:

> Formerly when the great mass of the people were voteless they had to do something violent in order to show what they felt; today the elector's bullet is his ballot. Let no one be deceived, therefore, because in this present struggle everything is peaceful and orderly, in contrast to the disorderliness of other great struggles of the past.

We wondered if the man who said these words could fail to realise that voteless women, deprived of every constitutional means of righting their grievances, were also obliged to do something violent in order to show how they felt. His opening address removed all doubt on that score.

Sir Rufus Isaacs has a clear-cut, hawk-like face, deep eyes, and a somewhat world worn air. The first words he spoke were so astoundingly unfair that I could hardly believe that I heard them aright. He began his address to the jury by telling them that they must not, on any account, connect the act of the defendants with any political agitation.

> I am very anxious to impress upon you from the moment we begin to deal with the facts of this case, that all questions of whether a woman is entitled to the Parliamentary franchise,

whether she should have the same right of franchise as a man, are questions which are in no sense involved in the trial of this issue. . . . Therefore, I ask you to discard altogether from the consideration of the matters which will be placed before you any viewpoint you may have on this no doubt very important political issue.

Nevertheless Sir Rufus added in the course of his remarks that he feared that it would not be possible to keep out of the conduct of the case various references to political events, and of course the entire trial, from beginning to end, showed clearly that the case was what Mr. Tim Healey, Mrs. Pethick Lawrence's counsel, called it, a great State Trial.

Proceeding, the attorney general described the W. S. P. U., which he said he thought had been in existence since 1907, and had used what were known as militant methods. In 1911 the association had become annoyed by the prime minister because he would not make women's suffrage what was called a government question. In November, 1911, the prime minister announced the introduction of a manhood suffrage bill. From that time on the defendants set to work to carry out a campaign which would have meant nothing less than anarchy. Women were to be induced to act together at a given time, in different given places, in such numbers that the police should be paralysed by the number of persons breaking the law, in order, to use the defendant's own words, "to bring the government to its knees."

After designating the respective positions held by the four defendants in the W. S. P. U., Sir Rufus went on to relate the events which resulted in the smashing of plate glass windows valued at some two thousand pounds, and the imprisonment of over two hundred women who were incited to their deeds by the conspirators in the dock. He entirely ignored the motive of the acts in question, and he treated the whole affair as if the women had been burglars. This inverted statement of the matter, though accurate enough as to facts, was such as might have been given by King John of the signing of Magna Charta.

A very great number of witnesses were examined, a large number of them being policemen, and their testimony, and our cross examination disclosed the startling fact that there exists in England a special band of secret police entirely engaged in political work. These men, seventy-five in number, form what is known as the political branch of the Criminal Investigation Department of the Police. They go about in disguise, and their sole duty is to shadow Suffragettes and other political workers. They follow certain political workers from their homes to their places of business, to their social pleasures, into tea rooms and restaurants, even to the theatre. They pursue unsuspecting people in taxicabs, sit beside them in omnibuses. Above all they take down speeches. In fact the system is exactly like the secret police system of Russia.

Mr. Pethick Lawrence and I spoke in our own defence, and Mr. Healey M. P. defended Mrs. Pethick Lawrence. I cannot give our speeches in full, but I should like to include as much of them as will serve to make the entire situation clear to the reader.

Mr. Lawrence spoke first at the opening of the case. He began by giving an account of the suffrage movement and why he felt the enfranchisement of women appeared to him a question so grave that it warranted strong measures in its pursuit. He sketched briefly the history of the Women's Social and Political Union, from the time when Christabel Pankhurst and Annie Kenney were thrown out of Sir Edward Grey's meeting and imprisoned for asking a political question, to the torpedoing of the Conciliation Bill.

> The case that I have to put before you is that neither the conspiracy nor the incitement is ours; but that the conspiracy is a conspiracy of the Cabinet who are responsible for the government of this country; and that the incitement is the incitement of the Ministers of the Crown.

And he did this most effectually not only by telling of the disgraceful trickery and deceit with which the government had misled the suffragists in the matter of suffrage bills, but by giving the plain words in which members of the Cabinet had advised the women that they would never get the vote until they had learned to fight for it as men had fought in the past.

When it came my turn to speak, realising that the average man is profoundly ignorant of the history of the women's movement—because the press has never adequately or truthfully chronicled the movement—I told the jury, as briefly as I could, the story of the forty years' peaceful agitation before my daughters and I resolved that we would give our lives to the work of getting the vote for women, and that we should use whatever means of getting the vote that were necessary to success.

We founded the Women's Social and Political Union in 1903.

Our first intention was to try and influence the particular political Party, which was then coming into power, to make this question of the enfranchisement of women their own question and to push it. It took some little time to convince us—and I need not weary you with the history of all that has happened—but it took some little time to convince us that that was no use; that we could not secure things in that way. Then in 1905 we faced the hard facts. We realised that there was a Press boycott against Women's Suffrage. Our speeches at public meetings were not reported, our letters to the editors, were not published, even if we implored the editors; even the things relating to Women's Suffrage in Parliament were not recorded. They said the subject was not of sufficient public interest to be reported in the Press, and they were not prepared to report it. Then with regard to the men politicians in 1905: we realised how shadowy were the fine phrases about democracy, about human equality, used by the gentlemen who were then coming into power. They meant to ignore the women—there was no doubt whatever about that.

For in the official documents coming from the Liberal party on the eve of the 1905 election, there were sentences like this: 'What the country wants is a simple measure of Manhood Suffrage.' There was no room for the inclusion of women. We knew perfectly well that if there was to be franchise reform at all, the Liberal party which was then coming into power did not mean Votes for Women, in spite of all the pledges of members; in spite of the fact that a majority of the House of Commons, especially on the Liberal side, were pledged to it—it did not mean that they were going to put it into practice. And so we found some way of forcing their attention to this question.

Now I come to the facts with regard to militancy. We realised that the plans we had in our minds would involve great sacrifice on our part, that it might cost us all we had. We were at that time a little organisation, composed in the main of working women, the wives and daughters of working men. And my daughters and I took a leading part, naturally, because we thought the thing out, and, to a certain extent, because we were of better social position than most of our members, and we felt a sense of responsibility.

I described the events that marked the first days of our work, the scene in Free Trade Hall, Manchester, when my daughter and her companion were arrested for the crime of asking a question of a politician, and I continued:

> What did they do next? (I want you to realise that no step we have taken forward has been taken until after some act of repression on the part of our enemy, the government—because it is the government that is our enemy; it is not the Members of Parliament, it is not the men in the country; it is the government in power alone that can give us the vote. It is the government alone that we regard as our enemy, and the whole of our agitation is directed to bringing just as much pressure as necessary upon those people who can deal with our grievance.) The next step the women took was to ask questions during the course of meetings, because, as I told you, these gentlemen gave them no opportunity of asking them afterwards.
>
> And then began the interjections of which we have heard, the interference with the right to hold public meetings, the interference with the right of free speech, of which we have heard, for which these women, these hooligan women, as they have been called—have been denounced. I ask you, gentlemen, to imagine the amount of courage which it needs for a woman to undertake that kind of work. When men come to interrupt women's meetings, they come in gangs, with noisy instruments, and sing and shout together, and stamp their feet. But when women have gone to Cabinet Ministers' meetings—only to interrupt Cabinet Ministers and nobody else—they have gone singly.
>
> And it has become increasingly difficult for them to get in, because as a result of the women's methods there has developed the system of admission by ticket and the exclusion of women—a thing which in my Liberal days would have been thought a very disgraceful thing at Liberal meetings. But this ticket system developed, and so the women could only get in with very great difficulty. Women have concealed themselves for thirty-six hours in dangerous positions, under the platforms, in the organs, wherever they could get a vantage point. They waited starving in the cold, sometimes on the roof exposed to a winter's night, just to get a chance of saying in the course of

a Cabinet Minister's speech, 'When is the Liberal Government going to put its promises into practice?' That has been the form militancy took in its further development.

I went over the whole matter of our peaceful deputations, and of the violence with which they were invariably met; of our arrests and the farcical police court trials, where the mere evidence of policemen's unsupported statements sent us to prison for long terms; of the falsehoods told of us in the House of Commons by responsible members of the government—tales of women scratching and biting policemen and using hatpins—and I accused the government of making these attacks against women who were powerless to defend themselves because they feared the women and desired to crush the agitation represented by our organisation.

Now it has been stated in this court that it is not the Women's Social and Political Union that is in the court, but that it is certain defendants. The action of the government, gentlemen, is certainly against the defendants who are before you here today, but it is also against the Women's Social and Political Union. The intention is to crush that organisation. And this intention apparently was arrived at after I had been sent to prison for two months for breaking a pane of glass worth, I am told, 2s. 3d., the punishment which I accepted because I was a leader of this movement, though it was an extraordinary punishment to inflict for so small an act of damages as I had committed. I accepted it as the punishment for a leader of an agitation disagreeable to the government; and while I was there this prosecution started.

They thought they would make a clean sweep of the people who they considered were the political brains of the movement. We have got many false friends in the Cabinet—people who by their words appear to be well-meaning towards the cause of Women's Suffrage. And they thought that if they could get the leaders of the union out of the way, it would result in the indefinite postponement and settlement of the question in this country. Well, they have not succeeded in their design, and even if they had got all the so-called leaders of this movement out of their way they would not have succeeded even then. Now why have they not put the union in the dock?

We have a democratic government, so-called. This Women's

Social and Political Union is not a collection of hysterical and unimportant wild women, as has been suggested to you, but it is an important organisation, which numbers amongst its membership very important people. It is composed of women of all classes of the community, women who have influence in their particular organisations as working women; women who have influence in professional organisations as professional women; women of social importance; women even of Royal rank are amongst the members of this organisation, and so it would not pay a democratic government to deal with this organisation as a whole.

They hoped that by taking away the people that they thought guided the political fortunes of the organisation they would break the organisation down. They thought that if they put out of the way the influential members of the organisation they, as one member of the Cabinet, I believe, said, would crush the movement and get it 'on the run.' Well, governments have many times been mistaken, gentlemen, and I venture to suggest to you that governments are mistaken again. I think the answer to the government was given at the Albert Hall meeting held immediately after our arrest. Within a few minutes, without the eloquence of Mrs. Pethick Lawrence, without the appeals of the people who have been called the leaders of this movement, in a very few minutes £10,000 was subscribed for the carrying on of this movement.

Now a movement like that, supported like that, is not a wild, hysterical movement. It is not a movement of misguided people. It is a very serious movement. Women, I submit, like our members, and women, I venture to say, like the two women, and like the man who are in the dock to-day, are not people to undertake a thing like this lightly. May I just try to make you feel what it is that has made this movement the gigantic size it is from the very small beginnings it had? It is one of the biggest movements of modern times. A movement which is not only an influence, perhaps not yet recognised, in this country, but is influencing the women's movement all over the world.

Is there anything more marvellous in modern times than the kind of spontaneous outburst in every country of this woman's movement? Even in China—and I think it somewhat of a disgrace to Englishmen—even in China women have won the vote, as an outcome of a successful revolution, with which, I dare say, members of His Majesty's Government sympathise—a bloody revolution.

One more word on that point. When I was in prison the second time, for three months as a common criminal for no greater offence than the issue of a handbill—less inflammatory in its terms than some of the speeches of members of the government who prosecute us here—during that time, through the efforts of a member of Parliament, there was secured for me permission to have the daily paper in prison, and the first thing I read in the daily Press was this: that the government was at that moment fêting the members of the Young Turkish Revolutionary Party, gentlemen who had invaded the privacy of the Sultan's home—we used to hear a great deal about invading the privacy of Mr. Asquith's residence when we ventured to ring his door bell—gentlemen who had killed and slain, and had been successful in their revolution, while we women had never thrown a stone—for none of us was imprisoned for stone throwing, but merely for taking the part we had then taken in this organisation.

There we were imprisoned while these political murderers were being *fêted* by the very government who imprisoned us, and were being congratulated on the success of their revolution. Now I ask you, was it to be wondered at that women said to themselves: 'Perhaps it is that we have not done enough. Perhaps it is that these gentlemen do not understand womenfolk. Perhaps they do not realise women's ways, and because we have not done the things that men have done, they may think we are not in earnest.'

And then we come down to this last business of all, when we have responsible statesmen like Mr. Hobhouse saying that there had never been any sentimental uprising, no expression of feeling like that which led to the burning down of Nottingham Castle. Can you wonder, then, that we decided we should have to nerve ourselves to do more, and can you understand why we cast about to find a way, as women will, that would not involve loss of human life and the maiming of human beings, because women care more about human life than men, and I think it is quite natural that we should, for we know what life costs. We risk our lives when men are born.

Now, I want to say this deliberately as a leader of this movement. We have tried to hold it back, we have tried to keep it from going beyond bounds, and I have never felt a prouder woman than I did one night when a police constable said to me, after one of these demonstrations, 'Had this been a man's demonstration, there would have been bloodshed long ago.' Well, my lord, there has not been any bloodshed except on the part of the women themselves—these so-called militant women. Violence has been done to us, and I who stand before you in this dock have lost a dear sister in the course of this agitation. She died within three days of coming out of prison, a little more than a year ago.

These are things which, wherever we are, we do not say very much about. We cannot keep cheery, we cannot keep cheerful, we cannot keep the right kind of spirit, which means success, if we dwell too much upon the hard part of our agitation. But I do say this, gentlemen, that whatever in future you may think of us, you will say this about us, that whatever our enemies may say, we have always put up an honourable fight, and taken no unfair means of defeating our opponents, although they have not always been people who have acted so honourably towards us.

We have assaulted no one; we have done no hurt to anyone; and it was not until 'Black Friday'—and what happened on 'Black Friday' is that we had a new Home Secretary, and there appeared to be new orders given to the police, because the police on that occasion showed a kind of ferocity in dealing with the women that they had never done before, and the women came to us and said: 'We cannot bear this'—it was not until then we felt this new form of repression should compel us to take another step. That is the question of 'Black Friday,' and I want to say here and now that every effort was made after 'Black Friday' to get an open public judicial inquiry into the doings of 'Black Friday,' as to the instructions given to the police.

That inquiry was refused; but an informal inquiry was held by a man, whose name will carry conviction as to his status and moral integrity on the one side of the great political parties, and a man of equal standing on the Liberal side. These two men were Lord Robert Cecil and Mr. Ellis Griffith. They held a private inquiry, had women before them, took their evidence, examined that evidence, and after hearing it said that they believed what the women had told them was substantially true, and that they thought there was good cause for that inquiry to be held. That was embodied in a report.

To show you our difficulties, Lord Robert Cecil, in a speech at the Criterion Restaurant, spoke on this question. He called upon the government to hold this inquiry, and not one word of that speech was reported in any morning paper. That is the sort of thing we have had to face, and I welcome standing here, if only for the purpose of getting these facts out, and I challenge the attorney general to institute an inquiry into these proceedings—not that kind of inquiry of sending their inspectors to Holloway and accepting what they are told by the officials—but to open a public inquiry, with a jury, if he likes, to deal with our grievances against the government and the methods of this agitation.

I say it is not the defendants who have conspired, but the government who have conspired against us to crush this agitation; but however the matter may be decided, we are content to abide by the verdict of posterity. We are not the kind of people who like to brag a lot; we are not the kind of people who would bring ourselves into this position unless we were convinced that it was the only way. I have tried—all my life I have worked for this question—I have tried arguments, I have tried persuasion.

I have addressed a greater number of public meetings, perhaps, than any person in this court, and I have never addressed one meeting where substantially the opinion of the meeting—not a ticket meeting, but an open meeting, for I have never addressed any other kind of a meeting—has not been that where women bear burdens and share responsibilities like men they should be given the privileges that men enjoy. I am convinced that public opinion is with us—that it has been stifled—wilfully stifled—so that in a public Court of Justice one is glad of being allowed to speak on this question.

The attorney general's summing up for the prosecution was very largely a defence of the Liberal Party and its course in regard to woman suffrage legislation. Therefore, Mr. Tim Healey, in his defence of Mrs. Pethick Lawrence, did well to lay stress on the political character of the conspiracy charge and trial. He said:

> It is no doubt a very useful thing when you have political opponents to be able to set the law in motion against them. I have not the smallest doubt it would be a very convenient thing, if they had the courage to do it, to shut up the whole of His Majesty's Opposition while the present government is in office—to lock up all the men of lustre and distinction in our public forum and on our public platforms—all the Carsons, F. E. Smiths, Bonar Laws, and so on. It would be a most convenient thing to end the whole thing, as it would be to end women's agitation in the form of the indictment. Gentlemen of the jury, whatever words have been spoken by mutual opponents, whatever instructions have been addressed, not to feeble females, but to men who boast of drilling and of arms, they have not had the courage to prosecute anybody, except women, by means of an indictment.
>
> Yet the government of my learned friend have selected two dates as cardinal dates, and they ask you to pass judgment upon the prisoners at the bar, and to say that, without rhyme or reason, taking the course suggested without provocation, these responsible, well-bred, educated, university people, have suddenly, in the words of the indictment, wickedly and with malice aforethought engaged in these criminal designs.
>
> Gentlemen of the jury, the first thing I would ask in that connection is this: What is there in the course of this demand put forward by women which should have excited the treatment at the hands of His Majesty's Ministers which this movement, according to the documents which are in evidence before me, has received? I should suppose that the essence of all government is the smooth conduct of affairs, so that those who enjoy high station, great emoluments, should not be parties against whom the accusation of provoking civic strife and breeding public turmoil should be brought.
>
> What do we find? We find that, in regard to the treatment of the demand which had always been put forward humbly, respectably, respectfully, in its origin, by those who have received trade unionists, anti-vaccinators, deceased wife's sisters, and all other forms of political demand, and who have received them humbly and yielded to them, we find that when these people

advocating this particular form of civic reform request an audience, request admission, request even to have their petitions respectfully received, they have met, judicially, at all events, with a flat and solemn negative.

That is the beginning of this unhappy spirit bred in the minds of persons like the defendants, persons like those against whom evidence has been tendered—which has led to your being empanelled in that box to-day. And I put it to you when you are considering whether it is the incitement of my clients or the conduct of ministers that have led to these events—whether I cannot ask you to say that even a fair apportionment of blame should not rest upon more responsible shoulders, and whether you should go out of your way to say that these persons in the dock alone are guilty.

In closing Mr. Healey reverted to the political character of the trial:

The government have undertaken this prosecution to seclude for a considerable period their chief opponents. They hope there will be at public meetings which they attend no more inconvenient cries of 'Votes for Women.' I cannot conceive any other object which they could have in bringing the prosecution. I have expressed my regret at the loss which the shopkeepers, tradesmen and others have suffered. I regret it deeply. I regret that any person should bring loss or suffering upon innocent people. But I ask you to say that the law has already been sufficiently vindicated by the punishment of the immediate authors of the deed. What can be gained? Does justice gain? I almost hesitate to treat this as a legal inquiry. I regard it as a vindictive political act. Of all the astonishing acts that have ever been brought into a public court against a prisoner I cannot help feeling the charge against Mr. Pethick Lawrence is the most astonishing. He ventured to attend at some police courts and gave bail for women who had been arrested in endeavouring, as I understand, to present petitions to Parliament or to have resort to violence.

I do not complain of the way in which my learned friend has conducted the prosecution, but I do complain of the police methods—inquiring into the homes and the domestic circumstances of the prisoners, obtaining their papers, taking their newspaper, going into their banking account, bringing up their bankers here to say what is their balance; and I do say that in none of the prosecutions of the past have smaller methods belittled a great State trial, because, look at it as you will, you cannot get away from it that this is a great State trial.

It is not the women who are on trial. It is the men. It is the system of government which is upon its trial. It is this method of rolling the dice by fifty-four counts in an indictment without showing to what any bit of evidence is fairly attributable; the system is on its trial—a system whereby every innocent act in public life is sought to be enmeshed in a conspiracy.

The jury was absent for more than an hour, showing that they had some difficulty in agreeing upon a verdict. When they returned it was plain from their strained countenances that they were labouring under deep feeling. The foreman's voice shook as he pronounced the verdict, guilty as charged, and he had hard work to control his emotion as he added:

> Your Lordship, we unanimously desire to express the hope that, taking into consideration the undoubtedly pure motives that underlie the agitation that has led to this trouble, you will be pleased to exercise the utmost clemency and leniency in dealing with the case.

A burst of applause followed this plea. Then Mr. Pethick Lawrence arose and asked to say a few words before sentence was pronounced. He said that it must be evident, aside from the jury's recommendation, that we had been actuated by political motives, and that we were in fact political offenders. It had been decided in English Courts that political offenders were different from ordinary offenders, and Mr. Lawrence cited the case of a Swiss subject whose extradition was refused because of the political character of his offence. The court on that occasion had declared that even if the crime were murder committed with a political motive it was a political crime. Mr. Lawrence also reminded the judge of the case of the late Mr. W. T. Stead, convicted of a crime, yet because of the unusual motive behind the crime, was allowed first division treatment and full freedom to receive his family and friends. Last of all the case of Dr. Jameson was cited. Although his raid resulted in the death of twenty-one persons and the wounding of forty-six more, the political character of his offence was taken into account and he was made a first division prisoner.

They were men, fighting in a man's war. We of the W. S. P. U. were women, fighting in a woman's war. Lord Coleridge, therefore, saw in us only reckless and criminal defiers of law. Lord Coleridge said:

> You have been convicted of a crime for which the law would sanction, if I chose to impose it, a sentence of two years' imprisonment with hard labour. There are circumstances connected with your case which the jury have very properly brought to my attention, and I have been asked by you all three to treat you as first class misdemeanants. If, in the course of this case, I had observed any contrition or disavowal of the acts you have committed, or any hope that you would avoid repetition of them in future, I should have been very much prevailed upon by the arguments that have been advanced to me.

No contrition having been expressed by us, the sentence of the Court was that we were to suffer imprisonment, in the second division, for the term of nine months, and that we were to pay the costs of the prosecution.

Chapter 3

The sentence of nine months astonished us beyond measure, especially in view of certain very recent events, one of these being the case of some sailors who had mutinied in order to call attention to something which they considered a peril to themselves and to all seafarers. They were tried and found technically guilty, but because of the motive behind their mutiny, were discharged without punishment. Perhaps more nearly like our case than this was the case of the labour leader, Tom Mann, who, shortly before, had written a pamphlet calling upon His Majesty's soldiers not to fire upon strikers when commanded to do so by their superior officers. From the government's point of view this was a much more serious kind of inciting than ours, because if it had been responded to the authorities would have been absolutely crippled in maintaining order.

Besides, soldiers who refuse to obey orders are liable to the death penalty. Tom Mann was given a sentence of six months, but this was received, on the part of the Liberal Press and Liberal politicians, with so much clamour and protest that the prisoner was released at the end of two months. So, even on our way to prison, we told one another that our sentences could not stand. Public opinion would never permit the government to keep us in prison for nine months, or in the second division for any part of our term. We agreed to wait seven

Parliamentary days before we began a hunger strike protest.

It was very dreary waiting, those seven Parliamentary days, because we could not know what was happening outside, or what was being talked of in the House. We could know nothing of the protests and memorials that were pouring in, on our behalf, from Oxford and Cambridge Universities, from members of learned societies, and from distinguished men and women of all professions, not only in England but in every country of Europe, from the United States and Canada, and even from India. An international memorial asking that we be treated as political prisoners was signed by such great men and women as Prof. Paul Milyoukoff, leader of the Constitutional Democrats in the Duma; Signor Enrico Ferri, of the Italian Chamber of Deputies; Edward Bernstein, of the German Reichstag; George Brandes, Edward Westermarck, Madame Curie, Ellen Key, Maurice Maeterlinck, and many others.

The greatest indignation was expressed in the House, Keir Hardie and Mr. George Lansbury leading in the demand for a drastic revision of our sentences and our immediate transference to the first division. So much pressure was brought to bear that within a few days the Home Secretary announced that he felt it his duty to examine into the circumstances of the case without delay. He explained that the prisoners had not at any time been forced to wear prison clothes. Ultimately, which in this case means shortly before the expiration of the seven Parliamentary days, we were all three placed in the first division. Mrs. Pethick Lawrence was given the cell formerly occupied by Dr. Jameson and I had the cell adjoining.

Mr. Pethick Lawrence, in Brixton Gaol, was similarly accommodated. We all had the privilege of furnishing our cells with comfortable chairs, tables, our own bedding, towels, and so on. We had meals sent in from the outside; we wore our own clothing and had what books, newspapers and writing materials we required. We were not permitted to write or receive letters or to see our friends except in the ordinary two weeks' routine. Still we had gained our point that suffrage prisoners were politicals.

We had gained it, but, as it turned out, only for ourselves. When we made the inquiry, "Are all our women now transferred to the first division?" the answer was that the order for transference referred only to Mr. and Mrs. Pethick Lawrence and myself. Needless to say, we immediately refused to accept this unfair advantage, and after we had exhausted every means in our power to induce the Home Secretary to give the other suffrage prisoners the same justice that we had received, we adopted the protest of the hunger strike. The word flew swiftly through Holloway, and in some mysterious way travelled to Brixton, to Aylesbury, and Winson Green, and at once all the other suffrage prisoners followed our lead.

The government then had over eighty hunger strikers on their hands, and, as before, had ready only the argument of force, which means that disgusting and cruel process of forcible feeding. Holloway became a place of horror and torment. Sickening scenes of violence took place almost every hour of the day, as the doctors went from cell to cell performing their hideous office. One of the men did his work in such brutal fashion that the very sight of him provoked cries of horror and anguish. I shall never while I live forget the suffering I experienced during the days when those cries were ringing in my ears. In her frenzy of pain one woman threw herself from the gallery on which her cell opened. A wire netting eight feet below broke her fall to the iron staircase beneath, else she must inevitably have been killed. As it was she was frightfully hurt.

The wholesale hunger strike created a tremendous stir throughout England, and every day in the House the ministers were harassed with questions. The climax was reached on the third or fourth day of the strike, when a stormy scene took place in the House of Commons. The Under Home Secretary, Mr. Ellis Griffith, had been mercilessly questioned as to conditions under which the forcible feeding was being done, and as soon as this was over one of the suffragist members made a moving appeal to the prime minister himself to order the release of all the prisoners. Mr. Asquith, forced against his will to take part in the controversy, rose and said that it was not for him to interfere with the actions of his colleague, Mr. McKenna, and he added, in his own suave, mendacious manner: "I must point out this, that there is not one single prisoner who cannot go out of prison this afternoon on giving the undertaking asked for by the Home Secretary." Meaning an undertaking to refrain henceforth from militancy.

Instantly Mr. George Lansbury sprang to his feet and exclaimed:

"You know they cannot! It is perfectly disgraceful that the Prime Minister of England should make such a statement."

Mr. Asquith glanced carelessly at the indignant Lansbury, but sank into his seat without deigning to reply. Shocked to the depths of his soul by the insult thrown at our women, Mr. Lansbury strode up to the Ministerial bench and confronted the prime minister, saying again:

That was a disgraceful thing for you to say, Sir. You are beneath contempt, you and your colleagues. You call yourselves gentlemen, and you forcibly feed and murder women in this fashion. You ought to be driven out of office. Talk about protesting. It is the most disgraceful thing that ever happened in the history of England. You will go down to history as the men who tortured innocent women.

By this time the House was seething, and the indignant Labour member had to shout at the top of his big voice in order to be heard over the din. Mr. Asquith's pompous order that Mr. Lansbury leave the House for the day was probably known to very few until it appeared in print next day. At all events Mr. Lansbury continued his protest for five minutes longer, he cried:

You murder, torture and drive women mad, and then you tell them they can walk out. You ought to be ashamed of yourself. You talk about principle—you talk about fighting in Ulster—you, too—(turning to the Unionist benches)—You ought to be driven out of public life. These women are showing you what principle is. You ought to honour them for standing up for their womanhood. I tell you, Commons of England, you ought to be ashamed of yourselves.

The Speaker came to Mr. Asquith's rescue at last and adjured Mr. Lansbury that he must obey the prime minister's order to leave the House, saying that such disorderly conduct would cause the House to lose respect. "Sir," exclaimed Mr. Lansbury, in a final burst of righteous rage, "it has lost it already."

This unprecedented explosion of wrath and scorn against the government was the sensation of the hour, and it was felt on all sides that the release of the prisoners, or at least cessation of forcible feeding, which amounted to the same thing, would be ordered. Every day the Suffragettes marched in great crowds to Holloway, serenading the prisoners and holding protest meetings to immense crowds. The music and the cheering, faintly wafted to our straining ears, was inexpressibly sweet. Yet it was while listening to one of these serenades that the most dreadful moment of my imprisonment occurred. I was lying in bed, very weak from starvation, when I heard a sudden scream from Mrs. Lawrence's cell, then the sound of a prolonged and very violent struggle, and I knew that they had dared to carry their brutal business to our doors.

I sprang out of bed and, shaking with weakness and with anger, I set my back against the wall and waited for what might come. In a few moments they had finished with Mrs. Lawrence and had flung open the door of my cell. On the threshold I saw the doctors, and back of them a large group of wardresses. "Mrs. Pankhurst," began the doctor. Instantly I caught up a heavy earthenware water jug from a table hard by, and with hands that now felt no weakness I swung the jug head high.

"If any of you dares so much as to take one step inside this cell I shall defend myself," I cried. Nobody moved or spoke for a few seconds, and then the doctor confusedly muttered something about tomorrow morning doing as well, and they all retreated.

I demanded to be admitted to Mrs. Lawrence's cell, where I found my companion in a desperate state. She is a strong woman, and a very determined one, and it had required the united strength of nine wardresses to overcome her. They had rushed into the cell without any warning, and had seized her unawares, else they might not have succeeded at all. As it was she resisted so violently that the doctors could not apply the stethoscope, and they had very great difficulty in getting the tube down. After the wretched affair was over Mrs. Lawrence fainted, and for hours afterwards was very ill.

This was the last attempt made to forcibly feed either Mrs. Lawrence or myself, and two days later we were ordered released on medical grounds. The other hunger strikers were released in batches, as every day a few more triumphant rebels approached the point where the government stood in danger of committing actual murder. Mr. Lawrence, who was forcibly fed twice a day for more than ten days, was released in a state of complete collapse on July 1st. Within a few days after that the last of the prisoners were at liberty.

As soon as I was sufficiently recovered I went to Paris and had the joy of seeing again my daughter Christabel, who, during all the days of strife and misery, had kept her personal anxiety in the background and had kept staunchly at her work of leadership. The absence of Mr. and Mrs. Pethick Lawrence had thrown the entire responsibility of the editorship of our paper, *Votes for Women*, on her shoulders, but as she has invariably risen to meet new responsibility, she conducted the paper with skill and discretion.

We had much to talk about and to consider, because it was evident that militancy, instead of being dropped, as the other suffrage societies were constantly suggesting, must go on very much more vigorously than before. The struggle had been too long drawn out. We had to seek ways to shorten it, to bring it to such a climax that the government would acknowledge that something had to be done. We had already demonstrated that our forces were impregnable. We could not be conquered, we could not be terrified, we could not even be kept in prison. Therefore, since the government had their war lost in advance, our task was merely to hasten the surrender.

The situation in Parliament, as far as the suffrage question was concerned, was clean swept and barren. The third Conciliation Bill had failed to pass its second reading, the majority against it being fourteen.

Many Liberal members were afraid to vote for the bill because Mr. Lloyd-George and Mr. Lewis Harcourt had persistently spread the rumour that its passage, at that time, would result in splitting the Cabinet. The Irish Nationalist members had become hostile to the bill because their leader, Mr. Redmond, was an anti-suffragist, and had refused to include a woman suffrage clause in the Home Rule Bill. Our erstwhile friends, the Labour members, were so apathetic, or so fearful for certain of their own measures, that most of them stayed away from the House on the day the bill reached its second reading. So it was lost, and the militants were blamed for its loss! In June the government announced that Mr. Asquith's manhood suffrage bill would soon be introduced, and very soon after this the bill did appear. It simplified the registration machinery, reduced the qualifying period of residence to six months, and abolished property qualifications, plural voting and University representation.

In a word, it gave the Parliamentary franchise to every man above the age of twenty-one and it denied it to all women. Never in the history of the suffrage movement had such an affront been offered to women, and never in the history of England had such a blow been aimed at women's liberties. It is true that the prime minister had pledged himself to introduce a bill capable of being amended to include women's suffrage, and to permit any amendment that passed its second reading to become a part of the bill. But we had no faith in an amendment, nor in any bill that was not from its inception an official government measure. Mr. Asquith had broken every pledge he had ever made the women, and this new pledge impressed us not at all. Well we knew that he had given it only to cover his treachery in torpedoing the Conciliation Bill, and in the hope of placating the suffragists, perhaps securing another truce to militancy.

If this last was his hope he was most grievously disappointed. Signs were constantly appearing to indicate that women would no longer be contented with the symbolic militancy involved in window breaking. For example, traces were found in the Home Secretary's office at Whitehall of an attempt at arson. On the doorstep of another Cabinet Minister similar traces were found. Had the government acted upon these warnings, by giving women the vote, all the serious acts of militancy that have occurred since would have been averted. But like the heart of Pharaoh, the heart of the government hardened, and militant acts followed one another in rapid succession. In July the W. S. P. U. issued a manifesto which set forth our intentions in that regard. The manifesto read in part as follows:

> The leaders of the Women's Social and Political Union have so often warned the government that unless the vote were granted to women in response to the mild militancy of the past, a fiercer spirit of revolt would be awakened which it would be impossible to control. The government have blindly disregarded the warning, and now they are reaping the harvest of their unstatesmanlike folly.

This was issued immediately after a visit paid by Mr. Asquith to Dublin. The occasion had been intended to be one of great pomp and circumstance, a huge popular demonstration in honour of the sponsor of Home Rule, but the Suffragettes turned it into the most lamentable fiasco imaginable. From the hour of Mr. Asquith's attempted secret departure from London until his return he lived and moved in momentary dread of Suffragettes. Every time he entered or left a railway carriage or a steamer he was confronted by women. Every time he rose to speak he was interrupted by women. Every public appearance he made was turned into a riot by women. As he left Dublin a woman threw a hatchet into his motorcar, without, however, doing him any injury. As a final protest against his reception by Irishmen, the Theatre Royal was set on fire by two women. The theatre was practically empty at the time, the performance having been completed, and the damage done was comparatively small, yet the two women chiefly concerned, Mrs. Leigh and Miss Evans, were given the barbarous sentences of five years each in prison. These were the first women sentenced to penal servitude in the history of our movement.

Of course they did not serve their sentences. On entering Mountjoy Prison they put in the usual claim for first division treatment, and this being refused, they immediately adopted the hunger strike.

A number of Irish Suffragettes were in Mountjoy at this time for a protest made against the exclusion of women from the Home Rule Bill. They were in the first division, and they were almost on the eve of their release, but such is the indomitable spirit of militancy that these women entered upon a sympathetic hunger strike. They were released, but the government forbade the release of Mrs. Leigh and Miss Evans, that is, they ordered the authorities to retain the women as long as they could, by forcible feeding, be kept alive. After a struggle which, for fierceness and cruelty, is almost unparalleled in our annals, the two women fought their way out.

All during that summer militancy surged up and down throughout the kingdom. A series of attacks on golf links was instituted, not at all in a spirit of wanton mischief, but with the direct and very practical object of reminding the dull and self-satisfied English public that when the liberties of English women were being stolen from them was no time to think of sports. The women selected country clubs where prominent Liberal politicians were wont to take their week-end pleasures, and with acids they burned great patches of turf, rendering the golf greens useless for the time being. They burned the words, Votes for Women, in some cases, and always they left behind them reminders that women were warring for their freedom.

On one occasion when the court was at Balmoral Castle in Scotland, the Suffragettes invaded the Royal golf links, and when Sunday morning dawned all the marking flags were found to have been replaced by W. S. P. U. flags hearing inscriptions such as "Votes for Women means peace for Ministers," "Forcible feeding must be stopped," and the like. The golf links were frequently visited by Suffragettes in order to question recreant ministers. Two women followed the prime minister to Inverness, where he was playing golf with Mr. McKenna. Approaching the men one Suffragette exclaimed: "Mr. Asquith, you must stop forcible feeding—" She got no farther, for Mr. Asquith, turning pale with rage—perhaps—retreated behind the Home Secretary, who, quite forgetting his manners, seized the Suffragette, crying out that he was going to throw her into the pond. "Then we will take you with us," the two retorted, after which a very lively scuffle ensued, and the women were not thrown into the pond.

This golf green activity really aroused more hostility against us than all the window-breaking. The papers published appeals to us not to interfere with a game that helped weary politicians to think clearly, but our reply to this was that it had not had any such effect on

A Suffragette throwing a bag of flour at Mr. Asquith in Chester

the prime minister or Mr. Lloyd-George. We had undertaken to spoil their sport and that of a large class of comfortable men in order that they should be obliged to think clearly about women, and women's firm determination to get justice.

I made my return to active work in the autumn by speaking at a great meeting of the W. S. P. U., held in the Albert Hall. At that meeting I had the announcement to make that the six years' association of Mr. and Mrs. Pethick Lawrence with the W. S. P. U. had ended. Since personal dissensions have never been dwelt upon in the W. S. P. U., have never been allowed to halt the movement or to interfere for an hour with its progress, I shall not here say any more about this important dissension than I said at our first large meeting in Albert Hall after the holiday, on October 17th. That day a new paper was sold on the streets. It was called *The Suffragette*, it was edited by Christabel Pankhurst, and was henceforth to be the official organ of the union. Both in this new paper and in *Votes for Women*, the following announcement appeared:

Grave Statement by the Leaders

At the first reunion of the leaders after the enforced holiday, Mrs. Pankhurst and Miss Christabel Pankhurst outlined a new militant policy which Mr. and Mrs. Pethick Lawrence found themselves altogether unable to approve.

Mrs. Pankhurst and Miss Christabel Pankhurst indicated that they were not prepared to modify their intentions, and recommended that Mr. and Mrs. Pethick Lawrence should resume control of the Paper, *Votes for Women*, and should leave the Women's Social and Political Union.

Rather than make schism in the ranks of the union Mr. and Mrs. Pethick Lawrence consented to take this course.

This was signed by all four. That night at the meeting I further explained to the members that, hard as partings from old friends and comrades unquestionably were, we must remember that we were fighting in an army, and that unity of purpose and unity of policy are absolutely necessary, because without them the army is hopelessly weakened. I said:

It is better that those who cannot agree, cannot see eye to eye as to policy, should set themselves free, should part, and should be free to continue their policy as they see it in their own way, unfettered by those with whom they can no longer agree.

Continuing I said:

> I give place to none in appreciation and gratitude to Mr. and Mrs. Pethick Lawrence for the incalculable services that they have rendered the militant movement for Woman Suffrage, and I firmly believe that the women's movement will be strengthened by their being free to work for woman suffrage in the future as they think best, while we of the Women's Social and Political Union shall continue the militant agitation for Woman Suffrage initiated by my daughter and myself and a handful of women more than six years ago.

I then went on to survey the situation in which the W. S. P. U. now stood and to outline the new militant policy which he had decided upon. This policy, to begin with, was relentless opposition, not only to the party in power, the Liberal Party, but to all parties in the coalition. I reminded the women that the government that had tricked and betrayed us and was now plotting to make our progress towards citizenship doubly difficult, was kept in office through the coalition of three parties. There was the Liberal Party, nominally the governing party, but they could not live another day without the coalition of the Nationalist and the Labour parties. So we should say, not only to the Liberal Party but to the Nationalist Party and the Labour Party:

> So long as you keep in office an anti-suffrage government, you are parties to their guilt, and from henceforth we offer you the same opposition which we give to the people whom you are keeping in power with your support.

I said further:

> We have summoned the Labour Party to do their duty by their own programme, and to go into opposition to the government on every question until the government do justice to women. They apparently are not willing to do that. Some of them tell us that other things are more important than the liberty of women—than the liberty of working women. We say, 'Then, gentlemen, we must teach you the value of your own principles, and until you are prepared to stand for the right of women to decide their lives and the laws under which they shall live, you, with Mr. Asquith and company, are equally responsible for all that has happened and is happening to women in this struggle for emancipation.'

Outlining further our new and stronger policy of aggression, I said:

There is a great deal of criticism, ladies and gentlemen, of this movement. It always seems to me when the anti-suffrage members of the government criticise militancy in women that it is very like beasts of prey reproaching the gentler animals who turn in desperate resistance when at the point of death. Criticism from gentlemen who do not hesitate to order out armies to kill and slay their opponents, who do not hesitate to encourage party mobs to attack defenceless women in public meetings—criticism from them hardly rings true. Then I get letters from people who tell me that they are ardent suffragists but who say that they do not like the recent developments in the militant movement, and implore me to urge the members not to be reckless with human life.

Ladies and gentlemen, the only recklessness the militant suffragists have shown about human life has been about their own lives and not about the lives of others, and I say here and now that it has never been and never will be the policy of the Women's Social and Political Union recklessly to endanger human life. We leave that to the enemy. We leave that to the men in their warfare. It is not the method of women. No, even from the point of view of public policy, militancy affecting the security of human life would be out of place. *There is something that governments care far more for than human life, and that is the security of property, and so it is through property that we shall strike the enemy.* From henceforward the women who agree with me will say, 'We disregard your laws, gentlemen, we set the liberty and the dignity and the welfare of women above all such considerations, and we shall continue this war, as we have done in the past; and what sacrifice of property, or what injury to property accrues will not be our fault. It will be the fault of that Government who admit the justice of our demands, but refuses to concede them without the evidence, so they have told us, afforded to governments of the past, that those who asked for liberty were in earnest in their demands!'

I called upon the women of the meeting to join me in this new militancy, and I reminded them anew that the women who were fighting in the Suffragette army had a great mission, the greatest mission the world has ever known—the freeing of one-half the human race, and through that freedom the saving of the other half. I said to them:

> Be militant each in your own way. Those of you who can express your militancy by going to the House of Commons and refusing to leave without satisfaction, as we did in the early days—do so. Those of you who can express militancy by facing party mobs at Cabinet Ministers' meetings, when you remind them of their falseness to principle—do so. Those of you who can express your militancy by joining us in our anti-government by-election policy—do so. Those of you who can break windows—break them.
>
> Those of you who can still further attack the secret idol of property, so as to make the government realise that property is as greatly endangered by women's suffrage as it was by the Chartists of old—do so. And my last word is to the government: I incite this meeting to rebellion. I say to the government: You have not dared to take the leaders of Ulster for their incitement to rebellion. Take me if you dare, but if you dare I tell you this, that so long as those who incited to armed rebellion and the destruction of human life in Ulster are at liberty, you will not keep me in prison. So long as men rebels—and voters—are at liberty, we will not remain in prison, first division or no first division.

I ask my readers, some of whom no doubt will be shocked and displeased at these words of mine that I have so frankly set down, to put themselves in the place of those women who for years had given their lives entirely and unstintingly to the work of securing political freedom for women; who had converted so great a proportion of the electorate that, had the House of Commons been a free body, we should have won that freedom years before; who had seen their freedom withheld from them through treachery and misuse of power. I ask you to consider that we had used, in our agitation, only peaceful means until we saw clearly that peaceful means were absolutely of no avail, and then for years we had used only the mildest militancy, until we were taunted by Cabinet Ministers, and told that we should never get the vote until we employed the same violence that men had used in their agitation for suffrage.

After that we had used stronger militancy, but even that, by comparison with the militancy of men in labour disputes, could not possibly be counted as violent. Through all these stages of our agitation we had been punished with the greatest severity, sent to prison like common criminals, and of late years tortured as no criminals have been tortured for a century in civilised countries of the world. And during all these years we had seen disastrous strikes that had caused suffering and death, to say nothing at all of the enormous economic waste, and we had never seen a single strike leader punished as we had been. We, who had suffered sentences of nine months' imprisonment for inciting women to mild rebellion, had seen a labour leader who had done his best to incite an army to mutiny released from prison in two months by the government. And now we had come to a point where we saw civil war threatened, where we read in the papers every day reports of speeches a thousand times more incendiary than anything we had ever said. We heard prominent members of Parliament openly declaring that if the Home Rule Bill was passed Ulster would fight, and Ulster would be right. None of these men were arrested. Instead they were applauded. Lord Selborne, one of our sternest critics, referring to the fact that Ulstermen were drilling under arms, said publicly:

> The method which the people of Ulster are adopting to show the depths of their convictions and the intensity of their feelings will impress the imagination of the whole country.

But Lord Selborne was not arrested. Neither were the mutinous officers who resigned their commissions when ordered to report for duty against the men of Ulster who were actually preparing for civil war.

What does all this mean? Why is it that men's blood-shedding militancy is applauded and women's symbolic militancy punished with a prison cell and the forcible feeding horror? It means simply this, that men's double standard of sex morals, whereby the victims of their lust are counted as outcasts, while the men themselves escape all social censure, really applies to morals in all departments of life. Men make the moral code and they expect women to accept it. They have decided that it is entirely right and proper for men to fight for their liberties and their rights, but that it is not right and proper for women to fight for theirs.

★★★★★★

There is no question that a great deal of the animus directed against us during 1913 and 1914 by the government was due to sex bitterness stirred up by a series of articles written by Christabel Pankhurst and published in *The Suffragette*. These articles, a fearless and authoritative exposé of the evils of sexual immoralities and their blasting effect on innocent wives and children, have since been published in a book called *The Great Scourge, and how to end it*, issued by David Nutt.

✶✶✶✶✶✶

They have decided that for men to remain silently quiescent while tyrannical rulers impose bonds of slavery upon them is cowardly and dishonourable, but that for women to do that same thing is not cowardly and dishonourable, but merely respectable. Well, the Suffragettes absolutely repudiate that double standard of morals. If it is right for men to fight for their freedom, and God knows what the human race would be like today if men had not, since time began, fought for their freedom, then it is right for women to fight for their freedom and the freedom of the children they bear. On this declaration of faith the militant women of England rest their case.

Chapter 4

I had called upon women to join me in striking at the government through the only thing that governments are really very much concerned about—property—and the response was immediate. Within a few days the newspapers rang with the story of the attack made on letter boxes in London, Liverpool, Birmingham, Bristol, and half a dozen other cities. In some cases the boxes, when opened by postmen, mysteriously burst into flame; in others the letters were destroyed by corrosive chemicals; in still others the addresses were rendered illegible by black fluids. Altogether it was estimated that over 5,000 letters were completely destroyed and many thousands more were delayed in transit.

It was with a deep sense of their gravity that these letter-burning protests were undertaken, but we felt that something drastic must be done in order to destroy the apathy of the men of England who view with indifference the suffering of women oppressed by unjust laws. As we pointed out, letters, precious though they may be, are less precious than human bodies and souls. This fact was universally realised at the sinking of the *Titanic*. Letters and valuables disappeared forever, but their loss was forgotten in the far more terrible loss of the multitude of human lives. And so, in order to call attention to greater crimes against human beings, our letter burnings continued.

In only a few cases were the offenders apprehended, and one of the few women arrested was a helpless cripple, a woman who could move about only in a wheeled chair. She received a sentence of eight months in the first division, and, resolutely hunger striking, was forcibly fed with unusual brutality, the prison doctor deliberately breaking one of her teeth in order to insert a gag. In spite of her disabilities and her weakness the crippled girl persisted in her hunger strike and her resistance to prison rules, and within a short time had to be released. The excessive sentences of the other pillar box destroyers resolved themselves into very short terms because of the resistance of the prisoners, every one of whom adopted the hunger strike.

Having shown the government that we were in deadly earnest when we declared that we would adopt guerrilla warfare, and also that we would not remain in prison, we announced a truce in order that the government might have full opportunity to fulfil their pledge in regard to a woman suffrage amendment to the Franchise Bill. We did not, for one moment, believe that Mr. Asquith would willingly keep his word. We knew that he would break it if he could, but there was a bare chance that he would not find this possible. However, our principal reason for declaring the truce was that we believed that the prime minister would find a way of evading his promise, and we were determined that the blame should be placed, not on militancy, but on the shoulders of the real traitor.

We reviewed the history of past suffrage bills: In 1908 the bill had passed its second reading by a majority of 179; and then Mr. Asquith had refused to allow it to go on; in 1910 the Conciliation Bill passed its second reading by a majority of 110, and again Mr. Asquith blocked its progress, pledging himself that if the bill were reintroduced in 1911, in a form rendering it capable of free amendment, it would be given full facilities for becoming law; these conditions were met in 1911, and we saw how the bill, after receiving the increased majority of 167 votes, was torpedoed by the introduction of a government manhood suffrage bill. Mr. Asquith this time had pledged himself that the bill would be so framed that a woman suffrage amendment could be added, and he further pledged that in case such an amendment was carried through its second reading, he would allow it to become a part of the bill. Just exactly how the government would manage to wriggle out of their promise was a matter of excited speculation.

All sorts of rumours were flying about, some hinting at the resignation of the prime minister, some suggesting the possibility of a general election, others that the amended bill would carry with it a forced referendum on women's suffrage. It was also said that the intention of the government was to delay the bill so long that, after it was passed in the House, it would be excluded from the benefits of the Parliament Acts, according to which a bill, delayed of passage beyond the first two years of the life of a Parliament, has no chance of being considered by the Lords. In order to become a law without the sanction of the House of Lords, a bill must pass three times through the House of Commons. The prospect of a woman suffrage bill doing that was practically nil.

To none of the rumours would Mr. Asquith give specific denial, and in fact the only positive utterance he made on the subject of the Franchise Bill was that he considered it highly improbable that the House would pass a woman suffrage amendment. In order to discourage woman suffrage sentiment in the House, Mr. Lloyd-George and Mr. Lewis Harcourt again busied themselves with spreading pessimistic prophecies of a Cabinet split in case an amendment was carried. No other threat, they well knew, would so terrorize the timid back bench Liberals, who, in addition to their blind party loyalty, stood in fear of losing their seats in the general election which would follow such a split. Rather than risk their political jobs they would have sacrificed any principle. Of course the hint of a Cabinet split was pure buncombe, and it deceived few of the members. But it established very clearly one thing, and this was that Mr. Asquith's promise that the House should be left absolutely free to decide the suffrage issue, and that the Cabinet stood ready to bow to the decision of the House was never meant to be fulfilled.

The Franchise Bill unamended, by its very wording, specifically denied the right of any woman to vote. Sir Edward Grey moved an amendment deleting from the bill the word male, thus leaving room for a women's suffrage amendment. Two such amendments were moved, one providing for adult suffrage for men and women, and the other providing full suffrage for women householders and wives of householders. The latter postponed the voting age of women to twenty-five years, instead of the men's twenty-one. On January 24th, 1913, debate on the first of the amendments was begun. A day and a half had been allotted to consideration of Sir Edward Grey's amendment, which if carried would leave the way clear for consideration of the other two, to each of which one-third of a day was allotted.

We had arranged for huge meetings to be held every day during the debates, and on the day before they were to open we sent a deputation of working women, led by Mrs. Drummond and Miss Annie

Kenney, to interview Mr. Lloyd-George and Sir Edward Grey. We had asked Mr. Asquith to receive the deputation, but, as usual, he refused. The deputation consisted of the two leaders, four cotton mill operatives from Lancashire, four workers in sweated trades of London, two pit brow lassies, two teachers, two trained nurses, one shop assistant, one laundress, one boot and shoe worker and one domestic worker, twenty in all, the exact number specified by Mr. Lloyd-George. Some hundreds of working women escorted the deputation to the official residence of the Chancellor of the Exchequer and waited anxiously in the street to hear the result of the audience.

The result was, of course, barren. Mr. Lloyd-George glibly repeated his confidence in the "great opportunity" afforded by the Franchise Bill, and Sir Edward Grey, reminding the women of the divergence of view held by the members of Cabinet on the suffrage question, assured them that their best opportunity for success lay in an amendment to the present bill. The women spoke with the greatest candour to the two ministers and questioned them sharply as to the integrity of the prime minister's pledge to accept the amendments, if passed. To such depth of infamy had English politics sunk that it was possible for women openly to question the plighted word of the king's chief Minister! Mrs. Drummond, who stands in awe of no human being, in plain words invited the slippery Mr. Lloyd-George to clear his own character from obloquy. In the closing words of her speech she put the whole matter clearly up to him, saying:

> Now, Mr. Lloyd-George, you have doggedly stuck to your old age pensions, and the insurance act, and secured them, and what you have done for these measures you can do also for the women.

The House met on the following afternoon to debate Sir Edward Grey's permissive amendment, but no sooner had the discussion opened than a veritable bombshell was cast into the situation. Mr. Bonar Law arose and asked for a ruling on the constitutionality of a woman's suffrage amendment to the bill as framed. The Speaker, who, besides acting as the presiding officer of the House, is its official parliamentarian, replied that, in his opinion, such an amendment would make a huge difference in the bill, and that he would be obliged, at a later stage of the debates, to consider carefully whether, if carried, any woman suffrage amendment would not so materially alter the bill that it would have to be withdrawn. In spite of this sinister pronouncement, the House continued to debate the Grey amendment, which was ably supported by Lord Hugh Cecil, Sir John Rolleston, and others.

During the intervening weekend holiday two Cabinet councils were held, and when the House met on Monday the prime minister called upon the speaker for his ruling. The speaker declared that, in his opinion, the passage of any one of the woman suffrage amendments would so alter the scope of the Franchise Bill as practically to create a new bill, because the measure, as it was framed, did not have for its main object the bestowal of the franchise on a hitherto excluded class. Had it been so framed a woman suffrage amendment would have been entirely proper.

But the main object of the bill was to alter the qualification, or the basis of registration for a Parliamentary vote. It would increase the male electorate, but only as an indirect result of the changed qualifications. An amendment to the bill removing the sex barrier from the election laws was not, in the speaker's opinion, a proper one.

The prime minister then announced the intentions of the Cabinet, which were to withdraw the Franchise Bill and to refrain from introducing, during that session, a plural voting bill. Mr. Asquith blandly admitted that his pledge in regard to women's suffrage had been rendered incapable of fulfilment, and he said that he felt constrained to give a new pledge to take its place. There were only two that could be given. The first was that the government should bring in a bill to enfranchise women, and this the government would not do. The second was that the government agree to give full facilities as to time, during the next session of Parliament, to a private member's bill, so drafted as to be capable of free amendment. This was the course that the government had decided to adopt. Mr. Asquith had the effrontery to say in conclusion that he thought that the House would agree that he had striven and had succeeded in giving effect, both in letter and in spirit, to every undertaking which the government had given.

Two members only, Mr. Henderson and Mr. Keir Hardie had the courage to stand up on the floor of the House and denounce the g

overnment's treachery, for treachery it unquestionably was. Mr. Asquith had pledged his sacred honour to introduce a bill that would be capable of an amendment to include women's suffrage, and he had framed a bill that could not be so amended. Whether he had done the thing deliberately, with the plain intention of selling out the women, or whether ignorance of Parliamentary rules accounted for the failure of the bill was immaterial. The bill need not have been drawn in ignorance. The fount of wisdom represented by Mr. Speaker could have been consulted at the time the bill was under construction quite as easily as when it had reached the debating stage. Our paper said editorially, representing and perfectly expressing our member's views:

> Either the government are so ignorant of Parliamentary procedure that they are unfit to occupy any position of responsibility, or else they are scoundrels of the worst kind.

I am inclined to think that the verdict of posterity will lean towards the later conclusion. If Mr. Asquith had been a man of honour he would have reframed the Franchise Bill in such a way that it could have included a suffrage amendment, or else he would have made amends for his stupendous blunder—if it was a blunder—by introducing a government measure for women's suffrage. He did neither, but disposed of the matter by promising facilities for a private member's bill which he knew, and which everybody knew, could not possibly pass.

There was no chance for a private member's bill, even with facilities, because of a number of reasons, but principally because the torpedoing of the Conciliation Bill had destroyed utterly the spirit of conciliation in which Conservatives, Liberals and Radicals in the House of Commons, and militant and non-militant women throughout the Kingdom had set aside their differences of opinion and agreed to come together on a compromise measure. When the second Conciliation Bill, of 1911, was under discussion, Lord Lytton had said:

> If this bill does not go through, the woman suffrage movement will not be stopped, but the spirit of conciliation of which this bill is an expression will be destroyed, and there will he war throughout the country, raging, tearing, fierce, bitter strife, though nobody wants it.

Lord Lytton's words were prophetic. At this last brazen piece of trickery on the part of the government the country blazed with bitter wrath. All the suffrage societies united in calling for a government measure for women's suffrage to be introduced without delay. The idle promise of facilities for a private member's bill was rejected with contumely and scorn. The Liberal women's executive committee met, and a strong effort was made to pass a resolution threatening the withdrawal from party work of the entire federation, but this failed and the executive merely passed a feeble resolution of regret.

The membership of the Women's Liberal Federation was, at that time, close to 200,000, and if the executive had passed the strong resolution, refusing to do any more work for the party until a government measure had been introduced, the government would have been forced to yield. They could not have faced the country without the support of the women. But these women, many of them, were wives of men in the service, the paid service of the Liberal Party. Many of them were wives of Liberal members. They lacked the courage, or the intelligence, or the insight, to declare war as a body on the government. A large number of women, and also many men, did resign from the Liberal Party, but the defections were not serious enough to affect the government.

The militants declared, and proceeded instantly to carry out, unrelenting warfare. We announced that either we must have a government measure, or a Cabinet split—those men in the Cabinet calling themselves suffragists going out—or we would take up the sword again, never to lay it down until the enfranchisement of the women of England was won.

It was at this time, February, 1913, less than two years ago as I write these words, that militancy, as it is now generally understood by the public began—militancy in the sense of continued, destructive, guerilla warfare against the government through injury to private property. Some property had been destroyed before this time, but the attacks were sporadic, and were meant to be in the nature of a warning as to what might become a settled policy. Now we indeed lighted the torch, and we did it with the absolute conviction that no other course was open to us. We had tried every other measure, as I am sure that I have demonstrated to my readers, and our years of work and suffering and sacrifice had taught us that the government would not yield to right and justice, what the majority of members of the House of Commons admitted was right and justice, but that the government would, as other governments invariably do, yield to expediency.

Now our task was to show the government that it was expedient to yield to the women's just demands. In order to do that we had to make England and every department of English life insecure and unsafe. We had to make English law a failure and the courts farce comedy theatres; we had to discredit the government and Parliament in the eyes of the world; we had to spoil English sports, hurt business, destroy valuable property, demoralise the world of society, shame the churches, upset the whole orderly conduct of life—

That is, we had to do as much of this guerilla warfare as the people of England would tolerate. When they came to the point of saying to the government: "Stop this, in the only way it can be stopped, by giving the women of England representation," then we should extinguish our torch.

Americans, of all people, ought to see the logic of our reasoning. There is one piece of American oratory, beloved of schoolboys, which has often been quoted from militant platforms. In a speech now included among the classics of the English language your great statesman, Patrick Henry, summed up the causes that led to the American Revolution. He said:

> We have petitioned, we have remonstrated, we have supplicated, we have prostrated ourselves at the foot of the throne, and it has all been in vain. We must fight—I repeat it, sir, we must fight.

Patrick Henry, remember, was advocating killing people, as well as destroying private property, as the proper means of securing the political freedom of men. The Suffragettes have not done that, and they never will. In fact the moving spirit of militancy is deep and abiding reverence for human life. In the latter course of our agitation I have been called upon to discuss our policies with many eminent men, politicians, literary men, barristers, scientists, clergymen. One of the last named, a high dignitary of the Church of England, told me that while he was a convinced suffragist, he found it impossible to justify our doing wrong that right might follow. I said to him:

> We are not doing wrong—we are doing right in our use of revolutionary methods against private property. It is our work to restore thereby true values, to emphasise the value of human rights against property rights. You are well aware, sir, that property has assumed a value in the eyes of men, and in the eyes of the law, that it ought never to claim. It is placed above all human values. The lives and health and happiness, and even the virtue of women and children—that is to say, the race itself— are being ruthlessly sacrificed to the god of property every day of the world.

To this my reverend friend agreed, and I said:

> If we women are wrong in destroying private property in order

that human values may be restored, then I say, in all reverence, that it was wrong for the Founder of Christianity to destroy private property, as He did when He lashed the money changers out of the Temple and when He drove the Gaderene swine into the sea.

It was absolutely in this spirit that our women went forth to war. In the first month of guerilla warfare an enormous amount of property was damaged and destroyed. On January 31st a number of putting greens were burned with acids; on February 7th and 8th telegraph and telephone wires were cut in several places and for some hours all communication between London and Glasgow were suspended; a few days later windows in various of London's smartest clubs were broken, and the orchid houses at Kew were wrecked and many valuable blooms destroyed by cold. The jewel room at the Tower of London was invaded and a showcase broken.

The residence of H. R. H. Prince Christian and Lambeth Palace, seat of the Archbishop of Canterbury, were visited and had windows broken. The refreshment house in Regents Park was burned to the ground on February 12th and on February 18th a country house which was being built at Walton-on-the-Hill for Mr. Lloyd-George was partially destroyed, a bomb having been exploded in the early morning before the arrival of the workmen. A hat pin and a hair pin picked up near the house—coupled with the fact that care had been taken not to endanger any lives—led the police to believe that the deed had been done by women enemies of Mr. Lloyd-George.

Four days later I was arrested and brought up in Epsom police court, where I was charged with having "counselled and procured" the persons who did the damage. Admitted to bail for the night, I appeared next morning in court, where the case was fully reviewed. Speeches of mine were read, one speech, made at a meeting held on January 22nd, in which I called for volunteers to act with me in a particular engagement; and another, made the day after the explosion, in which I publicly accepted responsibility for all militant acts done in the past, and even for what had been done at Walton. At the conclusion of the hearing I was committed for trial at the May Assizes at Guildford. Bail would be allowed, it was stated, if I would agree to give the usual undertaking to refrain from all militancy or incitement to militancy.

I asked that the case be set for speedy trial at the Assizes then in progress. I was entirely willing, I said, to give an undertaking for a short period, for a week, or even two weeks, but I could not possibly do so for a much longer period, looking at the fact that a new session of Parliament began in March, and was vitally concerned with the interests of women. The request was refused, and I was ordered to be taken to Holloway. I warned the magistrate that I should at once adopt the hunger strike, and I told him that if I lived at all until the summer it would be a dying woman who would come up for trial.

Arriving at Holloway I carried out my intention, but within twenty-four hours I heard that the authorities had arranged that my trial should take place on April 1st, instead of at the end of June, and at the Central Criminal Court, London, instead of the Guildford Court. I then gave the required undertakings and was immediately released on bail.

Chapter 5

When I entered Old Bailey on that memorable Wednesday, April 2nd, 1913, to be tried for inciting to commit a felony, the court was packed with women. A great crowd of women who could not obtain the necessary tickets remained in the streets below for hours waiting news of the trial. A large number of detectives from Scotland Yard, and a still larger number of uniformed police were on duty both inside and outside the court. I could not imagine why it was considered necessary to have such a regiment of police on hand, for I had not, at that time, realised the state of terror into which the militant movement, in its new development, had thrown the authorities.

Mr. Bodkin and Mr. Travers Humphreys appeared to prosecute on behalf of the Crown, and I conducted my own case, in consultation with my solicitor, Mr. Marshall. The judge, Mr. Justice Lush, having taken his seat I entered the dock and listened to the reading of the indictment. I pled "not guilty," not because I wished to evade responsibility for the explosion,—I had already assumed that responsibility—but because the indictment accused me of having wickedly and maliciously incited women to crime. What I had done was not wicked of purpose, but quite the opposite of wicked. I could not therefore truthfully plead guilty. The trial having opened the judge courteously asked me if I would like to sit down. I thanked him, and asked if I might also have a small table on which to place my papers. By orders of the judge a table was brought me.

Mr. Bodkin opened the case by explaining the "Malicious Damages to Property Act" of 1861, under which I was charged, and after describing the explosion which had damaged the Lloyd-George house at Walton, said that I was accused of being in the affair an accessory before the fact. It was not suggested, he said, that I was present when the crime was committed, but it was charged that I had moved and incited, counselled and procured women whose names were unknown to carry out that crime. It would be for the jury to decide, after the evidence had been presented, whether the facts did not point most clearly to the conclusion that women, probably two in number, who committed the crime were members of the Women's Social and Political Union, which had its office in Kingsway in London, and of which the defendant was the head, moving spirit and recognised leader.

The blowing up of Mr. Lloyd-George's house was then described in detail. That the damage was intended as an act against Mr. Lloyd-George was clear, Mr. Bodkin said, from the malicious statements made against him by the prisoner. He produced a private letter written by me to a friend in which I had defended militancy, and said that not only had it become a duty but in the circumstances it had also become a political necessity. Said Mr. Bodkin:

> A letter of that kind proves very clearly several things. It shows that she is the leader. It shows her influence over the emotional members of this organisation. It shows that according to her, militancy can be withheld for a time and let loose upon society at another time. And it further shows that any person or any woman who wants to indulge in militancy, which is only a picturesque expression for committing crimes against society, has to communicate with her, and with her alone, by word of mouth or by letter. That is the proclamation which went out to the members of this organisation. The plain language of that letter is, 'If we don't get what we want, the government and their members will be responsible, and the government and the public will be bullied into giving us what we want.'

Many extracts from my speeches made in January and February were read, and the final speech made just before my arrest at Chelsea. But before they were read I said:

> I wish to lodge an objection now to the police reports of my speeches. They have been supplied to me, and the only report I accept is that of the journalist of Cardiff who is one of the witnesses. He has furnished a fairly accurate report of what I said in

that town. The police reports I do not accept. They are grossly inaccurate and ignorant and ungrammatical, and they convey an absolutely wrong impression of what I said in many respects.

Witnesses were then examined; the carter who heard and reported the explosion; the foreman in charge of the damaged house, who told the cost of the damages, and described the explosives, etc., found on the premises; several police officers who told of finding hairpins and a woman's rubber golosh in the house, and so on. Absolutely nothing was brought out that tended to show that the Suffragettes had anything to do with the affair. The judge noted this for he said to Mr. Bodkin:

> I am not quite sure how you present this case. There are two ways of looking at it. Do you only ask the jury to say that the defendant specifically counselled the perpetration of this crime, or do you also say that, looking at her speeches that you read—assuming you prove that they were uttered—that the language used being a general incitement to damage property, anyone who acted on this invitation and perpetrated this outrage would be incited by her to do it?

Mr. Bodkin replied that the latter assumption was correct. "I say that the speeches generally are incitement to all kinds of acts of violence against property, and that they present evidence of attacks against property and a particular individual, and that there is evidence in the speeches which have been read, and which will be proved, of admissions by Mrs. Pankhurst of having been connected with the particular outrage in a way which makes her in law an accessory before the fact."

"But you do not confine the case to the latter way of putting it?"

"No," replied Mr. Bodkin.

"Even if the jury are satisfied," said the judge, "that Mrs. Pankhurst was not directly connected with this outrage by counselling it, you still ask the jury to say that by counselling, as you say she had in the speeches, the destruction of property, especially that belonging to a particular gentleman, anybody who acted on that and committed this outrage would have been incited by her to do it?"

"Yes, my lord."

"I think, Mrs. Pankhurst, you now understand the way it is put?" asked the Judge.

"I understand it quite well, my lord," I replied.

Proceedings were resumed on the following day, and the examination of witnesses for the prosecution went on. At the close of the examination, the judge inquired whether I desired to call any witnesses. I replied:

"I do not desire to give evidence or to call any witnesses, but I desire to address Your Lordship."

I began by objecting to some of the things Mr. Bodkin had said in his speech which concerned me personally. He had referred to me—or at least his words conveyed the suggestion—that I was a woman riding about in my motor car inciting other women to do acts which entail imprisonment and great suffering, while I, perhaps indulging in some curious form of pleasure, was protected, or thought myself protected, from serious consequences.

I said that Mr. Bodkin knew perfectly well that I shared all the dangers the other women faced, that I had been in prison three times, serving two of the sentences in full, and being treated like an ordinary felon—searched, put in prison clothes, eating prison fare, given solitary confinement and conforming to all the abominable rules imposed upon women who commit crimes in England. I thought I owed it to myself, especially as the same suggestions—in regard to the luxury in which I lived, supported by the members of the W. S. P. U.—had been made, not only by Mr. Bodkin in court, but by members of the government in the House of Commons—I thought I owed it to myself to say that I owned no motorcar and never had owned one.

The car in which I occasionally rode was owned by the organisation and was used for general propaganda work. In that car, and in cars owned by friends I had gone about my work as a speaker in the Woman Suffrage movement. It was equally untrue, I said, that some of us were making incomes of £1,000 to £1,500 a year out of the suffrage movement, as had actually been alleged in the debates in the House in which members of Parliament were trying to decide how to crush militancy. No woman in our organisation was making any such income, or anything remotely like it. Myself, I had sacrificed a considerable portion of my income because I had to surrender a very important part of it in order to be free to do what I thought was my duty in the movement.

Addressing myself to my defence I told the court that it was a very serious condition of things when a large number of respectable and naturally law abiding people, people of upright lives, came to hold the law in contempt, came seriously to making up their minds that they were justified in breaking the law.

The whole of good government rests upon acceptance of the law, upon respect of the law, and I say to you seriously, my lord, and gentlemen of the jury, that women of intelligence, women of training, women of upright life, have for many years ceased to respect the laws of this country. It is an absolute fact, and when you look at the laws of this country as they effect women it is not to be wondered at.

At some length I went over these laws, laws that made it possible for the judge to send me, if found guilty, to prison for fourteen years, while the maximum penalty for offences of the most revolting kind against little girls was only two years' imprisonment. The laws of inheritance, the laws of divorce, the laws of guardianship of children—all so scandalously unjust to women, I sketched briefly, and I said that not only these laws and others, but the administration of the laws fell so far short of adequacy that women felt that they must be permitted to share the work of cleaning up the entire situation. I tried here to tell of certain dreadful things that I had learned as the wife of a barrister, things about some of the men in high places who are entrusted with the administration of the law, of a judge of assizes where many hideous crimes against women were tried, this judge himself being found dead one morning in a brothel, but the court would not allow me to go into personalities, as he called it, with regard to "distinguished people," and told me that the sole question before the jury was whether or not I was guilty as charged. I must speak on that subject and on no other.

After a hard fight to be allowed to tell the jury the reasons why women had lost respect for the law, and were making such a struggle in order to become law makers themselves, I closed my speech by saying:

> Over one thousand women have gone to prison in the course of this agitation, have suffered their imprisonment, have come out of prison injured in health, weakened in body, but not in spirit. I come to stand my trial from the bedside of one of my daughters, who has come out of Holloway Prison, sent there for two months' hard labour for participating with four other people in breaking a small pane of glass. She has hunger-struck in prison. She submitted herself for more than five weeks to the horrible ordeal of feeding by force, and she has come out of prison having lost nearly two stone in weight. She is so weak that she cannot get out of her bed. And I say to you, gentlemen,

that is the kind of punishment you are inflicting upon me or any other woman who may be brought before you.

I ask you if you are prepared to send an incalculable number of women to prison—I speak to you as representing others in the same position—if you are prepared to go on doing that kind of thing indefinitely, because that is what is going to happen. There is absolutely no doubt about it. I think you have seen enough even in this present case to convince you that we are not women who are notoriety hunters. We could get that, heaven knows, much more cheaply if we sought it. We are women, rightly or wrongly, convinced that this is the only way in which we can win power to alter what for us are intolerable conditions, absolutely intolerable conditions.

A London clergyman only the other day said that 60 *per cent.* of the married women in his parish were breadwinners, supporting their husbands as well as their children. When you think of the wages women earn, when you think of what this means to the future of the children of this country, I ask you to take this question very, very seriously. Only this morning I have had information brought to me which could be supported by sworn affidavits, that there is in this country, in this very city of London of ours, a regulated traffic, not only in women of full age, but in little children; that they are being purchased, that they are being entrapped, and that they are being trained to minister to the vicious pleasures of persons who ought to know better in their positions of life.

Well, these are the things that have made us women determined to go on, determined to face everything, determined to see this thing out to the end, let it cost us what it may. And if you convict me, gentlemen, if you find me guilty, I tell you quite honestly and quite frankly, that whether the sentence is a long sentence, whether the sentence is a short sentence, I shall not submit to it. I shall, the moment I leave this court, if I am sent to prison, whether to penal servitude or to the lighter form of imprisonment—because I am not sufficiently versed in the law to know what his lordship may decide; but whatever my sentence is, from the moment I leave this court I shall quite deliberately refuse to eat food—I shall join the women who are already in Holloway on the hunger strike. I shall come out of prison, dead or alive, at the earliest possible moment; and once out again, as soon as I am physically fit I shall enter into this fight again.

Life is very dear to all of us. I am not seeking, as was said by the Home Secretary, to commit suicide. I do not want to commit suicide. I want to see the women of this country enfranchised, and I want to live until that is done. Those are the feelings by which we are animated. We offer ourselves as sacrifices, just as your forefathers did in the past, in this cause, and I would ask you all to put this question to yourselves:—Have you the right, as human beings, to condemn another human being to death—because that is what it amounts to? Can you throw the first stone? Have you the right to judge women?

You have not the right in human justice, not the right by the constitution of this country, if rightly interpreted, to judge me, because you are not my peers. You know, every one of you, that I should not be standing here, that I should not break one single law—if I had the rights that you possess, if I had a share in electing those who make the laws I have to obey; if I had a voice in controlling the taxes I am called upon to pay, I should not be standing here. And I say to you it is a very serious state of things. I say to you, my lord, it is a very serious situation, that women of upright life, women who have devoted the best of their years to the public weal, that women who are engaged in trying to undo some of the terrible mistakes that men in their government of the country have made, because after all, in the last resort, men are responsible for the present state of affairs—I put it to you that it is a very serious situation.

You are not accustomed to deal with people like me in the ordinary discharge of your duties; but you are called upon to deal with people who break the law from selfish motives. I break the law from no selfish motive. I have no personal end to serve, neither have any of the other women who have gone through this court during the past few weeks, like sheep to the slaughter. Not one of these women would, if women were free, be lawbreakers. They are women who seriously believe that this hard path that they are treading is the only path to their enfranchisement.

They seriously believe that the welfare of humanity demands this sacrifice; they believe that the horrible evils which are ravaging our civilisation will never be removed until women get the vote. They know that the very fount of life is being poisoned; they know that homes are being destroyed; that because of bad education, because of the unequal standard of morals, even the mothers and children are destroyed by one of the vilest and most horrible diseases that ravage humanity.

There is only one way to put a stop to this agitation; there is only one way to break down this agitation. It is not by deporting us, it is not by locking us up in gaol; it is by doing us justice. And so I appeal to you gentlemen, in this case of mine, to give a verdict, not only on my case, but upon the whole of this agitation. I ask you to find me not guilty of malicious incitement to a breach of the law.

These are my last words. My incitement is not malicious. If I had power to deal with these things, I would be in absolute obedience to the law. I would say to women, 'You have a constitutional means of getting redress for your grievances; use your votes, convince your fellow-voters of the righteousness of your demands. That is the way to obtain justice.' I am not guilty of malicious incitement, and I appeal to you, for the welfare of the country, for the welfare of the race, to return a verdict of not guilty in this case that you are called upon to try.

After recapitulating the charge the judge, in summing up, said:

It is scarcely necessary for me to tell you that the topics urged by the defendant in her address to you with regard to provocation by the laws of the country and the injustice done to women because they are not given the vote as men are, have no bearing upon the question you have to decide.

The motive at the back of her mind, or at the back of the minds of those who actually did put the gunpowder there, would afford no defence to this indictment. I am quite sure you will deal with this case upon the evidence, and the evidence alone, without regard to any question as to whether you think the law is just or unjust. It has nothing to do with the case. I should think you will probably have no doubt that this defendant, if she did these things charged against her, is not actuated by the ordinary selfish motive that leads most of the criminals who are in this dock to commit the crimes that they do commit. She is none the less guilty if she did these things which are charged against her, although she believes that by means of this kind the condition of society will be altered.

The jury retired, and soon after the afternoon session of the court opened they filed in, and in reply to the usual question asked by the clerk of arraigns, said that they had agreed upon a verdict. Said the clerk:

"Do you find Mrs. Pankhurst guilty or not guilty?"

"Guilty," said the foreman, "with a strong recommendation to mercy."

I spoke once more to the judge.

The jury have found me guilty, with a strong recommendation to mercy, and I do not see, since motive is not taken into account in human laws, that they could do otherwise after your summing up. But since motive is not taken into account in human laws, and since I, whose motives are not ordinary motives, am about to be sentenced by you to the punishment which is accorded to people whose motives are selfish motives, I have only this to say: If it was impossible for a different verdict to be found; if it is your duty to sentence me, as it will be presently, then I want to say to you, as a private citizen, and to the jury as private citizens, that I, standing here, found guilty by the laws of my country, I say to you it is your duty, as private citizens, to do what you can to put an end to this intolerable state of affairs. I put that duty upon you. And I want to say, *whatever the sentence you pass upon me, I shall do what is humanly possible to terminate that sentence at the earliest possible moment. I have no sense of guilt. I feel I have done my duty. I look upon myself as a prisoner of war. I am under no moral obligation to conform to, or in any way accept, the sentence imposed upon me.* I shall take the desperate remedy that other women have taken. It is obvious to you that the struggle will be an unequal one, but I shall make it—I shall make it as long as I have an ounce of strength left in me, or any life left in me.

I shall fight, I shall fight, I shall fight, from the moment I enter prison to struggle against overwhelming odds; I shall resist the doctors if they attempt to feed me. I was sentenced last May in this court to nine months' imprisonment. I remained in prison six weeks. There are people who have laughed at the ordeal of hunger-striking and forcible feeding. All I can say is, and the doctors can bear me out, that I was released because, had I remained there much longer, I should have been a dead woman. I know what it is because I have gone through it. My own daughter has only just left it. (Sylvia Pankhurst, who was forcibly fed for five weeks, during an original sentence of two months imposed for breaking one window). There are women there still facing that ordeal, facing it twice a day.

Think of it, my lord, twice a day this fight is gone through. Twice a day a weak woman resisting overwhelming force, fights and fights as long as she has strength left; fights against women and even against men, resisting with her tongue, with her teeth, this ordeal. Last night in the House of Commons some alternative was discussed, or rather, some additional punishment. Is it not a strange thing, my lord, that laws which have sufficed to restrain men throughout the history of this country do not suffice now to restrain women—decent women, honourable women?

Well, my lord, I do want you to realise it. I am not whining about my punishment, I invited it. I deliberately broke the law, not hysterically or emotionally, but of set serious purpose, because I honestly feel it is the only way. Now, I put the responsibility of what is to follow upon you, my lord, as a private citizen, and upon the gentlemen of the jury, as private citizens, and upon all the men in this court—what are you, with your political powers, going to do to end this intolerable situation?

To the women I have represented, to the women who, in response to my incitement, have faced these terrible consequences, have broken laws, to them, I want to say I am not going to fail them, but to face it as they face it, to go through with it, and I know that they will go on with the fight whether I live or whether I die.

This movement will go on and on until we have the rights of citizens in this country, as women have in our Colonies, as they will have throughout the civilised world before this woman's war is ended.

That is all I have to say.

Mr. Justice Lush, in passing sentence, said:

It is my duty, Mrs. Emmeline Pankhurst, and a very painful duty it is, to pass what, in my opinion, is a suitable and adequate sentence for the crime of which you have been most properly convicted, having regard to the strong recommendation to mercy by the jury. I quite recognise, as I have already said, that

> the motives that have actuated you in committing this crime are not the selfish motives that actuate most of the persons who stand in your position, but although you blind your eyes to it, I cannot help pointing out to you that the crime of which you have been convicted is not only a very serious one, but, in spite of your motives, it is, in fact, a wicked one.
>
> It is wicked because it not only leads to the destruction of property of persons who have done you no wrong, but in spite of your calculations, it may expose other people to the danger of being maimed or even killed. It is wicked because you are, and have been, luring other people—young women, it may be—to engage in such crimes, possibly to their own ruin; and it is wicked, because you cannot help being alive to it if you would only think.
>
> You are setting an example to other persons who may have other grievances that they legitimately want to have put right by embarking on a similar scheme to yours, and trying to effect their object by attacking the property, if not the lives, of other people. I know, unfortunately—at least, I feel sure—you will pay no heed to what I say. I only beg of you to think of these things.

"I have thought of them," I interjected. The majesty of law, continued:

> Think, if only for one short hour, dispassionately. I can only say that, although the sentence I am going to pass must be a severe one, must be adequate to the crime of which you have been found guilty, if you would only realise the wrong you are doing, and the mistake you are making, and would see the error you have committed, and undertake to amend matters by using your influence in a right direction, I would be the first to use all my best endeavours to bring about a mitigation of the sentence I am about to pass.
>
> I cannot, and I will not, regard your crime as a merely trivial one. It is not. It is a most serious one, and, whatever you may think, it is a wicked one. I have paid regard to the recommendation of the jury. You yourself have stated the maximum sentence which this particular offence is by the legislature thought to deserve. The least sentence I can pass upon you is a sentence of three years' penal servitude.

As soon as the sentence was pronounced the intense silence which had reigned throughout the trial was broken, and an absolute pandemonium broke out among the spectators. At first it was merely a confused and angry murmur of "Shame!" "Shame!" The murmurs quickly swelled into loud and indignant cries, and then from gallery and court there arose a great chorus uttered with the utmost intensity and passion. "Shame!" "Shame!" The women sprang to their feet, in many instances stood on their seats, shouting "Shame!" "Shame!" as I was conducted out of the dock in charge of two wardresses. "Keep the flag flying!" shouted a woman's voice, and the response came in a chorus: "We will!" "Bravo!" "Three cheers for Mrs. Pankhurst!" That was the last I heard of the courtroom protest.

Afterwards I heard that the noise and confusion was kept up for several minutes longer, the judge and the police being quite powerless to obtain order. Then the women filed out singing the Women's Marseillaise—

March on, march on,
Face to the dawn,
The dawn of liberty.

The judge flung after their retreating forms the dire threat of prison for any woman who dared repeat such a scene. Threat of prison— to Suffragettes! The women's song only swelled the louder and the corridors of Old Bailey reverberated with their shouts. Certainly that venerable building had never in its checkered history witnessed such a scene. The great crowd of detectives and police who were on duty seemed actually paralysed by the audacity of the protest, for they made no attempt to intervene.

At three o'clock, when I left the court by a side entrance in Newgate Street, I found a crowd of women waiting to cheer me. With the two wardresses I entered a four wheeler and was driven to Holloway to begin my hunger strike. Scores of women followed in taxicabs, and when I arrived at the prison gates there was another protest of cheers for the cause and boos for the law. In the midst of all this intense excitement I passed through the grim gates into the twilight of prison, now become a battle-ground.

Chapter 6

Prison had indeed been for us a battle-ground ever since the time when we had solemnly resolved that, as a matter of principle, we would not submit to the rules that bound ordinary offenders against the law. But when I entered Holloway on that April day in 1913, it was with full knowledge that I had before me a far more prolonged struggle than any that the militant suffragists had hitherto faced. I have described the hunger strike, that terrible weapon with which we had repeatedly broken our prison bars. The government, at their wits' end to cope with the hunger strikers, and to overcome a situation which had brought the laws of England into such scandalous disrepute, had had recourse to a measure, surely the most savagely devised ever brought before a modern Parliament.

In March of that year, while I was waiting trial on the charge of conspiring to destroy Mr. Lloyd-George's country house, a bill was introduced into the House of Commons by the Home Secretary, Mr. Reginald McKenna, a bill which had for its avowed object the breaking down of the hunger strike. This measure, now universally known as the "Cat and Mouse Act," provided that when a hunger striking suffrage prisoner (the law was frankly admitted to apply only to suffrage prisoners) was certified by the prison doctors to be in danger of death, she could be ordered released on a sort of a ticket of leave for the purpose of regaining strength enough to undergo the remainder of her sentence. Released, she was still a prisoner, the prisoner, or the patient, or the victim, as you may choose to call her, being kept under constant police surveillance. According to the terms of the bill the prisoner was released for a specified number of days, at the expiration of which she was supposed to return to prison on her own account. Says the act:

> The period of temporary discharge may, if the Secretary of State thinks fit, be extended on a representation of the prisoner that the state of her health renders her unfit to return to prison. If such representation be made, the prisoner shall submit herself, if so required, for medical examination by the medical officer of the above mentioned prison, or other registered medical practitioner appointed by the Secretary of State.
> The prisoner shall notify to the Commissioner of Police of the Metropolis the place of residence to which she goes on her discharge. She shall not change her residence without giving one clear day's notice in writing to the commissioner, specifying the residence to which she is going and she shall not be temporarily absent from her residence for more than twelve hours without giving a like notice, etc.

The idea of militant suffragists respecting a law of this order is almost humorous, and yet the smile dies before the pity one feels for the minister whose confession of failure is embodied in such a measure. Here was a mighty government weakly resolved that justice to women it would not grant, knowing that submission of women it could not force, and so was willing to compromise with a piece of class legislation absolutely contrary to all of its avowed principles. Said Mr. McKenna, pleading in the House for the advancement of his odious measure:

> At the present time I cannot make these prisoners undergo their sentences without serious risk of death and I want to have power to enable me to compel a prisoner to undergo the sentence, and I want that power in all cases where the prisoner adopts the system of the hunger strike. At the present moment, although I have the power of release, I cannot release a prisoner without a pardon, and I have to discharge them for good. I want the power of releasing a prisoner without a pardon, with the sentence remaining alive. . . . I want to enforce the Law, and I want, if I can, to enforce it without forcible feeding, and without undergoing the risk of some one else's life.

Interrogated by several members, Mr. McKenna admitted that the "Cat and Mouse" bill, if passed, would not inevitably do away with forcible feeding, but he promised that the hateful and disgusting process would be resorted to only when "absolutely necessary." We shall see later how hypocritical this representation was.

Parliament, which had never had time to consider, beyond its initial stages, a women's suffrage measure, passed the Cat and Mouse Act through both houses within the limits of a few days. It was already law when I entered Holloway on April 3rd, 1913, and I grieve to state that many members of the Labour Party, pledged to support woman suffrage, helped to make it into law.

Of course the act was, from its inception, treated by the suffragists with the utmost contempt. We had not the slightest intention of assisting Mr. McKenna in enforcing unjust sentences against soldiers in the army of freedom, and when the prison doors closed behind me I adopted the hunger strike exactly as though I expected it to prove, as formerly, a means of gaining my liberty.

That struggle is not a pleasant one to recall. Every possible means of breaking down my resolution was resorted to. The daintiest and most tempting food was placed in my cell. All sorts of arguments were brought to bear against me—the futility of resisting the Cat and Mouse Act, the wickedness of risking suicide—I shall not attempt to record all the arguments. They fell against a blank wall of consciousness, for my thoughts were all very far away from Holloway and all its torments. I knew, what afterwards I learned as a fact, that my imprisonment was followed by the greatest revolutionary outbreak that had been witnessed in England since 1832. From one end of the island to the other the beacons of the women's revolution blazed night and day.

Many country houses—all unoccupied—were fired, the grand stand of Ayr race course was burned to the ground, a bomb was exploded in Oxted Station, London, blowing out walls and windows, some empty railroad carriages were blown up, the glass of thirteen famous paintings in the Manchester Art Gallery were smashed with hammers—these are simply random specimens of the general outbreak of secret guerilla warfare waged by women to whose liberties every other approach had been barricaded by the Liberal Government of free England. The only answer of the government was the closing of the British Museum, the National Gallery, Windsor Castle, and other tourist resorts. As for the result on the people of England, that was exactly what we had anticipated. The public were thrown into a state of emotion of insecurity and frightened expectancy.

Not yet did they show themselves ready to demand of the government that the outrages be stopped in the only way they could be stopped—by giving votes to women. I knew that it would be so. Lying in my lonely cell in Holloway, racked with pain, oppressed with increasing weakness, depressed with the heavy responsibility of unknown happenings, I was sadly aware that we were but approaching a far goal. The end, though certain, was still distant. Patience, and still more patience, faith and still more faith, well, we had called upon these souls' help before and it was certain that they would not fail us at this greatest crisis of all.

Thus in great anguish of mind and body passed nine terrible days, each one longer and more acutely miserable than the preceding. Towards the last, I was mercifully half unconscious of my surroundings. A curious indifference took possession of my over-wrought mind, and it was almost without emotion that I heard, on the morning of the tenth day, that I was to be released temporarily in order to recover my health. The governor came to my cell and read me my licence, which commanded me to return to Holloway in fifteen days, and meanwhile to observe all the obsequious terms as to informing the police of my movements. With what strength my hands retained I tore the document in strips and dropped it on the floor of the cell. I said:

> I have no intention of obeying this infamous law. You release me knowing perfectly well that I shall never voluntarily return to any of your prisons.

They sent me away, sitting bolt upright in a cab, unmindful of the fact that I was in a dangerous condition of weakness, having lost two stone in weight and suffered seriously from irregularities of heart action. As I left the prison I was gratefully aware of groups of our women standing bravely at the gates, as though enduring a long vigil. As a matter of fact, relays of women had picketed the place night and day during the whole term of my imprisonment. The first pickets were arrested, but as others constantly arrived to fill their places the police finally gave in and allowed the women to march up and down before the prison carrying the flag.

At the nursing home to which I was conveyed I learned that Annie Kenney, Mrs. Drummond, and our staunch friend, Mr. George Lansbury, had been arrested during my imprisonment, and that all three had adopted the hunger strike.

✶✶✶✶✶✶

Mr. Lansbury shortly before this had resigned his seat in Parliament and had gone to his constituents on the question of women's suffrage. Both the Liberal and the Conservative parties had united against him, with the result that a Unionist candidate was returned in his place. Mr. Lloyd-George publicly rejoiced in the result of this election, saying that Mr. Marsh, the Conservative candidate, had been his man. The Labour Party, in Parliament and out, meekly accepted this piece of Liberal chicanery without protest

✶✶✶✶✶✶

I also learned on my own account how desperately the government were striving to make their Cat and Mouse Act—the last stand in their losing campaign—a success. Without regard to the extra expense laid on the unfortunate tax payers of the country, the government employed a large extra force of police especially for this purpose. As I lay in bed, being assisted by every medical resource to return to life and health, these special police, colloquially termed "Cats," guarded the nursing home as if it were a besieged castle. In the street under my windows two detectives and a constable stood on guard night and day. In a house at right angles to my refuge three more detectives kept constant watch. In the mews at the rear of the house were more detectives, and diligently patrolling the road, as if in expectation of a rescuing regiment, two taxicabs, each with its *quota* of detectives, guarded the highways.

All this made recovery slow and difficult. But worse was to come. On April 30th, just as I was beginning to rally somewhat, came the news that the police had swooped down on our headquarters in Kingsway and had arrested the entire official force. Miss Barrett, associate editor of *The Suffragette*; Miss Lennox, the sub-editor; Miss Lake, business manager; Miss Kerr, office manager, and Mrs. Sanders, financial secretary of the Union, were arrested, although not one of them had ever appeared in any militant action. Mr. E. G. Clayton, a chemist, was also arrested, accused of furnishing the W. S. P. U. with explosive materials. The offices were thoroughly searched, and, as on a former occasion, stripped of all books and papers.

While this was being done another party of police, armed with a special warrant, proceeded to the printing office where our paper, *The Suffragette*, was published. The printer, Mr. Drew, was placed under arrest and the material for the paper, which was to appear on the following day, was seized. By one o'clock in the afternoon the entire plant and the headquarters of the Union were in the hands of the police, and to all appearances the militant movement—temporarily at least—was brought to a full stop. In my state of semi-prostration it at first seemed to me best to let the week's issue of the paper lapse, but on second thought I decided that even the appearance of surrender was not to be thought of.

How we managed it need not here be told, but we actually did, overnight, with hardly any material, except Christabel's leading article, and with hastily summoned helpers, get out the paper as usual, and side by side with the morning journals which bore front page stories of the suppression of the Suffragette organ, our paper sellers sold *The Suffragette*. The front page bore, instead of the usual cartoon, the single word in bold faced type—

RAIDED,

. . . the full story of the police search and the arrests being related in the other pages. Our headquarters, I may say in passing, remained closed less than forty-eight hours. We are so organised that the arrest of leaders does not seriously cripple us. Every one has an understudy, and when one leader drops out her substitute is ready instantly to take her place.

In this emergency there appeared as chief organiser in Miss Kenney's place, Miss Grace Roe, one of the young Suffragettes of whom I, as belonging to the older generation, am so proud. Faced by difficulties as great as the government could make them, Miss Roe at once showed herself to be equal to the situation, and to have the gift of unswerving loyalty combined with a strong and rapid judgment of things and people. Aiding her was Mrs. Dacre Fox, who surprised us all by her amazing ability to act as assistant editor of *The Suffragette*, manage a host of affairs in the office, and preside at our weekly meetings. Another member of the Union who came prominently to the front at the time of this crisis was Mrs. Mansel.

In two days' time the office was open and running quite as usual, no outward sign showing the grief and indignation felt for our imprisoned comrades. Most of them refused bail and instantly hunger struck appearing in court for trial three days later in a pitiful state. Mrs. Drummond was so obviously ill and in need of medical attention that she was discharged and was very soon afterwards operated upon. Mr. Drew, the printer, was forced to sign an undertaking not to publish the paper again. The others were sentenced to terms varying from six to eighteen months. Mr. Clayton was sentenced to twenty-one months, and after desperate resistance, during which he was forcibly fed many times, escaped his prison. The others, following the same example, starved their way to liberty, and have ever since been pursued at intervals and rearrested under the Cat and Mouse Act.

After my discharge, April 12th, I remained in the nursing home until partially restored, then, under the eyes of the police, I motored out to Woking, the ountry home of my friend, Dr. Ethel Smyth. This house, like the nursing home, was guarded by a small army of police. I never went to the window, I never took the air in the garden without being conscious of watching eyes. The situation became intolerable, and I determined to end it. On May 26th there was a great meeting at the London Pavilion, and I gave notice that I would attend it. Supported by Dr. Flora Murray, Dr. Ethel Smyth and my devoted Nurse Pine, I walked downstairs, to be confronted at the door by a detective, who demanded to know where I was going. I was in a weak state, much weaker than I had imagined, and in refusing the right of a man to question my movements I exhausted the last remnant of my strength and sank fainting in the arms of my friends. As soon as I re-

Re-arrest of Mrs. Pankhurst at Woking May 26, 1913

covered I got into the motor car. The detective instantly took his place beside me and told the chauffeur to drive to Bow Street Station. The chauffeur replied that he took his orders only from Mrs. Pankhurst, whereupon the detective summoned a taxicab and, placing me under arrest, took me to Bow Street.

Under the Cat and Mouse Act a paroled prisoner can be thus arrested without the formality of a warrant, nor does the time she has spent at liberty, in regaining her health, count off from her prison sentence. The magistrate at Bow Street was therefore quite within his legal rights when he ordered me returned to Holloway. I felt it my duty, nevertheless, to point out to him the inhumanity of his act. I said to him:

> I was released from Holloway on account of my health. Since then I have been treated exactly as if I were in prison. It has become absolutely impossible for any one to recover health under such conditions, and this morning I decided to make this protest against a state of affairs unparalleled in a civilised country.

The magistrate replied formally:

> You quite understand what the position is. You have been arrested on this warrant and all I have to do is to make an order recommending you to prison.

I said:

> I think that you should do so, with a full sense of responsibility. If I am taken to Holloway on your warrant I shall resume the protest I made before which led to my release, and I shall go on indefinitely until I die, or until the government decide, since they have taken upon themselves to employ you and other people to administer the laws, that they must recognise women as citizens and give them some control over the laws of this country.

It was a five days' hunger strike this time, because the extreme weakness of my condition made it impossible for me to endure a longer term. I was released on May 30th on a seven days' licence, and in a half-alive state was again carried to a nursing home. Less than a week later, while I was still bed-ridden, a terrible event occurred, one that should have shaken the stolid British public into a realisation of the seriousness of the situation precipitated by the Government. Emily Wilding Davison, who had been associated with the militant movement since 1906, gave up her life for the women's cause by throwing herself in the path of the thing, next to property, held most sacred to Englishmen—sport.

Miss Davison went to the races at Epsom, and breaking through the barriers which separated the vast crowds from the race course, rushed in the path of the galloping horses and caught the bridle of the king's horse, which was leading all the others. The horse fell, throwing his jockey and crushing Miss Davison in such shocking fashion that she was carried from the course in a dying condition. Everything possible was done to save her life. The great surgeon, Mr. Mansell Moullin, put everything aside and devoted himself to her case, but though he operated most skilfully, the injuries she had received were so frightful that she died four days later without once having recovered consciousness. Members of the Union were beside her when she breathed her last, on June 8th, and on June 14th they gave her a great public funeral in London. Crowds lined the streets as the funeral car, followed by thousands of women, passed slowly and sadly to St. George's Church, Bloomsbury, where the memorial services were held.

Emily Wilding Davison was a character almost inevitably developed by a struggle such as ours. She was a B. A. of London University, and had taken first class honours at Oxford in English Language and Literature. Yet the women's cause made such an appeal to her reason and her sympathies that she put every intellectual and social appeal aside and devoted herself untiringly and fearlessly to the work of the Union. She had suffered many imprisonments, had been forcibly fed and most brutally treated. On one occasion when she had barricaded her cell against the prison doctors, a hose pipe was turned on her from the window and she was drenched and all but drowned in the icy water while workmen were breaking down her cell door.

Miss Davison, after this experience, expressed to several of her friends the deep conviction that now, as in days called uncivilised, the conscience of the people would awaken only to the sacrifice of a human life. At one time in prison she tried to kill herself by throwing herself head-long from one of the upper galleries, but she succeeded only in sustaining cruel injuries. Ever after that time she clung to her conviction that one great tragedy, the deliberate throwing into the breach of a human life, would put an end to the intolerable torture of women. And so she threw herself at the king's horse, in full view of the king and queen and a great multitude of their Majesties' subjects, offering up her life as a petition to the king, praying for the release of suffering women throughout England and the world. No one can possibly doubt that that prayer can forever remain unanswered, for she took it straight to the Throne of the King of all the worlds.

The death of Miss Davison was a great shock to me and a very great grief as well, and although I was scarcely able to leave my bed I determined to risk everything to attend her funeral. This was not to be, however, for as I left the house I was again arrested by detectives who lay in waiting. Again the farce of trying to make me serve a three years' sentence was undertaken. But now the militant women had discovered a new and more terrible weapon with which to defy the unjust laws of England, and this weapon—the thirst strike—I turned against my gaolers with such effect that they were forced within three days to release me.

The hunger strike I have described as a dreadful ordeal, but it is a mild experience compared with the thirst strike, which is from beginning to end simple and unmitigated torture. Hunger striking reduces a prisoner's weight very quickly, but thirst striking reduces weight so alarmingly fast that prison doctors were at first thrown into absolute panic of fright. Later they became somewhat hardened, but even now they regard the thirst strike with terror. I am not sure that I can convey to the reader the effect of days spent without a single drop of water taken into the system. The body cannot endure loss of moisture. It cries out in protest with every nerve. The muscles waste, the skin becomes shrunken and flabby, the facial appearance alters horribly, all these outward symptoms being eloquent of the acute suffering of the entire physical being. Every natural function is, of course, suspended, and the poisons which are unable to pass out of the body are retained and absorbed. The body becomes cold and shivery, there is constant headache and nausea, and sometimes there is fever. The mouth and tongue become coated and swollen, the throat thickens and the voice sinks to a thready whisper.

When, at the end of the third day of my first thirst strike, I was sent home I was in a condition of jaundice from which I have never completely recovered. So badly was I affected that the prison authorities made no attempt to arrest me for nearly a month after my release. On July 13th I felt strong enough once more to protest against the odious Cat and Mouse Act, and, with Miss Annie Kenney, who was also at liberty "on medical grounds," I went to a meeting at the London Pavilion. At the close of the meeting, during which Miss Kenney's prison licence was auctioned off for £12, we attempted for the first time the open escape which we have so frequently since effected. Miss Kenney, from the platform, announced that we should openly leave the hall, and she forthwith walked coolly down into the audience. The police rushed in in overwhelming numbers, and after a desperate fight, succeeded in capturing her. Other detectives and policemen hurried to the side door of the hall to intercept me, but I disappointed them by leaving by the front door and escaping to a friend's house in a cab.

The police soon traced me to the house of my friend, the distinguished scientist, Mrs. Hertha Ayrton, and the place straightway became a besieged fortress. Day and night the house was surrounded, not only by police, but by crowds of women sympathisers.

On the Saturday following my appearance at the Pavilion we gave the police a bit of excitement of a kind they do not relish. A cab drove up to Mrs. Ayrton's door, and several well-known members of the Union alighted and hurried indoors. At once the word was circulated that a rescue was being attempted, and the police drew resolutely around the cab. Soon a veiled woman appeared in the doorway, surrounded by Suffragettes, who, when the veiled lady attempted to get into the cab, resisted with all their strength the efforts of the police to lay hands upon her. The cry went up from all sides: "They are arresting Mrs. Pankhurst!" Something very like a free fight ensued, occupying all the attention of the police who were not in the immediate vicinity of the cab. The men surrounding that rocking vehicle succeeded in tearing the veiled figure from the arms of the other women and piling into the cab ordered the chauffeur to drive full speed to Bow Street. Before they reached their destination, however, the veiled lady raised her veil—alas, it was not Mrs. Pankhurst, who by that time was speeding away in another taxicab in quite another direction.

Our ruse infuriated the police, and they determined to arrest me at my first public appearance, which was at the Pavilion on the Monday following the episode just related. When I reached the Pavilion I found it literally surrounded by police, hundreds of them. I managed to slip past the outside cordon, but Scotland Yard had its best men inside the hall, and I was not permitted to reach the platform. Surrounded by plain clothes men, batons drawn, I could not escape, but I called out to the women that I was being taken, and so valiantly did they rush to the rescue that the police had their hands full for nearly half an hour before they got me into a taxicab bound for Holloway. Six women were arrested that day, and many more than six policemen were temporarily incapacitated for duty.

By this time I had made up my mind that I would not only resist staying in prison, I would resist to the utmost of my ability going to prison. Therefore, when we reached Holloway I refused to get out of the cab, declaring to my captors that I would no longer acquiesce in the slow judicial murder to which the government were subjecting women. I was lifted out and carried into a cell in the convicted hospital wing of the gaol. The wardresses who were on duty there spoke with some kindness to me, suggesting that, as I was very apparently exhausted and ill, I should do well to undress and go to bed.

"No," I replied, "I shall not go to bed, not once while I am kept here. I am weary of this brutal game, and I intend to end it."

Without undressing, I lay down on the outside of the bed. Later in the evening the prison doctor visited me, but I refused to be examined. In the morning he came again, and with him the governor and the head wardress. As I had taken neither food nor water since the previous day my appearance had become altered to such an extent that the doctor was plainly perturbed. He begged me, "as a small concession," to allow him to feel my pulse, but I shook my head, and they left me alone for the day. That night I was so ill that I felt some alarm for my own condition, but I knew of nothing that could be done except to wait. On Wednesday morning the governor came again and asked me with an assumption of carelessness if it were true that I was refusing both food and water. "It is true," I said, and he replied brutally: "You are very cheap to keep." Then, as if the thing were not a ridiculous farce, he announced that I was sentenced to close confinement for three days, with deprivation of all privileges, after which he left my cell.

Twice that day the doctor visited me, but I would not allow him to touch me. Later came a medical officer from the Home Office, to which I had complained, as I had complained to the governor and the prison doctor, of the pain I still suffered from the rough treatment I had received at the pavilion. Both of the medical men insisted that I allow them to examine me, but I said:

> I will not be examined by you because your intention is not to help me as a patient, but merely to ascertain how much longer it will be possible to keep me alive in prison. I am not prepared to assist you or the government in any such way. I am not prepared to relieve you of any responsibility in this matter.

I added that it must be quite obvious that I was very ill and unfit to be confined in prison. They hesitated for a moment or two, then left me.

Wednesday night was a long nightmare of suffering, and by Thursday morning I must have presented an almost mummified appearance. From the faces of the governor and the doctor when they came into my cell and looked at me I thought that they would at once arrange for my release. But the hours passed and no order for release came. I decided that I must force my release, and I got up from the bed where I had been lying and began to stagger up and down the cell. When all strength failed me and I could keep my feet no longer I lay down on the stone floor, and there, at four in the afternoon, they found me, gasping and half unconscious. And then they sent me away. I was in a very weakened condition this time, and had to be treated with saline solutions to save my life.

I felt, however, that I had broken my prison walls for a time at least, and so this proved. It was on July 24th that I was released. A few days later I was borne in an invalid's chair to the platform of the London Pavilion. I could not speak, but I was there, as I had promised to be. My licence, which by this time I had ceased to tear up because it had an auction value, was sold to an American present for the sum of one hundred pounds. I had told the governor on leaving that I intended to sell the licence and to spend the money for militant purposes, but I had not expected to raise such a splendid sum as one hundred pounds. I shall always remember the generosity of that unknown American friend.

A great medical congress was being held in London in the summer of 1913, and on August 11th we held a large meeting at Kingsway Hall, which was attended by hundreds of visiting doctors. I addressed this meeting, at which a ringing resolution against forcible feeding was passed, and I was allowed to go home without police interference. It was, as a matter of fact, the second time during that month that I had spoken in public without molestation. The presence of so many distinguished medical men in London may have suggested to the authorities that I had better be left alone for the time being. At all events I was left alone, and late in the month I went, quite publicly, to Paris, to see my daughter Christabel and plan with her the campaign for the coming autumn. I needed rest after the struggles of the past five months, during which I had served, of my three years' prison sentence, not quite three weeks.

Chapter 7

The two months of the summer of 1913 which were spent with my daughter in Paris were almost the last days of peace and rest I have been destined since to enjoy. I spent the days, or some hours of them, in the initial preparation of this volume, because it seemed to me that I had a duty to perform in giving to the world my own plain statement of the events which have led up to the women's revolution in England. Other histories of the militant movement will undoubtedly be written; in times to come when in all constitutional countries of the world, women's votes will be as universally accepted as men's votes are now; when men and women occupy the world of industry on equal terms, as co-workers rather than as cut-throat competitors; when, in a word, all the dreadful and criminal discriminations which exist now between the sexes are abolished, as they must one day be abolished, the historian will be able to sit down in leisurely fashion and do full justice to the strange story of how the women of England took up arms against the blind and obstinate Government of England and fought their way to political freedom.

I should like to live long enough to read such a history, calmly considered, carefully analysed, conscientiously set forth. It will be a better book to read than this one, written, as it were, in camp between battles. But perhaps this one, hastily prepared as it has been, will give the reader of the future a clearer impression of the strenuousness and the desperation of the conflict, and also something of the heretofore undreamed of courage and fighting strength of women, who, having learned the joy of battle, lose all sense of fear and continue their struggle up to and past the gates of death, never flinching at any step of the way.

Every step since that meeting in October, 1912, when we definitely declared war on the peace of England, has been beset with danger and difficulty, often unexpected and undeclared. In October, 1913, I sailed in the French liner, *La Provence*, for my third visit to the United States.

My intention was published in the public press of England, France and America. No attempt at concealment of my purpose was made, and in fact, my departure was witnessed by two men from Scotland Yard. Some hints had reached my ears that an attempt would be made by the Immigration officers at the port of New York to exclude me as an undesirable alien, but I gave little credit to these reports. American friends wrote and cabled encouraging words, and so I passed my time aboard ship quite peacefully, working part of the time, resting also against the fatigue always attendant on a lecture tour.

We came to anchor in the harbour of New York on October 26th, and there, to my astonishment, the Immigration authorities notified me that I was ordered to Ellis Island to appear before a Board of Special Inquiry. The officers who served the order of detention did so with all courtesy, even with a certain air of reluctance. They allowed my American travelling companion, Mrs. Rheta Childe Dorr, to accompany me to the island, but no one, not even the solicitor sent by Mrs. O. H. P. Belmont to defend me, was permitted to attend me before the Board of Special Inquiry. I went before these three men quite alone, as many a poor, friendless woman, without any of my resources, has had to appear. The moment of my entrance to the room I knew that extraordinary means had been employed against me, for on the desk behind which the board sat I saw a complete *dossier* of my case in English legal papers.

These papers may have been supplied by Scotland Yard, or they may have been supplied by the government. I cannot tell, of course. They sufficed to convince the Board of Special Inquiry that I was a person of doubtful character, to say the least of it, and I was informed that I should have to be detained until the higher authorities at Washington examined my case. Everything was done to make me comfortable, the rooms of the commissioner of Immigration being turned over to me and my companion. The very men who found me guilty of moral obloquy—something of which no British jury has ever yet accused me—put themselves out in a number of ways to make my detention agreeable. I was escorted all over the island and through the quarters assigned detained immigrants, whose right to land in the United States is in question. The huge dining-rooms, the spotless kitchens and the admirably varied bill of fare interested and impressed me. Nothing like them exists in any English institution.

I remained at Ellis Island two and a half days, long enough for the Commissioner of Immigration at Washington to take my case to the President who instantly ordered my release. Whoever was responsible for my detention entirely overlooked the advertising value of the incident. My lecture tour was made much more successful for it and I embarked for England late in November with a very generous American contribution to our war chest, a contribution, alas, that I was not permitted to deliver in person.

The night before the White Star liner *Majestic* reached Plymouth

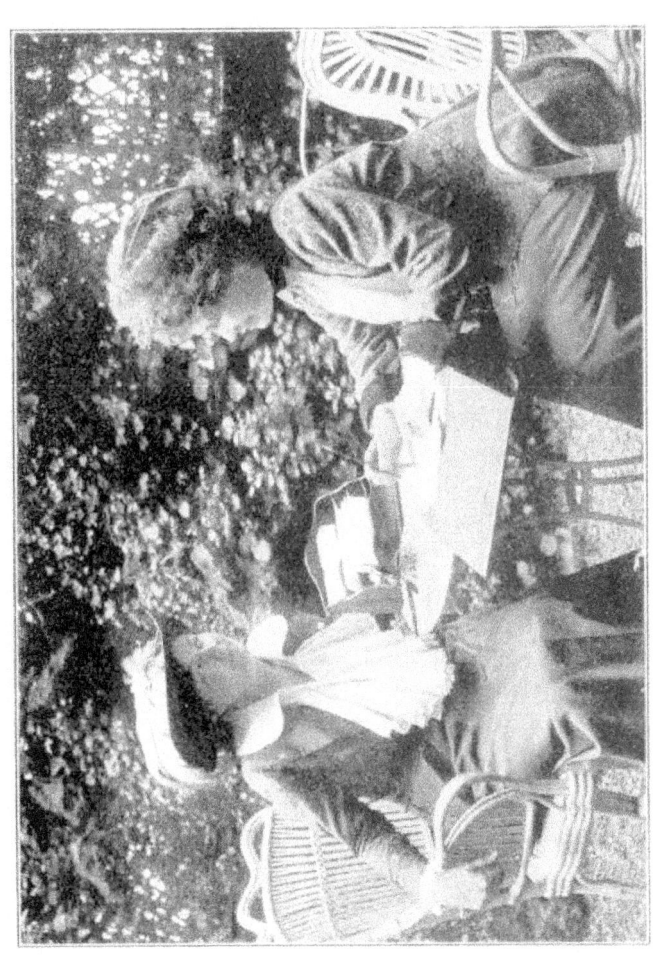

Mrs. Pankhurst and Christabel in the garden of Christabel's home in Paris

a wireless message from headquarters informed me that the government had decided to arrest me on my arrival. The arrest was made, under very dramatic conditions, the next day shortly before noon. The steamer came to anchor in the outer harbour, and we saw at once that the bay, usually so animated with passing vessels, had been cleared of all craft. Far in the distance the tender, which on other occasions had always met the steamer, rested at anchor between two huge grey warships. For a moment or two the scene halted, the passengers crowding to the deckrails in speechless curiosity to see what was to happen next. Suddenly a fisherman's dory, power driven, dashed across the harbour, directly under the noses of the grim war vessels.

Two women, spray drenched, stood up in the boat, and as it ploughed swiftly past our steamer the women called out to me: "The Cats are here, Mrs. Pankhurst! They're close on you—" Their voices trailed away into the mist and we heard no more. Within a minute or two a frightened ship's boy appeared on deck and delivered a message from the purser asking me to step down to his office. I answered that I would certainly do nothing of the kind, and next the police swarmed out on deck and I heard, for the fifth time that I was arrested under the Cat and Mouse Act. They had sent five men from Scotland Yard, two men from Plymouth and a wardress from Holloway, a sufficient number, it will be allowed, to take one woman from a ship anchored two miles out at sea.

Following my firm resolve not to assist in any way the enforcing of the infamous law, I refused to go with the men, who thereupon picked me up and carried me to the waiting police tender. We steamed some miles up the Cornish coast, the police refusing absolutely to tell me whither they were conveying me, and finally disembarked at Bull Point, a government landing-stage, closed to the general public. Here a motorcar was waiting, and accompanied by my bodyguard from Scotland Yard and Holloway, I was driven across Dartmoor to Exeter, where I had a not unendurable imprisonment and hunger strike of four days. Everyone from the governor of the prison to the wardresses were openly sympathetic and kind, and I was told by one confidential official that they kept me only because they had orders to do so until after the great meeting at Empress Theatre, Earls Court, London, which had been arranged as a welcome home for me. The meeting was held on the Sunday night following my arrest, and the great sum of £15,000 was poured into the coffers of militancy. This included the £4,500 which had been collected during my American tour.

Several days after my release from Exeter I went openly to Paris to confer with my daughter on matters relating to the campaign about to open, returning to attend a W. S. P. U. meeting on the day before my license expired. Nevertheless the boat train carriage in which I travelled with my doctor and nurse was invaded at Dover town by two detectives who told me to consider myself under arrest. We were making tea when the men entered, but this we immediately threw out of the window, because a hunger strike always began at the instant of arrest. We never compromised at all, but resisted from the very first moment of attack.

The reason for this uncalled for arrest at Dover was the fear on the part of the police of the bodyguard of women, just then organised for the expressed purpose of resisting attempts to arrest me. That the police, as well as the government were afraid to risk encountering women who were not afraid to fight we had had abundant testimony. We certainly had it on this occasion, for knowing that the bodyguard was waiting at Victoria Station, the authorities had cut off all approaches to the arrival platform and the place was guarded by battalions of police. Not a passenger was permitted to leave a carriage until I had been carried across the arrival platform between a double line of police and detectives and thrown into a forty horse power motorcar, guarded within by two plain clothes men and a wardress, and without by three more policemen.

Around this motorcar were twelve taxi-cabs filled with plain clothes men, four to each vehicle, and three guarding the outside, not to mention the driver, who was also in the employ of the police department. Detectives on motorcycles were on guard at various points ready to follow any rescuing taxicab.

Arrived at Holloway I was again lifted from the car and taken to the reception room and placed on the floor in a state of great exhaustion. When the doctor came in and told me curtly to stand up I was obliged to tell him that I could not stand. I utterly refused to be examined, saying that I was resolved to make the government assume full responsibility for my condition. I declared:

> I refuse to be examined by you or any prison doctor, and I do this as a protest against my sentence, and against my being here at all. I no longer recognise a prison doctor as a medical man in the proper sense of the word. I have withdrawn my consent to be governed by the rules of prison; I refuse to recognise the

authority of any prison official, and I therefore make it impossible for the government to carry out the sentence they have imposed upon me.

Wardresses were summoned, I was placed in an invalid chair and so carried up three flights of stairs and put into an unwarmed cell with a concrete floor. Refusing to leave the chair I was lifted out and placed on the bed, where I lay all night without removing my coat or loosening my garments. It was on a Saturday that the arrest had been made, and I was kept in prison until the following Wednesday morning. During all that time no food or water passed my lips, and I added to this the sleep strike, which means that as far as was humanly possible I refused all sleep and rest. For two nights I sat or lay on the concrete floor, resolutely refusing the oft repeated offers of medical examination. "You are not a doctor," I told the man. "You are a government torturer, and all you want to do is to satisfy yourself that I am not quite ready to die."

The doctor, a new man since my last imprisonment, flushed and looked extremely unhappy. "I suppose you do think that," he mumbled.

On Tuesday morning the governor came to look at me, and no doubt I presented by that time a fairly bad appearance. At least I gathered as much from the alarmed expression of the wardress who accompanied him. To the governor I made the simple announcement that I was ready to leave prison and that I intended to leave very soon, dead or alive. I told him that from that moment I should not even rest on the concrete floor, but should walk my cell until I was released or until I died from exhaustion. All day I kept to this resolution, pacing up and down the narrow cell, many times stumbling and falling, until the doctor came in at evening to tell me that I was ordered released on the following morning. Then I loosened my gown and lay down, absolutely spent, and fell almost instantly into a death-like sleep. The next morning a motor ambulance took me to the Kingsway headquarters where a hospital room had been arranged for my reception. The two imprisonments in less than ten days had made terrible drafts on my strength, and the coldness of the Holloway cell had brought on a painful neuralgia. It was many days before I recovered even a tithe of my usual health.

These two arrests resulted exactly as the government should have known that they would result, in a great outbreak of fresh militancy.

As soon as the news spread that I had been taken at Plymouth a huge fire broke out in the timber yards at Richmond Walk, Devenport, and an acre and a half of timber, beside a pleasure fair and a scenic railway adjacent, to the value of thousands of pounds was destroyed. No one ever discovered the cause of the fire, the greatest that ever occurred in the neighbourhood, but tied to one of the railings was a copy of the *Suffragette* and to another railing two cards, on one of which was written a message to the government:

> How dare you arrest Mrs. Pankhurst and allow Sir Edward Carson and Mr. Bonar Law to go free?

The second card bore the words:

> Our reply to the torture of Mrs. Pankhurst, and her cowardly arrest at Plymouth.

Besides this fire, which waged fiercely from midnight until dawn, a large unoccupied house at Bristol was destroyed by fire; a fine residence in Scotland, also unoccupied, was badly damaged by fire; St. Anne's Church in a suburb of Liverpool was partly destroyed; and many pillar boxes in London, Edinburgh, Derby and other cities were fired. In churches all over the kingdom our women created consternation by interpolating into the services reverently spoken prayers for prisoners who were suffering for conscience' sake. The reader no doubt has heard of these interruptions, and if so he has read of brawling, shrieking women, breaking into the sanctity of religious services, and creating riot in the House of God. I think the reader should know exactly what does happen when militants, who are usually religious women, interrupt church services. On the Sunday when I was in Holloway, following my arrest at Dover, certain women attending the afternoon service at Westminster Abbey, chanted in concert the following prayer:

> God save Emmeline Pankhurst, help us with Thy love and strength to guard her, spare those who suffer for conscience' sake. Hear us when we pray to Thee.

They had hardly finished this prayer when vergers fell upon them and with great violence hustled them out of the abbey. One kneeling man, who happened to be near one of the women, forgot his Christian intercessions long enough to beat her in the face with his fists before the vergers came.

Similar scenes have taken place in churches and cathedrals throughout England and Scotland, and in many instances the women have been most barbarously treated by vergers and members of the congregations. In other cases the women not only have been left unmolested, but have been allowed to finish their prayers amid deep and sympathetic silence. Some clergymen have even been brave enough to add a reverent amen to these prayers for women in prison, and it has happened that clergymen have voluntarily offered prayers for us. The Church as a whole, however, has undoubtedly failed to live up to its obligation to demand justice for women, and to protest against the torture of forcible feeding. During the year just closing we sent many deputations to Church authorities, the bishops, one after another having been visited in this manner. Some of the bishops, including the reactionary Archbishop of Canterbury, refused to accord the desired interview, and when that happened, the answer of the deputation was to sit on the doorstep of the Episcopal residence until surrender followed—as it invariably did.

As Holloway Gaol is within his diocese, the Bishop of London was visited by the W. S. P. U. and the demand was made that the bishop himself should witness forcible feeding in order to realise the horror of the proceeding. He did visit two of the tortured women, but he did not see them forcibly fed, and when he came out he gave the public an account of his interview with them which was in effect the government's version of the facts. The W. S. P. U. was naturally indignant, while all the government's friends hailed the bishop as a supporter of the policy of torture. Only those who have suffered the pain and agony, not to speak of the moral humiliation of forcible feeding can realise the depths of the iniquity which the Bishop of London was manoeuvred by the government to whitewash. It may be true, as the bishop comforted himself by saying, that the victims of forcible feeding suffered the more because they struggled under the process.

But, as Mary Richardson wrote in the *Suffragette*, to expect a victim not to struggle was the same as telling her that she would suffer less if she did not jump on getting a cinder in her eye. Miss Richardson declared:

> The principle is the same. One struggles because the pain is excruciating, and the nerves of the eyes, ears and face are so tortured that it would be impossible not to resist to the uttermost. One struggles, also, because of another reason—a moral

reason—for forcible feeding is an immoral assault as well as a painful physical one, and to remain passive under it would give one the feeling of sin; the sin of concurrence. One's whole nature is revolted; resistance is therefore inevitable.

I think it proper here to explain also the policy upon which we embarked in 1914 of taking our cause directly to the king. The reader has perhaps heard of Suffragette "insults" to King George and Queen Mary, and it is but just that he should hear a direct account of how these "insults" are offered. Several isolated attempts had been made to present petitions to the king, once when he was on his way to Westminster to open Parliament, and again on an occasion when he paid a visit to Bristol. On the latter occasion the woman who tried to present the petition was assaulted by one of the king's equerries, who struck her with the flat of his sword.

We finally resolved on the policy of direct petition to the king because we had been forced to abandon all hope of successful petitioning to his ministers. Tricked and betrayed at every turn by the Liberal government, we announced that we would not again put even a pretence of confidence in them. We would carry our demand for justice to the throne of the monarch. Late in December, 1913, while I was in prison for the second time since my return to England, a great gala performance was given at Covent Garden, the opera being the *Jeanne d'Arc* of Raymond Rôze. The king and queen and the entire court were present, and the scene was expected to be one of unusual brilliance. Our women took advantage of the occasion to make one of the most successful demonstrations of the year. A box was secured directly opposite the Royal Box, and this was occupied by three women, beautifully gowned.

On entering they had managed, without attracting the slightest attention, to lock and barricade the door, and at the close of the first act, as soon as the orchestra had disappeared, the women stood up, and one of them, with the aid of a megaphone, addressed the king. Calling attention to the impressive scenes on the stage, the speaker told the king that women were today fighting, as Joan of Arc fought centuries ago, for human liberty, and that they, like the maid of Orleans, were being tortured and done to death, in the name of the king, in the name of the Church, and with the full knowledge and responsibility of established government. At this very hour the leader of these fighters in the army of liberty was being held in prison and tortured by the king's authority.

The vast audience was thrown into a panic of excitement and horror, and amid a perfect turmoil of cries and adjurations, the door of the box was finally broken down and the women ejected. As soon as they had left the house others of our women, to the number of forty or more, who had been sitting quietly in an upper gallery, rose to their feet and rained suffrage literature on the heads of the audience below. It was fully three quarters of an hour before the excitement subsided and the singers could go on with the opera.

The sensation caused by this direct address to royalty inspired us to make a second attempt to arouse the king's conscience, and early in January, as soon as Parliament re-assembled, we announced that I would personally lead a deputation to Buckingham Palace. The plan was welcomed with enthusiasm by our members and a very large number of women volunteered to join the deputation, which was intended to make a protest against three things—the continued disfranchisement of women; the forcible feeding and the cat and mouse torture of those who were fighting against this injustice; and the scandalous manner in which the government, while coercing and torturing militant women, were allowing perfect freedom to the men opponents of Home Rule in Ireland, men who openly announced that they were about to carry out a policy, not merely of attacking property, but of destroying human life.

I wrote a letter to the king, conveying to him "the respectful and loyal request of the Women's Social and Political Union that Your Majesty will give audience to a deputation of women." The letter went on:

> The deputation desire to submit to Your Majesty in person their claim to the Parliamentary vote, which is the only protection against the grievous industrial and social wrongs that women suffer; is the symbol and guarantee of British citizenship; and means the recognition of women's equal dignity and worth, as members of our great Empire.
>
> The deputation will further lay before Your Majesty a complaint of the medieval and barbarous methods of torture whereby Your Majesty's ministers are seeking to repress women's revolt against the deprivation of citizen rights—a revolt as noble and glorious in its spirit and purpose as any of those past struggles for liberty which are the pride of the British race.

We have been told by the unthinking—by those who are heedless of the constitutional principles upon which is based our loyal request for an audience of Your Majesty in person—that our conversation should be with Your Majesty's ministers.

We repudiate this suggestion. In the first place, it would not only be repugnant to our womanly sense of dignity, but it would be absurd and futile for us to interview the very men against whom we bring the accusations of betraying the Women's Cause and torturing those who fight for that Cause.

In the second place, we will not be referred to, and we will not recognise the authority of men who, in our eyes, have no legal or constitutional standing in the matter, because we have not been consulted as to their election to Parliament nor as to their appointment as Ministers of the Crown.

I then cited as a precedent in support of our claim to be heard by the king in person, the case of the Deputation of Irish Catholics, which, in the year 1793, was received by King George III in person. I further said:

Our right as women to be heard and to be aided by Your Majesty is far stronger than any such right possessed by men, because it is based upon our lack of every other constitutional means of securing the redress of our grievances. We have no power to vote for Members of Parliament, and therefore for us there is no House of Commons. We have no voice in the House of Lords. But we have a king, and to him we make our appeal.

Constitutionally speaking, we are, as voteless women, living in the time when the power of the monarch was unlimited. In that old time, which is passed for men though not for women, men who were oppressed had recourse to the king—the source of power, of justice, and of reform.

Precisely in the same way we now claim the right to come to the foot of the throne and to make of the king in person our demand for the redress of the political grievance which we cannot, and will not, any longer tolerate.

Because women are voteless, there are in our midst today sweated workers, white slaves, outraged children, and innocent mothers and their babes stricken by horrible disease. It is for the sake and in the cause of these unhappy members of our sex, that we ask of Your Majesty the audience that we are confident will be granted to us.

It was some days before we had the answer to this letter, and in the meantime some uncommonly stirring and painful occurrences attracted the public attention.

CHAPTER 8

For months before my return to England from my American lecture tour, the Ulster situation had been increasingly serious. Sir Edward Carson and his followers had declared that if Home Rule government should be created and set up in Dublin, they would—law or no law—establish a rival and independent Government in Ulster. It was known that arms and ammunition were being shipped to Ireland, and that men—and women too, for that matter—were drilling and otherwise getting ready for civil war. The W. S. P. U. approached Sir Edward Carson and asked him if the proposed Ulster Government would give equal voting rights to women. We frankly declared that in case the Ulster men alone were to have the vote, that we should deal with "King Carson" and his colleagues exactly in the same manner that we had adopted towards the British Government centred at Westminster.

Sir Edward Carson at first promised us that the rebel Ulster Government, should it come into existence, would give votes to Ulster women. This pledge was later repudiated, and in the early winter months of 1914 militancy appeared in Ulster. It had been raging in Scotland for some time, and now the imprisoned Suffragettes in that country were being forcibly fed as in England. The answer to this was, of course, more militancy. The ancient Scottish church of Whitekirk, a relic of pre-Reformation days, was destroyed by fire. Several unoccupied country houses were also burned.

It was about this time, February, 1914, that I undertook a series of meetings outside London, the first of which was to be held in Glasgow, in the St. Andrews Hall, which holds many thousands of people. In order that I might be free on the night of the meeting, I left London unknown to the police, in a motor car. In spite of all efforts to apprehend me I succeeded in reaching Glasgow and in getting to the platform of St. Andrews' where I found myself face to face with an enormous, and manifestly sympathetic audience.

As it was suspected that the police might rush the platform, plans had been made to offer resistance, and the bodyguard was present in force. My speech was one of the shortest I have ever made. I said:

> I have kept my promise, and in spite of His Majesty's Government I am here tonight. Very few people in this audience, very few people in this country, know how much of the nation's money is being spent to silence women. But the wit and ingenuity of women is overcoming the power and money of the British Government. It is well that we should have this meeting tonight, because today is a memorable day in the annals of the United Kingdom of Great Britain and Ireland. Today in the House of Commons has been witnessed the triumph of militancy—men's militancy—and tonight I hope to make it clear to the people in this meeting that if there is any distinction to be drawn at all between militancy in Ulster and the militancy of women, it is all to the advantage of the women.
>
> Our greatest task in this women's movement is to prove that we are human beings like men, and every stage of our fight is forcing home that very difficult lesson into the minds of men, and especially into the minds of politicians. I propose tonight at this political meeting to have a text. Texts are usually given from pulpits, but perhaps you will forgive me if I have a text tonight. My text is: 'Equal justice for men and women, equal political justice, equal legal justice, equal industrial justice, and equal social justice.' I want as clearly and briefly as I can to make it clear to you tonight that if it is justifiable to fight for common ordinary equal justice, then women have ample justification, nay, have greater justification, for revolution and rebellion, than ever men have had in the whole history of the human race. Now that is a big contention to make, but I am going to prove it. You get the proof of the political injustice—

As I finished the word "injustice," a steward uttered a warning shout, there was a tramp of heavy feet, and a large body of police burst into the hall, and rushed up to the platform, drawing their truncheons as they ran. Headed by detectives from Scotland Yard, they surged in on all sides, but as the foremost members attempted to storm the platform, they were met by a fusillade of flower-pots, tables, chairs, and other missiles. They seized the platform railing, in order to tear it down, but they found that under the decorations barbed wires were concealed. This gave them pause for a moment.

Meanwhile, more of the invading host came from other directions.

The bodyguard and members of the audience vigorously repelled the attack, wielding clubs, batons, poles, planks, or anything they could seize, while the police laid about right and left with their batons, their violence being far the greater. Men and women were seen on all sides with blood streaming down their faces, and there were cries for a doctor. In the middle of the struggle, several revolver shots rang out, and the woman who was firing the revolver—which I should explain was loaded with blank cartridges only—was able to terrorise and keep at bay a whole body of police.

I had been surrounded by members of the bodyguard, who hurried me towards the stairs from the platform. The police, however, overtook us, and in spite of the resistance of the bodyguard, they seized me and dragged me down the narrow stair at the back of the hall. There a cab was waiting. I was pushed violently into it, and thrown on the floor, the seats being occupied by as many constables as could crowd inside.

The meeting was left in a state of tremendous turmoil, and the people of Glasgow who were present expressed their sense of outrage at the behaviour of the police, who, acting under the government's instructions, had so disgraced the city. General Drummond, who was present on the platform, took hold of the situation and delivered a rousing speech, in which she exhorted the audience to make the Government feel the force of their indignation.

I was kept in the Glasgow police-cells all night, and the next morning was taken, a hunger and thirst striking prisoner, to Holloway, where I remained for five memorable days. This was the seventh attempt the government had made to make me serve a three years' term of penal servitude on a conspiracy charge, in connection with the blowing up of Mr. Lloyd-George's country house. In the eleven and a half months since I had received that sentence I had spent just thirty days in prison. On March 14th I was again released, still suffering severely, not only from the hunger and thirst strike, but from injuries received at the time of my brutal arrest in Glasgow.

The answer to that arrest had been swift and strong. In Bristol, the scene of great riots and destruction when men were fighting for votes, a large timber-yard was burnt. In Scotland a mansion was destroyed by fire. A milder protest consisted of a raid upon the house of the Home Secretary, in the course of which eighteen windows were broken.

The greatest and most startling of all protests hitherto made was the attack at this time on the Rokeby "Venus" in the National Gallery.

Mary Richardson, the young woman who carried out this protest, is possessed of a very fine artistic sense, and nothing but the most compelling sense of duty would have moved her to the deed. Miss Richardson being placed on trial, made a moving address to the court, in the course of which she said that her act was premeditated, and that she had thought it over very seriously before it was undertaken. She added:

> I have been a student of art, and I suppose care as much for art as anyone who was in the gallery when I made my protest. But I care more for justice than I do for art, and I firmly believe than when a nation shuts its eyes to justice, and prefers to have women who are fighting for justice ill-treated, mal-treated, and tortured, that such action as mine should be understandable; I don't say excusable, but it should be understood.
> I should like to point out that the outrage which the government has committed upon Mrs. Pankhurst is an ultimatum of outrages. It is murder, slow murder, and premeditated murder. That is how I have looked at it....
> How you can hold women up to ridicule and contempt, and put them in prison, and yet say nothing to the government for murdering people, I cannot understand....
> The fact is that the nation is either dead or asleep. In my opinion there is undoubted evidence that the nation is dead, because women have knocked in vain at the door of administrators, archbishops, and even the king himself. The government have closed all doors to us. And remember this—a state of death in a nation, as well as in an individual, leads to one thing, and that is dissolution. I do not hesitate to say that if the men of the country do not at this eleventh hour put their hand out and save Mrs. Pankhurst, before a few more years are passed they will stretch out their hand in vain to save the Empire.

In sentencing Miss Richardson to six month's imprisonment the magistrate said regretfully that if she had smashed a window instead of an art treasure he could have given her a maximum sentence of eighteen months, which illustrates, I think, one more queer anomaly of English law.

A few weeks later another famous painting, the Sargent portrait of Henry James, was attacked by a Suffragette, who, like Miss Richardson, was sent through the farce of a trial and a prison sentence which she did not serve. By this time practically all the picture galleries and other public galleries and museums had been closed to the public. The Suffragettes had succeeded in large measure in making England unattractive to tourists, and hence unprofitable to the world of business. As we had anticipated, the reaction against the Liberal Government began to manifest itself. Questions were asked daily, in the press, in the House of Commons, everywhere, as to the responsibility of the government in the Suffragette activities. People began to place that responsibility where it belonged, at the doors of the government, rather than at our own.

Especially did the public begin to contrast the treatment meted out to the rebel women with that accorded to the rebel men of Ulster. For a whole year the government had been attacking the women's right of free speech, by their refusal to allow the W. S. P. U. to hold public meetings in Hyde Park. The excuse given for this was that we advocated and defended a militant policy. But the government permitted the Ulster militants to advocate their war policy in Hyde Park, and we determined that, with or without the government's permission, we should, on the day of the Ulster meeting, hold a suffrage meeting in Hyde Park. General Drummond was announced as the chief speaker at this meeting, and when the day came, militant Ulster men and militant women assembled in Hyde Park. The militant men were allowed to speak in defence of bloodshed; but General Drummond was arrested before she had uttered more than a few words.

Another proof that the government had a law of leniency for militant men and a law of persecution for militant women was shown at this time by the case of Miss Dorothy Evans, our organiser in Ulster. She and another Suffragette, Miss Maud Muir, were arrested in Belfast charged with having in their possession a quantity of explosives. It was well known that there were houses in Belfast that secreted tons of gunpowder and ammunition for the use of the rebels against Home Rule, but none of those houses were entered and searched by the police. The authorities reserved their energies in this direction for the headquarters of the militant women. Naturally enough the two suffrage prisoners, on being arraigned in court, refused to be tried unless the government proceeded also against the men rebels. The prisoners throughout the proceedings kept up such a disturbance that the trial could not properly go on. When the case was called Miss Evans rose and protested loudly, saying:

I deny your jurisdiction entirely until there are in the dock beside us men who are well known leaders of the Ulster militant movement.

Miss Muir joined Miss Evans in her protest and both women were dragged from the court. After an hour's adjournment the trial was resumed, but the women again began to speak, and the case was hurried through in the midst of indescribable din and commotion. The women were sent to prison on remand, and after a four days' hunger and thirst strike were released unconditionally.

The result of this case was a severe outbreak of militancy, three fires destroying Belfast mansions within a few days. Fires blazed almost daily throughout England, a very important instance being the destruction of the Bath Hotel at Felixstowe, valued at £35,000. The two women responsible for this were afterwards arrested, and as their trials were delayed, they were, although unconvicted prisoners, tortured by forcible feeding for several months. This occurred in April, a few weeks before the day appointed for our deputation to the king.

I had appointed May 21st for the deputation, in spite of the fact that the king had, through his ministers, refused to receive us. Replying to this I had written, again directly to the king, that we utterly denied the constitutional right of ministers, who not being elected by women were not responsible to them, to stand between ourselves and the throne, and to prevent us from having an audience of His Majesty. I declared further that we would, on the date announced, present ourselves at the gates of Buckingham Palace to demand an interview.

Following the despatch of this letter my life was made as uncomfortable and as insecure as the government, through their police department, could contrive. I was not allowed to make a public appearance, but I addressed several huge meetings from the balcony of houses where I had taken refuge. These were all publicly announced, and each time the police, mingling with crowds, made strenuous efforts to arrest me. By strategy, and through the valiant efforts of the bodyguard, I was able each time to make my speech and afterwards to escape from the house. All of these occasions were marked by fierce opposition from the police and splendid courage and resistance on the part of the women.

The deputation to the king was, of course, marked by the government as an occasion on which I could be arrested, and when, on the day appointed, I led the great deputation of women to the gates of

"Arrested at the king's gate!" May, 1914

Buckingham Palace, an army of several thousand police were sent out against us. The conduct of the police showed plainly that they had been instructed to repeat the tactics of Black Friday, described in an earlier chapter. Indeed, the violence, brutality and insult of Black Friday were excelled on this day, and at the gates of the King of England. I myself did not suffer so greatly as others, because I had advanced towards the palace unnoticed by the police, who were looking for me at a more distant point. When I arrived at the gates I was recognised by an inspector, who at once seized me bodily, and conveyed me to Holloway.

Before the deputation had gone forth, I had made a short speech to them, warning them of what might happen, and my final message was:

Whatever happens, do not turn back.

They did not, and in spite of all the violence inflicted upon them, they went forward, resolved, so long as they were free, not to give up the attempt to reach the palace. Many arrests were made, and of those arrested many were sent to prison. Although for the majority, this was the first imprisonment, these brave women adopted the hunger strike, and passed seven or eight days without food and water before they were released, weak and ill as may be supposed.

Chapter 9

In the weeks following the disgraceful events before Buckingham Palace the government made several last, desperate efforts to crush the W. S. P. U., to remove all the leaders and to destroy our paper, the *Suffragette*. They issued summonses against Mrs. Drummond, Mrs. Dacre Fox and Miss Grace Roe; they raided our headquarters at Lincolns Inn House; twice they raided other headquarters temporarily in use, not to speak of raids made upon private dwellings where the new leaders, who had risen to take the places of those arrested, were at their work for the organisation. But with each successive raid the disturbances which the government were able to make in our affairs became less, because we were better able, each time, to provide against them. Every effort made by the government to suppress the *Suffragette* failed, and it continued to come out regularly every week.

Although the paper was issued regularly, we had to use almost super-human energy to get it distributed. The government sent to all the great wholesale news agents a letter which was designed to terrorise and bully them into refusing to handle the paper or to sell it to the retail news agents. Temporarily, at any rate, the letter produced in many cases the desired effect, but we overcame the emergency by taking immediate steps to build up a system of distribution which was worked by women themselves, independently of the newspaper trade. We also opened a "Suffragette Defence Fund," to meet the extra expense of publishing and distributing the paper.

Twice more the government attempted to force me to serve the three years' term of penal servitude, one arrest being made when I was being carried to a meeting in an ambulance. Wholesale arrests and hunger strikes occurred at the same time, but our women continued their work of militancy, and money flowed into our Protest and Defence Fund. At one great meeting in July the fund was increased by nearly £16,000.

But now unmistakable signs began to appear that our long and bitter struggle was drawing to a close. The last resort of the government of inciting the street mobs against us had been little successful, and we could see in the temper of the public abundant hope that the reaction against the government, long hoped for by us, had actually begun.

Every day of the militant movement was so extraordinarily full of events and changes that it is difficult to choose a point at which this narrative should be brought to a close. I think, however, that an account of a recent debate which took place in the House of Commons will give the reader the best idea of the complete breakdown of the government in their effort to crush the women's fight for liberty.

On June 11th, when the House of Commons had gone into a Committee of Supply, Lord Robert Cecil moved a reduction of 100 pounds on the Home Office vote, thus precipitating a discussion of militancy. Lord Robert said that he had read with some surprise that the government were not dissatisfied with the measures which they had taken to deal with the violent suffragists, and he added with some asperity that the government took a much more sanguine view of the matter than anybody else in the United Kingdom. The House, Lord Robert went on to declare, would not be in a position to deal with the case satisfactorily unless they realised the devotion of the followers to their leaders, who were almost fully responsible for what was going on. Ministerial cheers greeted this utterance, but they ceased suddenly when the speaker went on to say that these leaders could never have induced their followers to enter upon a career of crime but for the serious mistakes which had been made over and over again by the

Government.

Among these mistakes Lord Robert cited the shameful treatment of the women on Black Friday, the policy of forcible feeding and the scandal of the different treatment accorded Lady Constance Lytton and "Jane Warton." There were Opposition cheers at this, and they were again raised when Lord Robert deplored the terrible waste of energy, and "admirable material" involved in the militant movement. Although Lord Robert Cecil deemed it unjust as well as futile for Suffragist Members to withhold their support from the woman suffrage movement on account of militancy he himself was in favour of deportation for Suffragettes. At this there were cries of "Where to?" and "Ulster!"

Mr. McKenna replied by first calling attention to the fact that in the militant movement they had a phenomenon "absolutely without precedent in our history." Women in numbers were committing crimes, beginning with window breaking, and proceeding to arson, not with the motives of ordinary criminals, but with the intention of advertising a political cause and of forcing the public to grant their demands. Mr. McKenna continuing said:

"The number of women who commit crimes of that kind is extremely small, but the number of those who sympathise with them is extremely large. One of the difficulties which the police have in detecting this form of crime and in bringing home the offence to the criminal is that the criminals find so many sympathisers among the well-to-do and thoroughly respectable classes that the ordinary administration of the law is rendered comparatively impossible. Let me give the House some figures showing the number of women who have been committed to prison for offences since the beginning of the militant agitation in 1906.

In that year the total number of commitments to prison was 31, all the persons charged being women. In 1909 the figure rose to 156; in 1911 to 188 (182 women and six men); and in 1912 to 290 (288 women and two men). In 1913 the number dropped to 183, and so far this year it has dropped to 108. These figures include all commitments to prison and re-arrests under the Cat and Mouse Act. What is the obvious lesson to be drawn? Up to 1912 the number of offences committed for which imprisonment was the punishment was steadily increasing, but since the beginning of last year—that is to say, since the new Act came into force—the number of individual offences has been very greatly reduced. On the other hand, we see that the seriousness of the offences is much greater."

This statement, that the number of imprisonments had decreased since the adoption of the Cat and Mouse Act, was of course, incorrect, or at best misleading. The fact was that the number of imprisonments decreased because, where formerly the militants went willingly to prison for their acts, they now escaped prison wherever possible. A comparatively small number of "mice" were ever rearrested by the police.

Mr. McKenna went on to say that he realised fully the growing sense of indignation against the militant suffragists and he added, "Their one hope is, rightly or wrongly, that the well advertised indignation of the public will recoil on the head of the government."

"And so it will," interpolated a voice.

"My honourable friend," replied Mr. McKenna, "says so it will. I believe that he is mistaken." But he gave no reasons for so believing. Referring to what he called the "recent grave rudenesses which have been committed against the king," Mr. McKenna said: "It is true that all subjects have the right of petitioning His Majesty, providing the petition is couched in respectful terms, but there is no right on the part of the subjects generally to personal audience for the purpose of the presentation of the petition or otherwise. It is the duty of the Home Secretary to present all such petitions to the king, and further to advise His Majesty what action should be taken. It was therefore ridiculous for any Suffragist to assert that there had been any breach of constitutional propriety on the part of the king in refusing, on the advice of the Home Secretary to receive the deputation."

Also, said Mr. McKenna, in view of the fact that the petition for an audience was sent by a person under sentence of penal servitude—myself—it was the plain duty of the Home Secretary to advise the king not to grant it. He referred to the incident, he said, only because it was illustrative of the militant's methods of advertising their cause. He gave them credit, he was bound to say, for a certain degree of intelligence in adopting their methods.

> No action has been so fruitful of advertisement as the recent absurdities which they have perpetrated in relation to the king.

Coming down to the question of methods of meeting and overcoming militancy, Mr. McKenna said that he had received an almost unlimited correspondence on the subject from every section of the public.

Four methods were suggested. The first is to let them die. (Hear, hear.) That is, I should say, at the present moment, the most popular (laughter), judging by the number of letters I have received. The second is to deport them. (Hear, hear.) The third is to treat them as lunatics. (Hear, hear.) And the fourth is to give them the franchise. (Hear, hear, and laughter.) I think that is an exhaustive list. I notice each one of them is received with a certain very moderate amount of applause in this House. I hope to give reason why at the present time I think we should not adopt any one of them.

The first suggestion was usually, not always, based on the assumption that the women would take their food if they knew that the alternative was death. Mr. McKenna read to the House in opposition to that view "the opinion of a great medical expert who had had intimate knowledge of the Suffragettes from the first." Mr. McKenna continued:

> We have to face the fact, therefore, that they would die. Let me say, also, with actual experience of dealing with suffragists, in many cases they have got in their refusal of food and water beyond the point when they could help themselves, and they have clearly done all that they could do to show their readiness to die. . . . There are those who hold another assumption. They think that after one or two deaths in prison militancy would cease. In my judgment there was never a greater delusion. I readily admit that this is the issue upon which I stand and upon which I feel I would fight to the end those who would adopt as their policy to let the prisoners die. So far from putting an end to militancy, I believe it would be the greatest incentive to militancy which could ever happen. For every woman who dies, there would be scores of women who would come forward for the honour, as they would deem it, of earning the crown of martyrdom.

"How do you know?" called out an Opposition member. The Home Secretary retorted;

> How do I know? I have had more to do with these women than the honourable member, much more. Those who hold that opinion leave out of account all recognition of the nature of these women. I do not speak in admiration of them. They are

hysterical fanatics, but, coupled with their hysterical fanaticism, they have a courage, part of their fanaticism, which undoubtedly stands at nothing, and the honourable member who thinks that they would not come forward, not merely to risk death, but to undergo it, for what they deem the greatest cause on earth is making, in my judgment, a profound mistake.... They would seek death, and I am sure that however strong public opinion outside might be today in favour of allowing them to die, when there were twenty, thirty, forty, or more deaths in prison, you would have a violent reaction of public opinion, and the honourable gentleman who now so glibly says 'Let them die' would be among the first to blame the government for what he would describe as the inhuman attitude they had adopted.

That policy could not be adopted without an Act of Parliament. For the reason I have given I have not asked Parliament to remove from prison officials the responsibility under which they now rest for doing their best to keep those committed to their charge alive. But, supposing this legal responsibility were removed from the prison officials, let honourable members for a moment transport themselves in imagination to a prison cell and conceive of a prison doctor, a humane man, standing by watching a woman slowly being done to death by starvation and thirst, knowing that he could help her and that he could keep her alive. Did they think that any doctor would go on with such action, or that we should be able to retain medical men under such conditions in our service? I do not believe it. The doctor would think, as I should think if I saw a woman lying there, 'What has been this woman's offence?' It may have been obstructing the police, coupled with the obstinacy derived from fanaticism which leads her to refuse food and water. Obstructing the police and she is to die! I could not distinguish, and no Home Secretary could ever say, that this woman should be left to die and that that woman should not. Once we were committed to a policy of allowing them to die if they did not take their food we should have to go on with it, and we should have woman after woman whose only offence may have been obstructing the police, breaking a window, or even burning down an empty house, dying because she was obstinate. I do not believe that that is a policy which on consideration will ever recommend itself to the British people, and I am bound to say for myself I could never take a hand in carrying that policy out. (Cheers.)

Lord Robert Cecil's favourite remedy of deportation Mr. McKenna dismissed on the grounds that this would be merely removing the difficulty to some other country than Great Britain. If the suggested distant island were treated as a prison the women would hunger strike there as they did in English prisons. If the island were not treated as a prison, the Suffragettes' rich friends would come and rescue them in yachts.

The suggestion that the militants be treated as lunatics was also dismissed as impossible. Admitting that he had tried to get them certified as lunatics and had failed because the medical profession would not consent to such a course, Mr. McKenna said that he could not, contrary to the advice of the doctors, get certification by Act of Parliament. "There remains," said Mr. McKenna, "the last proposal, that we should give them the franchise."

"That is the right one," exclaimed Mr. William Redmond, but the Home Secretary replied:

> Whatever may be said as to the merits or demerits of that proposal, it is clearly not one I can discuss now in Committee of Supply. I am not responsible, as Home Secretary, for the state of the law on the franchise, nor is there any occasion for me to express or conceal my own opinions on the point; but I certainly do not think, and I am sure the Committee will agree with me, that that could be seriously treated as a remedy for the existing state of lawlessness.

Coming at last to the constructive part of his speech Mr. McKenna told the House of Commons that the government had one last resort, which was to take legal proceedings against subscribers to the funds of the W. S. P. U. The funds of the society, he said, were undoubtedly beyond the arm of the British law. But the government were in hopes of stopping future subscriptions, he concluded:

> We are now not without hope that we have evidence which will enable us to proceed against the subscribers (loud cheers) in civil action, and if we succeed the subscribers will become personally liable for all the damage done. (Cheers.) It is a question of evidence. . . I have further directed that the question should be considered whether the subscribers could not be

proceeded against criminally as well as by civil action. (Cheers.) We have only been able to obtain this evidence by our now not infrequent raids upon the offices, and such property as we can get at of the society. . . . A year ago a raid was made on the offices of the society, but we obtained no such evidence. If we succeed in making the subscribers personally responsible individually for the whole damage done I have no doubt that the insurance companies will quickly follow the example set them by the government, and in turn bring actions to recover the cost which has been thrown upon them. If that is done I have no doubt the days of militancy are over.

The militants live only by the subscriptions of rich women (cheers) who themselves enjoy all the advantages of wealth secured for them by the labour of others (cheers) and use their wealth against the interests of society, paying their unfortunate victims to undergo all the horrors of a hunger and thirst strike in the commission of a crime. Whatever feelings we may have against the wretched women who for 30s. and £2 a week go about the country burning and destroying, what must our feelings be for the women who give their money to induce the perpetration of these crimes and leave their sisters to undergo the punishment while they live in luxury? (Cheers.) If we can succeed against them we will spare no pains. If the action is successful in the total destruction of the means of revenue of the Women's Social and Political Union I think we shall see the last of the power of Mrs. Pankhurst and her friends. (Cheers.)

In the general debate which followed the government were obliged to listen to very severe criticisms of their past and present policy towards the militant women. Mr. Keir Hardie said in part:

We may not today discuss the question of the franchise, but surely it was possible for the Home Secretary, without any transgression on the rules of the House, to have held out just a ray of hope for the future as to the intentions of the government in regard to this most urgent question. On that point, may I say that I am not one of those who believe that a right thing should be withheld because some of the advocates of it resort to weapons of which we do not approve. That note has been sounded more than once, and if it be true, and it is true, that a section of the public outside are strongly opposed to this conduct, it is equally true that the bulk of the people look with a very calm and indifferent eye upon what is happening so long as the vote is withheld from women.

Mr. Hardie concluded by regretting that the House, instead of discussing Woman Suffrage, was discussing methods of penalising militant women.

Mr. Rupert Gwynne said:

Nobody is in a more ridiculous position than the members on the Treasury Bench. They cannot address a meeting, or go to a railway station, or even get into a taxicab, without having detectives with them. Even if they like it, we, the public do not, because we have to pay for it. It is not worth the expense that it costs to have a detective staff following Cabinet Ministers wherever they go, whether in a private or a public capacity. Further, if the Home Secretary is correct in saying that these women are prepared to die, and invite death, in order to advertise their devotion to their cause, does he really think they are going to mind if their funds are attached?

Another friend of the Suffragists, Mr. Wedgwood said:

We are dealing with a problem which is a very serious one indeed. To my mind, when you find a large body of public opinion, and a large number of people capable of going to these lengths, there is only one thing for a respectable House of Commons to do, and that is to consider very closely and clearly whether the complaints of those who complain are or are not justified. We are not justified in acting in panic. What it is our duty to do is to consider the rights and wrongs of these people who have acted in this way.
I attribute myself no value to the vote, but I do think that when we seriously consider the question of Woman Suffrage, which has not been done by this House up to the present, we should remember that when you see people capable of this amount of self-sacrifice, that the one duty of the House of Commons is not to stamp the iron heel upon them, but to see how far their cause is just, and to act according to justice.

When such a debate as this was possible in the House of Commons, it must be plain to every disinterested reader that militancy never set the cause of suffrage back, but on the contrary, set it forward at least half a century. When I remember how that same House of Commons, a few years ago, treated the mention of woman suffrage with scorn and contempt, how they permitted the most insulting things to be said of the women who were begging for their political freedom, how, with indecent laughter and coarse jokes they allowed suffrage bills to be talked out, I cannot but marvel at the change our militancy so quickly brought about. Mr. McKenna's speech was in itself a token of the complete surrender of the government.

Of course the promise of the Home Secretary that subscribers to our funds should, if possible, be held legally responsible for damage done to private property by the Suffragettes, was never meant to be adhered to. It was, in fact, a perfectly absurd promise, and I think that very few Members of Parliament were deceived by it. Our subscribers can always remain anonymous if they choose, and if it should ever be possible to attack them for our deeds, they would naturally take refuge behind that privilege.

Our battles are practically over, we confidently believe. For the present at least our arms are grounded, for directly the threat of foreign war descended on our nation we declared a complete truce from militancy. What will come out of this European war—so terrible in its effects on the women who had no voice in averting it—so baneful in the suffering it must necessarily bring on innocent children—no human being can calculate. But one thing is reasonably certain, and that is that the Cabinet changes which will necessarily result from warfare will make future militancy on the part of women unnecessary. No future government will repeat the mistakes and the brutality of the Asquith Ministry. None will be willing to undertake the impossible task of crushing or even delaying the march of women towards their rightful heritage of political liberty and social and industrial freedom.

What Forcible Feeding Means
By Frank Moxon.

In speaking on this serious question of Forcible Feeding I shall avoid anything which might in any way be regarded as of a sentimental nature. It is my wish to present to you a perfectly frank and full account of the medical aspect of this treatment. I feel that this is a very great responsibility for me to undertake, as it is a serious indictment, in my opinion, of my profession. It is my resolve, however, no matter what the consequences be, to protest with all my power, against the hideous torture that is going on in His Majesty's prisons, under the name of medical treatment.

Forcible feeding was first carried out on Suffragist prisoners in Winson Green Gaol, Birmingham, in October of the year 1909, at the time when the present Lord Gladstone was Home Secretary. It was then that Mr. Mansell Moullin, the eminent consulting surgeon to the London Hospital, came forward and expressed his disapproval by writing a letter to the *Times*. And I should like here to express my sincere gratitude for his fearless and outspoken criticism of this grave subject. It is one of the few bright spots to illuminate the otherwise disgraceful apathy and silence of the medical profession.

In October of this same year, Dr. Flora Murray organised and presented to Mr. Asquith a memorial signed by 117 doctors, protesting against the forcible feeding of prisoners. Since that time two further petitions have been presented, the one in June 1912, signed by 116 doctors, and the other in December 1913, signed by 226. Innumerable protest meetings have been held. The last large one, organised by the clergy, was held in the Queen's Hall, at the end of last year, when the Bishop of Kensington presided, and was supported by four other bishops and over 500 clergy of different denominations. Deputations by the score, formed of all classes of people, have approached the premier and the Home Secretary on this subject.

A debate was held in the House of Commons on March 18 of last year, when the large majority of the members expressed their abhorrence and strong disapproval of what was variously described as a disgusting, dangerous, degrading, and most objectionable operation. Both the medical and lay press, despite a shameful censorship, have, during these last four and a half years, been compelled to publish countless letters and articles of protest.

Two well-known journalists, Mr. Brailsford and Mr. Nevinson, severed their connection with one of the leading Liberal papers, on account of their disapproval of the support given to forcible feeding.

The Cat and Mouse Act was passed, and became law in April of last year, for the declared purpose of enabling Mr. McKenna to get rid of the necessity for forcible feeding, which he himself described on April 2, 1913, as "a most objectionable practice." Mr. McKenna it is true, on being pressed, admitted that he did not intend to give up the practice of forcible feeding altogether. But, despite his statement on this matter, no one if they have read the debate, can have any doubt that the House voted for this bill in the firm belief that it would in effect mean the end of forcible feeding. In fact, Mr. McKenna himself said that he thought that that would be the result.

It would not I think be out of place here briefly to discuss the ethics and customs of the medical profession. An article in the *British Medical Journal* for May 4, 1913, entitled, "The Hippocratic Oath," gives a very good idea of the ethics of the profession, as supposed to have been laid down by the celebrated Greek physician, Hippocrates:

> The first grand characteristic of Hippocratic medicine is the high conception of the duties and status of the physician.

This oath reads:

> I will follow that system of regimen which according to my ability and judgment I consider for the benefit of my patients, and abstain from whatever is deleterious and mischievous. I will give no deadly medicine to anyone if asked, nor suggest any such counsel. Into whatever houses I enter, I will go into them for the benefit of the sick, and will abstain from every voluntary act of mischief and corruption, and further, from the seduction of females or males, of freemen or slaves.

The following extract of Ruskin's views on the medical profession I also obtained from the *British Medical Journal*:

> Whatever his science, we would shrink from him in horror if we found him regard his patients merely as subjects to experiment on, much more if we found that receiving bribes from persons interested in their deaths, he was using his best skill to give poison in the mask of medicine.

It is asserted by some that medical etiquette demands that criticism levelled against the conduct of professional brethren should not be conducted in public, or in the lay press; that prison doctors by reason of their position as government officials, are prevented from entering into a discussion of the truth or falsity of any allegations against their professional brethren. I consider that in a grave matter such as the forcible feeding of sane and resisting prisoners, when one has strong reason to believe, despite ministerial statements to the contrary, that strong pressure is brought to bear on the prison doctors in order to induce them to carry out a procedure for the purpose of compelling prisoners to serve their sentences, that then it is not only permissible, but an obvious duty to protest against what I can only call a prostitution of the profession.

It becomes all the more necessary to appeal to the general public when the leading officials of the medical profession are so blinded in their misplaced anxiety for the maintenance of the law, as to forget the real duties of their calling, as so well defined in the aforementioned "Hippocratic Oath," or, again, when the medical press, like the lay press, does everything to discourage an open discussion. Even if it were true that prison doctors are prevented by their position from publicly defending themselves they are still by no means in such an isolated or difficult position as a general practitioner would be. And this for at least two reasons: first, because of their salaried position they are independent of public opinion, in so far as the earning of their living goes; and secondly, because they have the whole influence of the Home Office, Cabinet, Parliament, and Party Press, together with all the office and title-seeking satellites at their back.

This latter fact was well shown in the case of Lady Constance Lytton, to which I shall refer at a later period. Further, to mention but two cases: a late medical officer of the Birmingham Prison, Dr. Helby, did make a public statement in reference to the forcible feeding of Mary Leigh, and more lately Dr. Devon, one of the Prison Commissioners, defended his conduct of these cases in a public lecture.

An editorial in the *British Medical Journal* stated:

> The prison doctors are faced with a divided duty, that which they owe to their patients, and that which they owe to their official superiors, and that the Home Office has no right to place them in this cruel dilemma.

Now if these words imply anything, they imply an admission that the prison doctors are persisting with an operation, which if their patients were not also prisoners, they would not hesitate to desist from.

In the statutory rules and orders for medical officers of local convict and general prisons, there is nothing which can he construed in any way to suggest that a prison doctor must adopt or carry out any treatment which he as a medical man does not in his own discretion think advisable, or according to strict medical custom. He is not a subordinate officer, and only has to obey the governor in so far that he must conform to the general rules and regulations of the prison, which also apply to the governor himself, as laid down in the Prison act of 1865. On the other hand, the governor cannot have any punishments carried out on the prisoners, *e.g.* flogging, solitary confinement, hard labour, etc., unless and until the medical officer certifies those prisoners as fit to undergo it; nor may he refuse to allow a prisoner even tobacco or wine if the doctor thinks them necessary.

Mr. McKenna has endeavoured to show that according to the ruling of the late Lord Chief Justice, in the case of Leigh v. Gladstone, the prison doctor is compelled to forcibly feed prisoners. This is not the case The ruling referred to was as follows:

> He should rule as a matter of law, that it was the duty of the prison officials to preserve the health of the prisoners, and *a fortiori* to preserve their lives, and he would therefore ask the jury whether the means adopted were proper for this purpose.

"The means adopted" referred to the forcible feeding of Mrs. Leigh, an action having been brought by the latter, claiming damages for assault against the Home Secretary, governor and prison doctor for carrying out this operation by force. The jury certainly gave their verdict for the prison officials, but I humbly submit that no lay jury is in the position, as regards medical knowledge, to rule as to whether a certain medical treatment is either right or satisfactory. They certainly are not qualified to lay it down that doctors *must forcibly feed any* patient. It is entirely a matter for the doctor to decide according to each individual case.

The Lord Chief Justice also said in his summing up that:

> It was said that the treatment had failed. That had nothing to do with the case; for there was evidence that it (forcible feeding) had been successfully continued for two and a half years, and they had heard that two other ladies had completed their full sentence, although fed by force.

Now this is not a full and fair presentation of facts: as I shall refer to later on, I also have known of a lunatic that was forcibly fed for two or more years, but that does not prove that it is, therefore, right or possible to successfully forcibly feed a sane and resisting person. As for the reference to cases that had *completed* their sentences although forcibly fed, you will note that no mention is made of the length of the sentence, nor of the condition of health on release of those who had so been treated, and you must agree that these are both most important factors in considering the question as to whether forcible feeding is either useful or humane medical treatment.

It has been made much of that when a certain eminent surgeon was cross-examined in the abovementioned action in the High Court, he admitted that should a private patient decline to take food, thereby endangering life, he would not hesitate to order such a patient to be fed by forcible means. To do this surgeon full justice, it is necessary to first examine in detail the actual and full facts in regard to what is called forcible feeding. I shall go into this later on.

I do not think I can do better than now quote the following extracts, taken from a book published in 1912, entitled *The Criminal and the Community*, and written by the former Medical Officer of Glasgow Prison, Dr. Devon, who has since become one of His Majesty's Prison Commissioners:

> So far as the Act of Parliament is concerned the treatment of the sick lies wholly in his (the doctor's) discretion, and there is no power granted to any authority to interfere with or overturn his decision. The Act of Parliament refers the sick, not to the commissioner, but to the surgeon of the prison. If the patient requires treatment the medical officer may prescribe any regimen which he considers applicable to the case, and the governor has the instructions carried out. In certain physical disease resort to artificial feeding may be necessary, but prisoners suffering from these diseases are not fit for prison discipline,

and should be treated in a hospital outside. If the women (referring to the suffrage prisoners) required to be fed artificially, it by no means follows that it was a proper thing to do so in prison. It certainly was indiscreet, and it is difficult to see how, if it were justifiable to resort to this measure (forcible feeding) in order to save the life of a prisoner, it would be argued that a medical officer would not be equally justified in cutting off the injured or diseased arm of a prisoner, in spite of his protestations, in order to save his life. It is one thing to place the liberties of men, and another thing altogether to place their lives in the hands of officials. At no time will an honourable man do all that the law permits him to do, for his standard of conduct is higher than, and in advance of the law.

I only wish that the writer of these noble sentiments had stuck to them; for he is reported to have answered when asked if he thought he could keep Miss Ethel Moorhead in prison until the end of her sentence:

Frankly, no! but I will keep her until she is in such a condition that she will be unable to do anything.

To settle the question as to whether the prison medical officers have really any divided duty, as suggested by the editor of the *British Medical Journal* and others, I wrote on November 5 of last year (1913) to Mr. McKenna asking the following question:

Is it the duty of the prison doctor to obey the command of the prison officials or yourself in regard to medical treatment, *e.g.*, forcible feeding, if he (the doctor) considers it useless from a medical point of view?

He replied through Sir Edward Troup as follows:

The question whether any individual prisoner who refuses food should be artificially fed or allowed to continue to starve *is purely a medical one* for the medical officer of the prison in his discretion to decide. No 'commands' are given him upon this subject by the Secretary of State, or the prison authorities. If the medical officer thinks that continued voluntary starvation would be more beneficial, or less likely to cause death than forcible feeding, he is under no obligation to adopt the latter alternative.

You will, I think, agree then that this letter does in fact most explicitly state that the prison doctors have no divided duty; that the responsibility for the continuance of forcible feeding does, in fact, rest on their shoulders.

I have said that there is strong reason to suppose that ministerial pressure is brought to bear on the medical officers to carry out forcible feeding. If you read the debate on forcible feeding held on March 18, 1913, you will find in paragraph 886 that Mr. McKenna said:

> Without an amendment of the law as it now stands, *it is the duty* of the medical officer of a prison to feed a prisoner who starves, unless an attempt to feed such a prisoner is likely to be seriously injurious to the prisoner's health.

Again, in paragraph 887 he says:

> If the prisoner's health were normal it would be *the duty* of the medical officer, when they starved, to keep them alive by forcible feeding.

In paragraph 903, Mr. Ellis Griffiths said:

> As I understand, what Mr. McKenna said was, that if there were prisoners who abstained from food, and who could, according to medical advice, be safely forcibly fed, in those circumstances if he neglected to forcibly feed them and they died, he would be liable to be charged with manslaughter.

And further on he says:

> What Mr. McKenna said was, that if a prisoner died while being forcibly fed, the then Home Secretary would be liable.

On October 10, 1913, the Home Office issued a statement to the Press, in which were the following words:

> Instructions have been given to the prison authorities to take all proper precautions, *including, if necessary, artificial feeding,* to prevent prisoners from endangering their lives or health by this voluntary starvation.

You see that the Home Secretary's contention, or his version of the law is that if a prisoner is certified medically as fit to be forcibly fed, then the doctor would be guilty of manslaughter if he refused to carry it out, and the patient died. If on the other hand, the prisoner died as the result of forcible feeding, then he, the Home Secretary would be responsible. Sir A. Cripps, now a Law Lord, said in the House that:

> He believed that (Mr. McKenna's) notion that he is bound to have recourse to forcible feeding in those cases is absolutely without foundation.

Sir A. Cripps was most emphatic on this point. Now I say that a false ruling of the law is held over the doctor's head as a virtual threat; the government, and the law officers endeavour, for the sole purpose of upholding and maintaining the efficiency of the law, to make the doctors believe that not only is it their duty to forcibly feed prisoners who starve, but that they would be liable to punishment and dismissal if they refused to do it. The government and the law officers pursue this policy because they know that the alternative to torture is that the law would utterly break down before the just demands of the women. Now it perhaps does seem a difficulty to some that men like these prison doctors should be placed in such a position, but their duty is perfectly clear. They have nothing whatever to do with the government's difficulties. They are, or should be, solely concerned with the health of their patients, and I am perfectly convinced that if they would but remember that their patients are patients before they are prisoners, and that if they had not been encouraged in their wretched work by physicians to Royalty, they would not hesitate to admit that an operation which produces such disastrous results, and which so utterly fails in its expressed purpose, can only be considered as a torture.

As medical men, whether prison doctors or not, we must consider this serious question in its relationship to health. It is no part of our function to consider whether our patient is or is not guilty of an offence against the law, neither are we justified in using or suggesting any treatment which cannot be upheld or applied on medical grounds and medical grounds only. That is to say, it must be proved to be of use for the purpose of curing disease, preventing ill-health or alleviating pain. Ours is a noble profession and we must see to it that if the State calls for our aid, our independence in medical affairs is not invaded. We are the protectors of the body: it is our honourable lot to see that the vessel if marred or damaged is repaired, or at least made clean for the better protection and passage of the spirit.

It is perhaps not generally known that a prisoner is said to have no liberty, so that if the medical officer considers an operation necessary, he may carry it out without the permission of the patient, with this proviso: that if the operation be a serious one, he must first consult with another medical practitioner. It must be noted, however, that it is not stated whether that other medical practitioner is to be independent or not, of the Home Office.

I do not for a moment believe or suggest that advantage would be taken of this to carry out *any* operation merely for the whim or fancy of doing so, and in point of fact the Prisons are not equipped with the necessary instruments, wards, and nurses to enable the medical officers to carry out surgical operations efficiently. But at the same time we cannot forget that it has given them the power to carry out the operation of forcible feeding.

Now we have the authority of Dr. Devon, a Prison Commissioner, for saying that when a prisoner is reported sick or asks to see the doctor he is automatically freed from the ordinary rules, and that "where artificial feeding may be necessary, prisoners are not fit for prison discipline and should be treated in a hospital outside." Further, this same commissioner has said that:

> The specialist can perform no operation without the consent of the patient or his friends, even though he believe that operation is necessary for the saving of life.

Now these Suffrage Prisoners *are* reported sick, and *are* transferred to the prison hospital (which, as a matter of fact, is not a real hospital, for there are no fully trained hospital nurses in charge), and therefore, according to this Prison Commissioner, are automatically freed from the ordinary rules as applied to prisoners. Then in the name of all that is just how can it be considered right to perform an operation without the consent of the patient, even although that patient be in prison hospital? I do submit in all sincerity that it is an iniquities thing that a sane and conscious prisoner should be forced to undergo any operation against his will, and when you consider that in regard to this operation of forcible feeding as carried out in His Majesty's Prisons, an assault is made on the prisoner by the prison officials to enable the doctor to carry it out, it is then even more unpardonable.

In some cases it takes from four to eight wardresses and two or more doctors to accomplish this degrading and revolting procedure. I am quite prepared to agree that the medical officer would be guilty if they took no measures in an endeavour to prevent their patients dying from starvation. I am even prepared to admit that it was excusable, and perhaps natural at first, that artificial feeding should be tried as one of those measures. I cannot, however, agree that an assault may be made on a prisoner, and an operation carried out which practically in every case proves useless, and only makes that prisoner's condition more serious, and suffering immeasurably greater.

There seems to be much misunderstanding as to what is the true definition of forcible feeding, for the terms forcible feeding, and artificial feeding, are frequently used in a synonymous sense. The Home Secretary is ashamed of, and fights shy of the word "forcible "preferring whenever possible to use the nicer sounding word "artificial." The Bishops, too, prefer to speak of artificial feeding.

There are various means of carrying out (what would be rightly called) artificial feeding. They are (1) By a feeding cup; (2) By means of a spoon or bottle, as with a baby; (3) By a rubber tube with a funnel attached, the tube being passed through the nose; (4) By a larger rubber tube, with funnel attached, passed through the mouth; (5) By means of enemata. By forcible feeding we mean any of the above procedures, when in addition the patient actively resists their being carried out, thereby necessitating the use of attendants to overcome struggling, and a gag to force open the mouth.

Artificial feeding is a comparatively easy operation in skilled hands. It may be required when a patient is too ill to eat, or swallow, or when as the result of injury or of disease of the mouth or gullet, the power of swallowing is either difficult or impossible. I knew and used to feed an old demented man in an asylum. He had been fed by means of a tube passed through the mouth into the stomach for several years. He was unable to swallow because as the result of an attempt at suicide, he had severed his gullet. But then he offered no resistance; in fact, he used to welcome the approach of the doctors at the hour of feeding.

Other cases I have known of in hospitals, where as I have said, the patient is too ill, but both willing and anxious to have food administered in this way. You will remember that both Mr. Masterman and Mr. McKenna stated in the House, that forcible feeding was an ordinary medical procedure as frequently carried out in our hospitals. We will suppose it was ignorance on their part. It certainly was not true. On the other hand, forcible feeding is carried out in lunatic asylums; both the maniac, and the melancholic may have to be so fed, but the resistance here, though it may be sometimes violent in the case of the maniac, is nevertheless *purposeless* and variable.

Peterson says that:

It is only in rare instances that feeding is not effected in some other way, before the use of the tube becomes imperative.

That forcible feeding as carried out on the Suffragist prisoners is something different to that in asylums is I think very clearly shown by a letter dated October 12, 1912, in the *British Medical Journal*, written by a physician to the Bethlehem Royal Hospital for the insane. He said that:

> There be something wrong if so many have to be released, more than 2,000 instances of tube feeding every year take place in the Bethlehem Hospital without any untoward symptoms.

I would suggest that when this physician speaks of 2,000 instances a year, that "instances" does not mean separate cases. It means that several patients were forcibly fed, the number of operations collectively totalling 2,000. Other doctors with experience of forcible feeding in asylums have written in a similar strain. Dr. Charles Mercier, an eminent mental specialist, said in a recent letter to *The Times* that "everyone agrees that the measures hitherto adopted are futile." I presume that he will agree that forcible feeding is here included. He suggests that:

> The authorities are mistaken in supposing there would be any considerable outcry if any of the criminals in prison were allowed to die.

I ask what is this callous suggestion but an admission that forcible feeding in his opinion, is a failure, and if it is a failure, what is it but a torture? I consider that this is a great admission for one whom I should not be surprised to hear, was the "medical expert who had very wide experience of forcible feeding in lunatic asylums" to whom Mr. McKenna referred in paragraph 894 of the Parliamentary Debates for March 18, 1913. Apparently these mental experts cannot grasp the difference between insane people with their purposeless and variable resistance to the taking of food, and sane people such as these noble and heroic women, whose resistance is a matter of conscience and principle, and is persisted in to the end, women who are imbued with a deep moral and unbending spirit and are prepared to face death in fighting for a cause which they hold as dear as life itself. That even these mental experts have not much faith in their pet hobby, is shown in a book on mental diseases written by Dr. Clouston, for he gives as unfavourable indications in the prognosis of melancholia and mania, "the persistent refusal of food, requiring forcible feeding."

The dangers and effects of forcible feeding have been greatly minimised, but here again the deductions have been mostly drawn from the results of artificial feeding, as I have described it, and from the forcible feeding of lunatics. That there are dangers and very serious effects I shall show by first quoting from authorities on this subject, and secondly by detailing some of the actual fatalities that have happened as a direct result of the forcible feeding of Suffragist Prisoners. In Quain's *Dictionary of Medicine* we are told that:

> If a patient is shouting during the passage of the tube, it readily goes into the mouth or larynx.
>
> Nasal feeding if long continued may lead to ulceration of the mucous membranes of the nose.
>
> The jaw may be dislocated or fractured if force is used to open the mouth too rapidly against the powerful muscles of the jaw.
>
> That a patient with a small pharynx may become very cyanosed during the feeding (that is mouth-feeding) and that regurgitation can be easily effected by the patient.
>
> If a patient vomits fluids into the mouth by the side of the tube, food may be drawn into the air passages and asphyxia result.

In an Epitome of mental diseases by James Shaw, we are told that:

> By the nasal method an alarming amount of dyspnoea, discomfort and cyanosis is produced even when the tube has not passed into the larynx.

In a book entitled *Mind and its Disorders*, we read:

> If the patient regurgitates gastric contents by the side of the tube into the pharynx, the tube and gag must at once be withdrawn for it is impossible for him to swallow the fluid under such circumstances and the only other way of disposing of it is to inhale it.

Professor Oppenheim of Berlin says:

> We cannot be too emphatic in advising avoidance of forced feeding. Some of the worst cases of neurasthenia which I have seen have developed as the direct result.

Sir Richard Douglas Powell, late President of the Medical Society, who, nevertheless, supported the forcible feeding of Suffragist Prisoners, stated that:

Forcible feeding was not wholly free from possibilities of accident with those who resist.

Heart trouble, indigestion, and insanity, to mention but a few are some other results of this abominable treatment, and it must be remembered that pain and suffering, by their influence on nutritional processes tend directly to prevent the return of tissues and organs to their normal state.

The first case I shall refer to is that of Miss Farmer who was fed in Winson Green Prison on June 23, 1909, after fasting for 36 hours. Miss Farmer stated on oath that she was fed through the nose, and *did not struggle or make any resistance.*

> The food, however, did not seem to pass into my stomach, but rose in my throat, choking me so that I coughed and spluttered all the time. I was in great stress and torment. When the tube was withdrawn I was violently sick, and for a long time afterwards coughed uncontrollably at intervals, making a very extraordinary whistling, screaming, crowing sort of sound, and bringing back quantities of the fluid with which I had been fed. The medical officer in the evening said, 'Well, I will not feed you tonight.' I was unable to lie down or sleep that night, owing to the pain in my chest and side, and shortness of breath. The next day the governor told me I was to be released. I arrived at my mother's home in Wales in the afternoon of that day. A doctor was at once called in, and I was found to have a high temperature, and to be suffering from pneumonia and pleurisy. (Publicly sworn to on February 19, 1914, at Richmond, Surrey.)

A second case of the inhalation of food into the lungs is that of Miss Lilian Lenton. I use the term "inhale" because of the technical quibble of the Home Office. For when it was stated that food was forced into Miss Lenton's lungs, the Home Office, while being in the position to deny that food was "forced in" were not able and, in fact, did not deny that food had got into the air passages. According to the prison medical officers, as stated in a White Paper ordered to be printed by the House of Commons on this case, we are told that:

> The patient was forcibly fed on a Sunday morning at about 11 a.m. by a nasal tube, after abstinence from food for three days. . . . .about an ounce of food was regurgitated at the conclu-

sion of the feeding, and the tube was withdrawn at once. . . . at about 1.45 p.m., we (the doctors) were called in and found her in a collapsed condition, and came to the conclusion that her life was in imminent danger. . . . I (the doctor) came to the conclusion that she was suffering from pleurisy which *may* have been present before. She was removed from the prison about six o'clock.

To complete what I consider as the self-convicting evidence of the prison officials in this case, I must add that Miss Lenton's solicitor had an interview with her on the day previous to her being forcibly fed, and stated that he found her in good spirits and normal health.

A third case of a similar kind is that of Miss Ethel Moorhead, who was forcibly fed in Edinburgh in the early part of this year. Describing the operation Miss Moorhead states that:

When the tube was rammed down my nostril and into the stomach I convulsively choked and coughed until it was over. I had an attack of coughing immediately afterwards. I continued coughing, and almost immediately began to feel pain in my side, and had difficulty in breathing. The pain in my side grew rapidly Worse, also the difficulty in breathing. Two nurses sat up with me, and the priest was sent for. Next morning I was examined by the doctors and released.

Miss Moorhead's medical attendant certified her as suffering on release, from double pneumonia.

A male suffragist prisoner who was forcibly fed was driven out of his mind and removed to an asylum by the prison authorities. There was no family history of insanity. It fortunately happened to be an extremely good family history on the side of both the father and the mother. I say fortunately, because Mr. McKenna suggested that it might be bad. It was a pure case of the terrible things that may happen.

Anyone who has read Lady Constance Lytton's book, *Prison and Prisoners*, will not doubt that the paralysis from which she is now suffering is the direct result of the tortures which she so heroically went through when being forcibly fed as Jane Warton. The denials of the Home Office in connection with the medical treatment under which Lady Constance Lytton suffered are not worth the paper on which they are written. The statements that "the doctor gave her a slap on the cheek" and did not examine her heart before forcibly feeding her, are damning evidence for our contention that this is not medical treatment but torture pure and simple.

I feel that the accusation that Lady Constance Lytton's statements are not true ought to be stoutly and strenuously denied. It seems to be a commonly accepted state of affairs that when the Home Office finds itself in the wrong, through the misbehaviour or folly maybe of one of its officials, the difficulty is got over by simply telling the public either that the charges have no foundation, or that the individual who accuses is a liar. When will the public rise to the fact that officialdom will never admit itself in the wrong, for an admission of wrong would weaken discipline, so it is said. Therefore, the stronger and more vehement the denial of any accusation which has been made against the government or its officials, the more likely is that accusation to be true.

I will here, therefore, give a more full account of the treatment that the Home Office officials meted out to Lady Constance Lytton. In regard to the first charge, namely, that the doctor slapped her face, I think it best to quote the actual words as related in the book, *Prison and Prisoners:*

> I choked the moment it (the tube) touched my throat until it had got down. Then the food was poured in very quickly; it made me sick a few seconds after it was down, and the action of the sickness made my body and legs double up, but the wardresses instantly pressed back my head and the doctor leant on my knees. The horror of it was more than I can describe. I was sick over the doctor and wardresses, and it seemed a long time before they took the tube out.
>
> As the doctor left he gave me a slap on the cheek, not violently, but as it were, to express his contemptuous disapproval, and he seemed to take it for granted that my distress was assumed.

Anyone who reads the obviously true and uncoloured account of Lady Constance Lytton's experiences in prison, will, I think, know whether to believe her or the Home Office, when matters relating to those experiences are in dispute.

As for the second charge, namely, about the examination of the heart, Lord Lytton, a brother, wrote to the *Times* on March 30, 1910, stating among other things, that no account of denial can get over the following facts:—

> (1) Lady C. Lytton, when imprisoned in Newcastle after refusing to answer the medical questions put to her, and adopting

the hunger strike, received a careful and thorough medical examination, which disclosed symptoms of "serious heart disease," and on these grounds she was released as unfit to submit to forcible feeding.

(2) Three months later "Jane Warton" when imprisoned at Liverpool, also refused to answer medical questions, or to take prison food. On this occasion she was entered in the prison books as having refused medical examination, and was forcibly fed eight times. Such medical examination as took place during the forcible feeding failed, according to the medical officer's report, to disclose any symptoms of heart disease, and she was eventually released on the grounds of loss of weight and general physical weakness.

Now Sir Edward Troup, in a letter in answer to these charges, stated that an enquiry had been made by the Prison Commissioners into the truth of the charges brought by Lady Constance Lytton against the officers of the prison, and as a result of that enquiry he (Home Secretary) is satisfied that those charges are without foundation, and that there is no justification for Lady Constance Lytton's account of her experience whilst she was in prison; and, further, "that the statement that the medical officer was guilty of slapping his patient's face is *utterly devoid of truth, and can only be the outcome of the imagination.*"

Now I prefer to believe that Lady Constance Lytton was speaking the truth, and that her statements are accurate in every detail, and no denials on the part of the Home Office will alter my conviction that this is so.

This case is an excellent example of the easy manner in which the Home Office so readily dismisses any statements against its officials as being untruthful.

Before I leave this case I wish to draw your attention to several important facts as related by Lady Constance Lytton in regard to the actual procedure of forcible feeding.

(1) She states that "she was sick whilst the throat-tube was in the stomach, and that she was sick over the doctor, etc., and it seemed a long time before the tube was withdrawn."

Now vomiting whilst the tube is in position in the gullet is extremely dangerous, because the food which is regurgitated by the side of the tube cannot escape, and is almost bound to be drawn into the windpipe and lungs when a breath is taken (a danger which, as I have already pointed out, actually happened in the cases of Miss Fanner, Miss Ethel Moorhead, and Miss Lilian Lenton). Here, then, the tube should have been withdrawn *immediately* on vomiting taking place, and not some time after.

(2) "The doctor lent on my knees."

This, too, is a dangerous procedure, and not permissible, according to medical experts, on the question of forcible feeding.

(3) "The doctor gave me a slap on the cheek."

It is hardly necessary to voice one's disgust at such a cowardly and ungentlemanly act.

Dr. Price, of Walton, who wrote the report of Lady Constance Lytton's case to the Home Office, stated in conversation with her sister that "he had been obliged to feed her through the mouth up to the date of her release"; he further stated that, "unlike some other Suffragettes, she had shown no violence beyond refusing to take her food, but that in all his experience he had never seen such a bad case of forcible feeding."

When asked what he meant by a "bad case," he said: "She was practically asphyxiated every time." This same doctor also stated that Lady Constance Lytton lost weight at the rate of 2 lbs. a day, and that consequently he had been obliged to advise her being released.

The following facts as given by this prison doctor should be noted:—

(1) Forcible feeding was carried out through the mouth, which is considered by most as more dangerous than through the nose.

(2) No resistance was offered by the patient.

(3) The patient was practically asphyxiated every time.

(4) Despite forcible feeding, the patient lost weight.

(5) That despite forcible feeding, the patient (who did not serve her sentence) had to be released.

Many cases of death as the result of forcible feeding are recorded, and there is little doubt that many more never reach the public ear. In the past year (1913) two cases were recorded in the press: the one, a man named Ed. J. Taunton, who died at the Cotton Hill Hospital for Mental Diseases, Stafford, the jury found that death was due to syncope accelerated by the forcible feeding; the other, a man named James McGavigan, who died in the Letterkenny Asylum, Co. Donegal, half an hour after being forcibly fed, and in this case it is recorded that the man made no resistance to the operation.

I could fill a book with the grave results of this terrible and vile torture, but time does not permit me to give any more here.

As proof that forcible feeding is not only a dangerous but a useless procedure, I will remind you of the fact that out of 160 cases of forcible feeding, involving about 130 different individuals, up to October of last year, (1914), 78 were released before the expiry of their sentences, and the remainder were cases which survived forcible feeding only by the fact of their short sentences.

Mr. McKenna himself had to admit that out of a total of 60 suffragist prisoners, 12 *per cent*, had to be released despite forcible feeding, and you must here bear in mind the fact that these numbers only covered a period of less than three months at the beginning of last year, 1913, and that 23 prisoners out of the total of 66, were still in prison at the time of the Home Secretary's statement, many of whom were later on released. Another factor also applies to these 66 prisoners, namely, that many of them were only sentenced for a few days, so that either no necessity arose for forcible feeding, or at the most it was only necessary to carry it out for two or three days. When you consider all these important items, you will readily understand that 12 *per cent*, of failures was, in fact, a fictitious figure.

We do indeed live in a cruel and barbarous world, a world which is too often ready, nay, eager to abuse and smite those with whom it does not agree, and so it is with this question of forcible feeding. Our opponents indignantly cry out that these women are common criminals, fanatics, or an unsexed people, and having dubbed them thus, they are content to say, "Well, even if forcible feeding is a torture, it is their own fault that they suffer, for they have only to give up their resistance, and all will be well." Yes, so can anyone who is a rebel. So could the martyrs of ages past; so could Christ have avoided crucifixion. It only means the giving up of one's principles.

Try and consider the agony of mind when these women are thrown into the prison cells to await their time for forcible feeding. Think what endurance is necessary to refuse food, knowing full well that your turn for forcible feeding is drawing closer and closer. Try and imagine what it must be to hear the screams and groans of a fellow-sufferer, growing louder and louder as she resists the efforts of the wardresses to hold her down, and then as the groans become weaker and weaker, to realise that at last the resistance has been overcome, and the doctors have done their work, and then to realise that the footsteps of wardresses and doctors were approaching your cell, and that your time had come. Try and imagine the mental agony as the doctor tells you that "unless food is taken in the proper way, very stern measures will be adopted, and you will be kept until you are a skeleton and a nervous and mental wreck, and then you will be sent to an institution where they look after mental wrecks." I say that this is torture worthy of the time of the Inquisition.

To crown, as it were, the iniquities of the Home Office, it would seem that in addition to "mechanical restraint," which means the holding and strapping down of violent patients, "chemical restraint" is now being resorted to, to enable the doctors to carry out the operation of forcible feeding more easily.

Some six or seven weeks since I saw Miss Phyllis Brady, and recorded my agreement with Dr. Flora Murray's suspicion that drugs had been administered to her while in prison.

As a result of these steps an independent pathological laborator reported that bromine was found in the excretions.

Mr. McKenna, in the House of Commons on Thursday, March 19, gave the following reply in answer to a question on the subject:

> The statements referred to were entirely without foundation. Neither bromide nor any other hypnotic drug had been given to Miss Brady in Holloway.

Since this Miss Brady has again been in Holloway Prison, and on her release Dr. Flora Murray took steps to substantiate her belief that drugs had been administered.

Moreover, it is now reported that by the same clinical means it has been proved that bromides have also been administered to two other prisoners, namely, Miss Mary Richardson and Miss Kitty Marion. The following is an extract from Dr. Murray's report:

> Her doctors are in a position to prove, by means of independent pathological reports, that five days after her release (Miss Richardson's) she was still excreting bromine.

I consider that this drugging is a further outrage on these noble women, and it cannot be too strongly pointed out how dangerous and deleterious a matter this drugging is for the health of these prisoners.

By this means their muscular power is weakened, and their senses dulled to such an extent, that resistance to the operation of forcible feeding is reduced to a most dangerous point. The paralysing effect that these drugs have on the sensibility of the throat, makes vomiting an extremely dangerous thing, for food may be more easily inhaled into the lungs, if regurgitated, and at the same time it would be more difficult to expel the food from the air passages on account of the diminishment of the reflex act of coughing.

Digestion is also seriously interfered with, and the heart and respiration depressed. The mind is dulled, and this latter fact, coupled with the general lowering of nutrition and muscular weakness, is likely to have a serious and permanent effect on the nervous and mental state of the patient.

In closing, I must also remind you of a further serious matter in connection with the forcible feeding of Miss Mary Richardson. Some time since Miss Richardson was released suffering from appendicitis, she was, however, again arrested, and despite the warning of her medical advisers, that the appendix trouble was still existent, forcible feeding and drugging was again resorted to until in the end the prison doctors had again to advise her release, on the grounds that an operation for appendicitis was urgently necessary; it is to be noted that the Home Office have released her for only six weeks.

Now the real facts are that Mr. McKenna has released Miss Richardson not only to have an operation, but because the prison doctors have advised him that to forcibly feed her any longer would mean her death. If this is not so, why was the operation for appendicitis advised after and not before forcible feeding was carried out, for surely a serious abdominal operation would stand a better chance of success before rather than after four weeks of forcible feeding and drugging.

The authorities have preferred first, to bring Miss Mary Richardson to the point of death, and then to release her on the pretext that it is only because an operation for appendix trouble is required.

The facts I have given you on this question of forcible feeding should leave no doubt in your minds that this operation can only be considered as a torture pure and simple, and this being so, it is your and my duty to stop at nothing which may be thought necessary to put an end to it.

Why We are Militant
Delivered by Mrs. Pankhurst in New York City, October 21, 1913

I know that in your minds there are questions like these; you are saying:

Woman Suffrage is sure to come; the emancipation of humanity is an evolutionary process, and how is it the women of Great Britain, instead of trusting to that evolution, instead of educating the masses of people of their country, instead of educating their own sex to prepare them for citizenship, how is it that those militant women in England are using violence and upsetting the business arrangements of their country in their undue impatience to attain their end?

Well, ladies and gentlemen, let me try to explain to you the situation.

Although you have a great deal of democracy, a great deal of representative government there, England is the most conservative country on earth; why, your forefathers found that out a great many years ago. If you had parsed your life in England as I have, you would know that there are certain word which certainly, during the last two generations, certainly until about ten years ago, aroused a feeling of horror and fear in the minds of the mass of the people. The word revolution, for instance, was identified in England, with all kind of horrible ideas. The idea of change, the idea of unsettling the established order of things.

Now, in America it is the proud boast of some of the most conservative men and women that I have met that they are descended from the heroes of the revolution. You have an organisation, I believe, called the Daughters of the Revolution, whose members put an interpretation upon the word revolution which is quite different from the interpretation given to it in Great Britain. Perhaps that will help, you to realise how extremely difficult it is in Great Britain to get anything done. All my life I have heard people talking in advocacy of reforms which it was self-evident would be for the good of the people, and yet it has all ended in talk; they are still talking about these reforms, and unless something happens of a volcanic nature they will go on talking about them until the end of time. Nothing ever has been got out of the British Parliament without something very nearly approaching a revolution. You need something dynamic in order to force legislation through the House of Commons; in fact, the whole machinery of government in England may almost be said to be an elaborate arrangement for not doing anything.

Now, you may say in answer to that, that there been some social legislation in England in it years.

The extensions of the franchise to the men of my country have been preceded by very great violence, by something like a revolution, by something like civil war. In 1832, you know we were on the edge of a civil war and on the edge revolution, and it was at the point of the sword—no, not at the point of the sword—it was after the practice of arson on so large a scale that half the city of Bristol was burned down in a single night, it was because more and greater violence and arson were feared that the Reform Bill of 1832 was allowed to pass into law.

In 1867, John Bright urged the people of London to crowd the approaches to the Houses bf Parliament in order to show their determination, and he said that if they did that no Parliament, however obdurate, could resist their just demands. Rioting went on all over the country, and as the result of that rioting, as the result of that unrest, which resulted in the pulling down of the Hyde Park railings, as a result of the fear of more rioting and violence that the Reform Act of 1867 was put upon the statute books.

In 1884 came the turn of the agricultural labourer; Joseph Chamberlain, who afterwards became a very conservative person and a radical, threatened that, unless the vote was given to the agricultural labourer, he would march 100,000 men from Birmingham to know the reason why, rioting was threatened and feared, and so the agricultural labourers got the vote.

Meanwhile, during the '80s, women, like men, were asking for the franchise. Appeals, larger and more numerous than for any other reform, were presented in support of Woman Suffrage. Meetings of the great corporations, great town councils, and city councils, parsed resolutions asking that women should have the vote. More meetings were held, and larger, for Woman Suffrage than were held for votes for men, and yet the women, did not get it. Men got the vote because they were and would be violent. The women did not get it because they were constitutional and law-abiding. Why, isn't it evident to everyone that, people who are patient where government is concerned may go on being patient. Why should anyone trouble to help them? I take to myself some shame that through all those years, at any rate from the early '80's, when I first came into the Suffrage movement, I did not learn my political lessons.

I believed, as many women still in England believe, that women could get their way in some mysterious manner, by purely woman's methods. We have been so accustomed, we women, to accept one standard for men and another standard for women, that we have even applied that variation of standard to the injury of our political welfare.

In the twentieth century women, having had better opportunities of education, and having had some training in politics, having in political life come so near to the superior being as to see that he was not altogether such a fount of wisdom as we had supposed, that he had his human weaknesses as we had, the twentieth century women began to say to themselves:

> Is it not time, since our methods have failed and the men's have succeeded, that we should take a leaf out of their political book?'

We were led to that conclusion, we older women, by the advice of the young—you know there is a French proverb which says, "*If youth knew; if age could*," but I think that we ought to reverse it, and when you can bring together youth and age, as we have done, and get them to adopt the same methods and take the same point of view, then you are on the high road to success.

Well, we in Great Britain, on the eve of the General Election of 1905, a mere handful of us—why, you could almost count us on the fingers of both hands—set out on the wonderful adventure of forcing the greatest government of modern times to give the women the vote. Only a few in number; we were not strong in influence, and we had hardly any money, and yet we quite gaily made our little banners with the words "Votes for Women" upon them, and we set out to win the enfranchisement of the women of our country.

The Suffrage movement was almost dead. The women had lost

heart. You could not get a Suffrage meeting that was attended by members of the general public. We used to have about 24 adherents in the front row. We. carried our resolutions and heard no more about them.

Two women changed that in a twinkling of an eye at a great Liberal demonstration in Manchester, where a Liberal leader. Sir Edward Grey, was explaining the programme to be carried out during the Liberals' next turn of office. The two women put the fateful question, "When are you going to give votes to women?" and refused to sit down until they had been answered. These two women were sent to gaol, and from that day to this the women's movement, both militant and constitutional, has never looked back. We had little more than one moribund society for Woman Suffrage in those days. Now we have about 46 societies for Woman Suffrage, composed both of men and women, and they are large in membership, they are rich in money, and their ranks are swelling every day that passes. That is how militancy has put back the clock of Woman Suffrage in Great Britain.

Now, some of you have said how wicked it is (the commissioners told me that on Saturday afternoon), how wicked it is to attack the property of private individuals who have done us no harm. Well, you know there is a proverb which says that *you cannot make omelettes without breaking eggs.* I wish we could.

I want to say here and now that the only justification for violence, the only justification for damage to property, the only justification for risk to the comfort of other human beings is the fact that you have tried all other available means and have failed to secure justice, and as a law-abiding person—and I am by nature a law-abiding person, as one hating violence, hating disorder—I want to say that from the moment we began our militant agitation to this day I have felt absolutely guiltless in this matter.

I tell you that in Great Britain there is no other way. We can show intolerable grievances. The Chancellor of the Exchequer, Mr. Lloyd George, who is no friend of the woman's movement, although a professed one, said a very true thing when speaking of the grievances of his own country, of Wales, He said:

> There comes a time in the life of human beings suffering from intolerable grievances when the only way to maintain their, self respect is to revolt against that injustice.

Well, I say, the time is long past when it became necessary for

Women to revolt in order to maintain their self respect in Great Britain. The women who are waging this war are women who would fight, if it . were only for the idea of liberty—if it were only that they might be free citizens of a free country—I myself would fight for that idea alone. But we have, in addition to this love of freedom, intolerable grievances to redress.

We do not feel the weight of those grievances in our persons. I think it is very true that people who are crushed by personal wrong are not the right people to fight for reforms. The people who can fight best are the people who have happy lives themselves, the fortunate ones. At any rate, in our revolution it is the happy women, the fortunate women, the women who have drawn prizes in the lucky bag of life, in the shape of good fathers, good husbands and good brothers, they are the women who are fighting this battle. They are fighting it for the sake of others more helpless than themselves, and it is of the grievances of those helpless ones that I want to say a few words tonight to make you understand the meaning of our militant campaign.

Those grievances are so pressing that, so far from it being a duty to be patient and to wait for evolution, in thinking of those grievances the idea of patience is intolerable, and we feel that patience is something akin to crime when our patience involves continued suffering on the part of the oppressed.

We are fighting to get the power to alter bad laws; but some people say to us:

> Go to the representatives in the House of Commons, point out to them that these laws are bad, and you will find them quite ready to alter them.

Ladies and gentlemen, there are women in my country who have spent long and useful lives trying to get reforms, and because of their voteless condition they are unable even to get the attention, to get the ear of Members of Parliament, much less are they able to secure those reforms.

Our marriage and divorce. laws are a disgrace to civilisation. I sometimes wonder, looking back from the serenity of past middle age, at the courage of women . I wonder that women have the courage to take upon themselves the responsibilities of marriage and motherhood when I see how little protection the law of my country affords them. I wonder that a woman will face the ordeal of childbirth with the knowledge that after she has risked her life to bring a child into the world she has absolutely no parental rights over the future of that child. Think what trust women have in men when a woman will marry a man, knowing, if she has knowledge of the law, that if that man is not all she in her love for him thinks him, that he may even bring a strange woman into the house, bring his mistress into the house to live with her, and she cannot get legal relief from such a marriage as that.

How often is women's trust misplaced, and yet how whole-hearted and how touching that trust must be when a woman, in order to get love and companionship will run such terrible risks in entering into marriage. Yet women have done it, and as we get to know more of life we militant Suffragists have nerved ourselves and forced ourselves to learn something of how other people live. As we get that knowledge we realise how political power, how political influence, which would enable us to get better laws, would make it possible for thousands upon thousands of unhappy women today to have lived happier lives.

Well, you may say the laws may be inadequate, the laws may be bad, but human nature, after all, is not much influenced by laws, and upon the whole people live fairly happy lives. Well, for those who are fortunate it is very comfortable to have that idea, but if you will really look at life as we find it in our centralised civilisation in Europe, you will find that after all the law is a great educator, and if men are brought up to think the law allows them to behave badly to those who should be nearest and dearest to them, the worst kind of man is very apt to take full advantage of all the laxity of the law.

What have we been hearing of so much during the last few years: It is very remarkable thing, ladies and gentlemen, that along with this woman's movement, along with this woman's revolt, you are having a great uncovering of social sores. We are having light let into dark places, whether it is in the United States or whether it is in the old countries of Europe, you find the social ills from which humanity suffers are very much the same. Every civilised country has been discussing how to deal with that most awful slavery, the white slave traffic.

When I was a very tiny child the great American people were divided into hostile sections on the question of whether it was right that one set of human beings of one colour should buy and sell human beings of another colour, and you have had a bloody war to settle that question. I tell you that throughout the civilised world today there is a slavery more awful than negro slavery in its worst form ever was. It is called the white slave traffic, but in awful traffic there are slaves of every shade of colour, and they are all of one sex.

Well, in my country we have been having legislation to deal with it. We have, had a White Slave Act, and under that Act of Parliament, in that Act of Parliament, they have put clauses that are called flogging clauses. Certain men are to be flogged if they are convicted and found guilty under that Act of Parliament, and the British House of Commons, composed of men of all shades of mottled colour, waxed highly eloquent on the need of flogging these so-called tigers of the human race, men engaged in the white slave traffic.

Well, we women looked on and we read their speeches, but in our hearts we said:

> Why don't they decide to go to the people for .whom the white slave traffic exists? What is the use of dealing with the emissaries, with the slave hunters, with the purveyors? Why don't they go to the very seat of the evil; why don't they attack the customers? If there was no demand there would be no traffic, because business does not exist if there is no demand for it?

And so we women said:

> It's no use, gentlemen, trying to put us off with sentimental legislation on the white slave traffic. We don't trust you to settle it; we want to have a hand in settling it ourselves, because we think we know how.

And we have a right to distrust that legislation. They passed the act very, very quickly; they put it on the statute books, and we have seen it in operation, and we know that the time of Parliament and the time of the nation was wasted on a piece of legislation which I fear was never intended to ha taken very seriously; something to keep the women quiet, something to lull us into a sense of security, something to make us believe that now, at least, the government were really grappling with the situation.

Well, and so we attacked this great evil. We said:

> How can we expect real legislation to deal with the white slave traffic on a small scale when the government of the country is the biggest white slave trading firm that we have got.

And it is true, because you know, although we have suppressed such regulation of vice in England, we have got it in full swing in the great dependencies that we own all over the world, and we have only to turn to India and look to every place where our army is stationed to find the government, which is in no way responsible to women, dealing, taking part in that awful trade, in absolute cold bloodedness where native women are concerned, all, forsooth, in the name of the health of the men of our forces.

Well, we have been speaking out, ladies and gentlemen; we have been saying to our nation and the, rulers of our nation:

> We will not have the health of one-half of the community, their pretended health, maintained at the expense of the degradation and sorrow and misery of the other half.

I want to ask you whether, in all the revolutions of the past, in your own revolt against , British rule, you had deeper or greater reasons for revolt than women have today?

Take the industrial side of the question: have men's wages for a hard day's work ever been so low and inadequate as are women's wages today? Have men ever had to suffer from the laws more injustice than women suffer? Is there a single reason which men have had for liberty that does not also apply to women?

Why, if you were talking to the men of any other nation you would not hesitate to reply in the affirmative. There is not a man in this meeting who has not felt sympathy with the uprising of the men of other lands when suffering from intolerable tyranny, when deprived of all representative rights. You are full of sympathy with men in Russia, You are full of sympathy with nations that rise against the domination of the Turk. You are full of sympathy with all struggling people striving for independence. How is it, then, that you have nothing but ridicule and contempt and reprobation for women who are fighting for exactly the same thing?

All my life I have tried to understand why it was that men who valued their citizenship as their dearest possession seemed to think citizenship ridiculous when it was to be applied to the women of their race. And I found an explanation, and it is the only one I can think of. it came tome when I was in a prison cell, remembering how I had seen men laugh at the idea of women going to prison. Why they would confess they could not bear a cell door to be shut upon themselves for .a single hour without asking to be let out. A thought came to me in my prison cell, and it was this: that to men women are not human beings like themselves. Some men think we are superhuman; they put us on pedestals; they revere us; they think we are too fine and too delicate to come down into the hurly-hurly of life. Other men think us sub-human; they think that we are a strange species unfortunately having to exist for the perpetuation of the race. They think that we are fit for drudgery, but that in some strange way our minds are not like theirs, our love for great things is not like theirs, and so we are a sort of sub-human species.

We are neither superhuman nor are we sub-human. We are just human beings like yourselves.

Our hearts burn within us when we read the great mottoes which celebrate the liberty of your country; when we go to France and we read the words, liberty, fraternity and equality, don't you think that we appreciate the meaning of. those words? And then when we wake to the knowledge that these things are not for us, they are only for our brothers, then there comes a sense of bitterness into the hearts of some women, and they say to themselves "Will men never; understand?" But so far as we in England are concerned, we have come to the conclusion that we are not going to leave men any illusions upon the question.

When we were patient, when we believed in argument and persuasion, they said:

> You don't really want it because if you did, you would do something unmistakable to show you were determined to have it.

And then when we did something unmistakeable they said:

> You are behaving so badly you show you are not fit for it.

Now, gentlemen, in your heart of hearts you do not believe that. You know perfectly well that there never was a thing worth, having that was not worth fighting for. You know perfectly well that if the situation were reversed, if you had no constitutional rights and we had all of them, if you had the duty of paying and obeying a: trying to look as pleasant as possible, and we were the proud citizens who could decide our fate and yours, because we knew what was good for you better than you knew for yourselves, you know perfectly well that you wouldn't stand it for a single day, and you would be perfectly justified in rebelling against such intolerable conditions.

Well, in Great Britain we have tried persuasion, we have tried the plan of showing (by going upon public bodies, where they allowed us to do work they hadn't much time to do themselves) that we were rather capable people. We did it in the hope that we should convince them and persuade them to do the right and proper thing. But we had all our labour for our pains, and now we are fighting for our rights, and we are growing stronger and better women in the process. We are getting more fit to use our rights because we have such difficulty in getting them.

And now may I say a word in answer to the people who criticise my coming to America

Always when human beings have been struggling for freedom they have looked to happier parts of the world for support and sympathy. In your hour of trouble you went to other peoples and asked them for help. It seems to me, looking into the past, into my recollections of history, that a great man named Benjamin Franklin went to France to ask the French people to help in the struggle for American independence. You didn't apologise for sending him, and I am sure he didn't apologise for going. There may have been people in France who said:

> Why does this pestilent, rebellious fellow come over trying to stir up people here in our peaceful country.

But, in the main, the people of France welcomed him. Their hearts thrilled at the idea of a brave and courageous struggle, and they sent money and they sent men to help to fight and win the independence of the American Republic.

Those who have been struggling for freedom' in other lands have come to you, and I can't help remembering that right through the struggle of the Irish people they sent lawbreakers to plead with you for help for lawbreakers in Ireland.

Yes, and like all political law breaking done by men the form their violence has taken has not been merely to break some shop windows or to set on fire the house of some rich plutocrat, but it has found its expression in the taking of human life, in the injury even of poor, dumb animals who could have no part in the matter. And yet you looked at that agitation in a large way. You said:

> In times of revolution and revolt you cannot curb the human spirit, you cannot bind men and women down to narrow rules of conduct which are proper. and right in times of peace.

And you sent your money and you sent help to cheer the Irish people in their struggle for greater freedom.

Why, then, should not I come to ask for help for British women? Whatever helps them is going to help women all over the world. It will be the hastening of your victory. It has not been necessary in the

United States for women to be militant in the sense that we are, and perhaps one of the reasons why it is not necessary and why it may never be necessary is that we are doing the militant work for you. And we are glad to do that work. We are proud to do, that work. If there are, any men who are fighters in this hall, any men who have taken part in warfare, I tell you, gentlemen, that amongst the other good things that you, consciously or unconsciously, have kept from women, you have kept the joy of battle.

We know the joy of battle. When, we have come out of the gates of Holloway at the point of death, battered, starved , forcibly fed as some of our women have been—their mouths forced open by iron gags—their bodies bruised, they have felt when the prison bars were broken and the doors have opened, even at the point of deaths they have felt the joy of battle and the exultation of victory.

People have said that women could never vote, never share in the government, because government rests upon force. We have proved that is not true. Government rests not upon force; government rests upon the consent of the governed; and the weakest woman, the very poorest woman, if she withholds her consent cannot be governed.

They sent me to prison, to penal servitude for three years. I came out of prison at the end of nine days, I broke my prison bars. Four times they took me back again; four times I burst the prison door open again. And I left England openly to come and visit America, with only three or four weeks of the three years' sentence of penal servitude served. Have we not proved, then, that they cannot govern human beings who without their consent?

And so we are glad that' we have had the fighting experience, we are glad to do all the fighting for all the women all over the world; and all that we ask of you is to back us up. We ask you to show that although, perhaps, you do not mean to fight as we do, that you understand the meaning of our fight; that you realise that we are women fighting for a great idea; that we wish the betterment of the human; race, and that we believe that, betterment is coming through the emancipation and uplifting of women.

Beware Suffragists
Cicely Hamilton

This is the cosy
Little home,
Whence no nice woman
Wants to roam.
She shuts the doors
And windows tight,
And never stirs
From morn to night.

This is the wife
All men would like
She never thinks
Nor rides a bike.

She cooks and cooks—
And all the while
She looks quite sweet,
Observe her smile!

These are the books
A wife should read
Of other books
She has no need.

Now turn your eyes
Another way.
A sadder picture
I'll display—
The female who
Is so depraved
She says she will not
Be enslaved.

Who thinks because
She earns her bread
By working with
Her hands or head,
She ought to have
Her little say
In making laws
She must obey.

Now here are some
Who want their rights
You see they all
Are perfect frights!
Their feet are huge,
Their stockings blue—
The Press says so:
It must be True.

(Much more like this
They seem to me—

But then reporters
Too can see.)

Here's one who's talking
To a crowd,
And talking to them
Very loud.
The crowd they jeer
And all make game;
She goes on talking
Just the same.

Then, bolder grown,
She waves her gamp
And strides along
With martial tramp;
She strides along
So very fast
That Palace Yard
She gains at last.

This man who runs
Is Jones, M.P.
He runs like mad,
As you can see.
Off flies his hat,
Out flies his coat —
He sees the woman
Who wants a vote.

But five policemen
Now have met
The ramping, tearing
Suffragette.
They do not faint,
Nor yet turn pale;
But grab and haul her
Off to jail.

Now in a cell
She sits and pines
And off thin skilly
Daily dines;
But still repeats,
As if by rote
"I want—I want—
I want a vote."

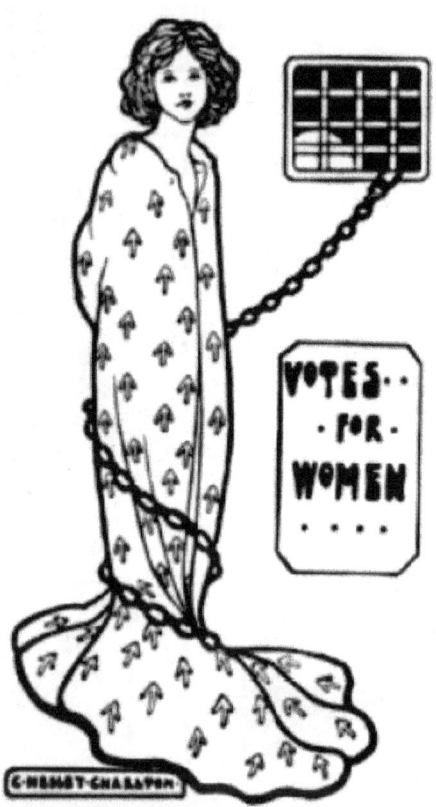

MORAL.

Take warning by
Her awful end.
And don't to poli-
Tics attend.
Don't earn your living—
If you can,
Have it earned for you
By a man.
Then sit at home
From morn till night,
And cook and cook
With all your might.

It may be slow—
But you can say,
"It's just as slow
In Holloway."

ALSO FROM LEONAUR
AVAILABLE IN SOFTCOVER OR HARDCOVER WITH DUST JACKET

A DIARY FROM DIXIE *by Mary Boykin Chesnut*—A Lady's Account of the Confederacy During the American Civil War

FOLLOWING THE DRUM *by Teresa Griffin Vielé*—A U. S. Infantry Officer's Wife on the Texas frontier in the Early 1850's

FOLLOWING THE GUIDON *by Elizabeth B. Custer*—The Experiences of General Custer's Wife with the U. S. 7th Cavalry.

LADIES OF LUCKNOW *by G. Harris & Adelaide Case*—The Experiences of Two British Women During the Indian Mutiny 1857. A Lady's Diary of the Siege of Lucknow by G. Harris, Day by Day at Lucknow by Adelaide Case

MARIE-LOUISE AND THE INVASION OF 1814 *by Imbert de Saint-Amand*—The Empress and the Fall of the First Empire

SAPPER DOROTHY *by Dorothy Lawrence*—The only English Woman Soldier in the Royal Engineers 51st Division, 79th Tunnelling Co. during the First World War

ARMY LETTERS FROM AN OFFICER'S WIFE 1871-1888 *by Frances M. A. Roe*—Experiences On the Western Frontier With the United States Army

NAPOLEON'S LETTERS TO JOSEPHINE *by Henry Foljambe Hall*—Correspondence of War, Politics, Family and Love 1796-1814

MEMOIRS OF SARAH DUCHESS OF MARLBOROUGH, AND OF THE COURT OF QUEEN ANNE VOLUME 1 by A. T. Thomson

MEMOIRS OF SARAH DUCHESS OF MARLBOROUGH, AND OF THE COURT OF QUEEN ANNE VOLUME 2 by A. T. Thomson

MARY PORTER GAMEWELL AND THE SIEGE OF PEKING *by A. H. Tuttle*—An American Lady's Experiences of the Boxer Uprising, China 1900

VANISHING ARIZONA *by Martha Summerhayes*—A young wife of an officer of the U.S. 8th Infantry in Apacheria during the 1870's

THE RIFLEMAN'S WIFE *by Mrs. Fitz Maurice*—*The Experiences of an Officer's Wife and Chronicles of the Old 95th During the Napoleonic Wars*

THE OATMAN GIRLS *by Royal B. Stratton*—The Capture & Captivity of Two Young American Women in the 1850's by the Apache Indians

AVAILABLE ONLINE AT **www.leonaur.com**
AND FROM ALL GOOD BOOK STORES

ALSO FROM LEONAUR
AVAILABLE IN SOFTCOVER OR HARDCOVER WITH DUST JACKET

THE WOMAN IN BATTLE by *Loreta Janeta Velazquez*—Soldier, Spy and Secret Service Agent for the Confederacy During the American Civil War.

BOOTS AND SADDLES by *Elizabeth B. Custer*—The experiences of General Custer's Wife on the Western Plains.

FANNIE BEERS' CIVIL WAR by *Fannie A. Beers*—A Confederate Lady's Experiences of Nursing During the Campaigns & Battles of the American Civil War.

LADY SALE'S AFGHANISTAN by *Florentia Sale*—An Indomitable Victorian Lady's Account of the Retreat from Kabul During the First Afghan War.

THE TWO WARS OF MRS DUBERLY by *Frances Isabella Duberly*—An Intrepid Victorian Lady's Experience of the Crimea and Indian Mutiny.

THE REBELLIOUS DUCHESS by *Paul F. S. Dermoncourt*—The Adventures of the Duchess of Berri and Her Attempt to Overthrow French Monarchy.

LADIES OF WATERLOO by *Charlotte A. Eaton, Magdalene de Lancey & Juana Smith*—The Experiences of Three Women During the Campaign of 1815: Waterloo Days by Charlotte A. Eaton, A Week at Waterloo by Magdalene de Lancey & Juana's Story by Juana Smith.

NURSE AND SPY IN THE UNION ARMY by *Sarah Emma Evelyn Edmonds*—During the American Civil War

WIFE NO. 19 by *Ann Eliza Young*—The Life & Ordeals of a Mormon Woman During the 19th Century

DIARY OF A NURSE IN SOUTH AFRICA by *Alice Bron*—With the Dutch-Belgian Red Cross During the Boer War

MARIE ANTOINETTE AND THE DOWNFALL OF ROYALTY by *Imbert de Saint-Amand*—The Queen of France and the French Revolution

THE MEMSAHIB & THE MUTINY by *R. M. Coopland*—An English lady's ordeals in Gwalior and Agra duringthe Indian Mutiny 1857

MY CAPTIVITY AMONG THE SIOUX INDIANS by *Fanny Kelly*—The ordeal of a pioneer woman crossing the Western Plains in 1864

WITH MAXIMILIAN IN MEXICO by *Sara Yorke Stevenson*—A Lady's experience of the French Adventure

AVAILABLE ONLINE AT **www.leonaur.com**
AND FROM ALL GOOD BOOK STORES

www.ingramcontent.com/pod-product-compliance
Lightning Source LLC
Chambersburg PA
CBHW031619160426
43196CB00006B/199